C000203308

THE KNIGHTS HOSPITALLER

THE KNIGHTS HOSPITALLER

Helen Nicholson

THE BOYDELL PRESS

First published 2001
The Boydell Press, Woodbridge

ISBN 0 85115 845 5

The Boydell Press is an imprint of Boydell & Brewer Ltd
PO Box 9 Woodbridge Suffolk IP12 3DF UK
and of Boydell & Brewer Inc.
PO Box 41026 Rochester NY 14604–4126 USA
website: http://www.boydell.co.uk

A catalogue record for this book is available
from the British Library

Library of Congress Cataloging-in-Publication Data
Nicholson, Helen.
The Knights Hospitaller/Helen Nicholson.
p. cm.
Includes bibliographical references (p.) and index.
ISBN 0–85115–845–5 (acid-free paper)
1. Knights of Malta – History. I. Title.
CR4723.N53 2002
271.'7912–dc21 2001035615

This publication is printed on acid-free paper

Typeset by Joshua Associates Ltd, Oxford
Printed in Great Britain by
St Edmundsbury Press Ltd, Bury St Edmunds, Suffolk

Contents

Illustrations

COLOUR PLATES

(between pages 84 and 85)

BLACK AND WHITE PLATES

FIGURES

Preface

THIS is a brief history of the Sovereign Military Order of Malta, better known to historians and the general public as the Knights Hospitaller. The Order began in Jerusalem in the second half of the eleventh century as a hospice for sick poor pilgrims. Within a century of its foundation it gained papal protection and a religious rule, and became a supra-national religious order. From caring for sick pilgrims it expanded its operations to guarding pilgrims on the roads of the Holy Land and to defending the crusader states in the Holy Land. After the loss of the crusader states the Order moved its centre of operations to the island of Rhodes; expelled from Rhodes by the Ottoman Turks at the beginning of 1523, it went on to settle on the island of Malta. After being expelled from Malta in 1798 by the forces of Napoleon Bonaparte the Order eventually settled in Rome, where its base remains to this day.

This study is intended to provide a reference work for scholars and students who come across the Hospitallers in the course of other reading or research. It is not intended to provide a comprehensive guide to the whole history of the Order. The study surveys the Order's activities against the Muslims in the Holy Land, Rhodes and Malta, with some consideration of the Order's organisation, religious life, economic activities and relations with European rulers. It has not been possible to include detailed studies of the Order's activities in the various states of Europe. Readers looking for more detail than can be provided here should refer to the 'Further Reading' section, at the end of the volume. This is arranged to provide easy reference to the various points in each chapter; notes have been kept to an essential minimum.

I have incurred many debts in the preparation of this volume. I am extremely grateful to my colleague Bill Zajac for assisting me in finding many of the essential books for this project and lending me books which would otherwise have been very difficult to obtain. I owe particular thanks to those who have generously supplied me with pictures and/or allowed me to reproduce them here: Professor Juan Fuguet Sans of Barcelona; Professor Denys Pringle of Cardiff; Edna and Eliezer Stern of the Israel Antiquities Authority; and Dr Theresa Vann of the Hill Monastic Manuscript Library, St John's University, Collegeville, Minnesota. I am also most grateful to the following institutions which have provided me with pictures and allowed me to reproduce them here: the Biblioteca Communale Augusta, Perugia; the Bibliothèque Nationale, Paris; the Israel Antiquities Authority; the National Maritime Museum, Greenwich; and the Bridgeman Art Library. In addition I thank Professor Alain Demurger of the University of the Sorbonne, Paris; Dr Edward Coleman of University College,

Dublin; Zsolt Hunyadi of the Central European University, Budapest, and Dr Ann Williams, retired, who supplied me with essential advice and contacts towards obtaining the illustrations in this book.

I am grateful to the staff of Cardiff University Library, the British Library, London, the Public Record Office, London, and the National Library of Malta for research facilities and assistance.

In 1999 the Academic Study Group on Israel and the Middle East gave me a grant towards a journey to Israel where I was able to meet fellow crusade historians and visit sites, which has been a great help in the preparation of this book.

I owe a debt to many other scholars, colleagues and friends: there are too many to list, but I should mention in particular Dr Anthony Luttrell, Dr Alan Forey and Professor Jonathan Riley-Smith, for allowing me to pick their brains on many occasions, and my colleagues Professors Peter Coss and Peter Edbury and Dr Kari Maund for supplying me with essential references. My husband Nigel Nicholson drew the maps and took the photographs of Rhodes and Malta. John Morgan produced the photographs of Crac des Chevaliers and Marqab. Professor Peter Edbury and Nigel Nicholson read the work through in the final stages and have saved me from many errors. My son Gawain, who has already made a small personal contribution to Hospitaller scholarship in his pamphlet 'Why the Turks attacked Malta', written at the age of six, has exercised admirable patience throughout the project. My students have contributed to this volume in various ways and I am grateful for their support, enthusiasm and constant flow of ideas.

Because this book is aimed at scholars and students who are not specialists on the history of the Order of the Hospital, I have tried to avoid technical terms where there is a modern English equivalent. Therefore I have used 'tongue' instead of *langue* and 'inn' instead of *auberge*, for example. In order to assist readers in finding places mentioned on modern maps, I have endeavoured to give both the medieval place names and the modern forms. All translations into English, unless otherwise indicated in the notes, are by the author.

The Masters of the Hospital of St John (The Sovereign Military Order of Malta)

–1120	Gerard
1120–1160	Raymond du Puy
1160–1162	Anger de Balben
1162	Arnold de Comps
1162–1170	Gilbert d'Assailly
1170–1172	Castus de Muralo
1172–1177	Jobert
1177–1187	Roger des Moulins
1188–1190	Armengarde de Aspe
1190–1192	Garnier de Nablūs
1192–1202	Geoffrey de Donjon
1202–1206	Alphonso of Portugal
1206–1207	Geoffrey le Rat
1207–1227	Garin de Montaigu
1228–1230	Bernard de Thercy
1230–1236	Guérin
1236–1239	Bertrand de Comps
1239–1242	Pierre de Viellebride
1243–1258	William de Châteauneuf
1258–1277	Hugh Revel
1277–1284	Nicholas Lorgne
1285–1293	John de Villiers
1294–1296	Odo de Pins
1296–1305	William de Villaret
1305–1317	Fulk de Villaret
1319–1346	Hélion de Villeneuve
1346–1353	Déodat de Gozon
1353–1355	Pierre de Corneillan
1355–1365	Roger des Pins
1365–1374	Raymond Bérenger
1374–1377	Robert de Juillac
1377–1396	Juan Fernández de Heredia
1396–1421	Philibert de Naillac
1421–1437	Antoni Fluviá
1437–1454	Jean Bonpart de Lastic
1454–1461	Jacques de Milly
1461–1467	Pedro Raimondo Zacosta
1467–1476	Giovanni Batista degli Orsini
1476–1503	Pierre d'Aubusson
1503–1512	Emery d'Amboise
1512–1513	Guy de Blanchefort
1513–1521	Fabrizio del Carretto
1521–1534	Philippe Villiers de l'Isle-Adam
1534–1535	Pierino del Ponte
1535–1536	Didiers de St Jalle
1536–1553	Juan de Omedes
1553–1557	Claude de la Sengle
1557–1568	Jean Parisot de la Valette
1568–1572	Pietro del Monte
1572–1581	Jean l'Évêque de la Cassière
1582–1595	Hugh Loubenx de Verdalle
1595–1601	Martin Garzes
1601–1622	Alof de Wignacort
1622–1623	Luiz Mendez de Vasconcellos
1623–1636	Antoine de Paule
1636–1657	Jean Paul de Lascaris Castellar
1657–1660	Martin de Redin
1660	Annet de Clermont de Chattes Gessan
1660–1663	Rafael Cotoner
1663–1680	Nicolas Cotoner
1680–1690	Gregorio Carafa
1690–1697	Adrien de Wignacort

1697–1720 Ramon Perellos y Roccaful
1720–1722 Marc'Antonio Zondadari
1722–1736 Antonio Manoel de Vilhena
1736–1741 Ramon Despuig
1741–1773 Emanuel Pinto de Fonseca
1773–1775 Francisco Ximenes de Texada
1775–1797 Emanuel de Rohan Polduc
1797–1798 Ferdinand von Hompesch
1798–1801 Tsar Paul I of Russia
1803–1805 Giovanni Battista Tommasi

There was then a series of lieutenant-masters, until:

1879–1905 Johann Baptist Ceschi a Santa Croce (lieutenant-master since 1872)
1905–1931 Galeas von Thun und Hohenstein
1931–1951 Ludovici Chigi Albani della Rovere

A series of lieutenant-masters followed, until:

1962–1988 Angelo de Mojana dei Signori di Cologna
1988– Andrew Bertie

The list of masters after 1801 is derived from H. J. A. Sire, *The Knights of Malta* (New Haven and London, 1994).

1

The Origins of the Hospital of St John in Jerusalem

JERUSALEM is a sacred city for the Jewish, Christian and Islamic faiths, and has been a focus for Christian pilgrimage since the early years of the Christian Church. Situated on a low hill with deep valleys to the east and west, and hemmed in by higher ground all round, its massive walls are testimony to the wars which have been fought over it throughout three millennia. Within these walls lie the Church of the Holy Sepulchre, built on the reputed site of Christ's empty tomb; the al-Aqsa mosque, which medieval Europeans believed was the site of the Temple of Solomon; and the Dome of the Rock, built on the site where Abraham intended to sacrifice his son Isaac (Genesis 22), and which medieval Europeans believed was the Temple where Christ had preached during His earthly ministry. Once inside the Old City of Jerusalem the unwary newcomer is quickly lost within a maze of tiny streets, some covered, many steeply sloping and stepped, edged with a bewildering array of small shops and filled with people – some strangers like themselves, others local people anxious to press upon them their wares or hospitality or guidance. The multiplicity of pilgrim accounts of Jerusalem surviving from the fourth century AD onwards bear witness to the constant demand from pilgrims for a reliable guide to the holy sites and a warning of the pitfalls for the unwary traveller arriving in this city which is both holy and strange to Europeans. From at least the beginning of the seventh century hospices existed which gave a safe welcome and shelter to pilgrims, pious travellers making a penitential journey to this sacred place.

As part of the Roman Empire, from the late third century AD Jerusalem came under the jurisdiction of the eastern Empire. From the time of the Emperor Constantine I (sole emperor 324–337) this was governed from Constantinople, formerly Byzantium. In 614 Jerusalem fell to the Sassanid ruler Chosroes or Khusro II of Persia (591–628), who carried off the relic of the True Cross. The city and the priceless relic were recaptured by the Byzantine emperor Heraclius (610–641). Yet the Byzantine Empire no longer had the resources to hold what had become a distant province, and in 638 Jerusalem fell to the advancing armies of Islam.

The Islamic faith demands that the followers of the Jewish and Christian faiths be allowed to practise their faiths without persecution, provided that they do not try to convert Muslims. Hence Muslim rulers of Jerusalem did not restrict Christian worship or pilgrimage except for a brief period under the maverick Caliph Hakim (al-Hakim Bi-amr Allah, 985–1021), who destroyed the Church of the Holy Sepulchre in 1009. Pilgrims continued to come to the city. Yet during the eleventh century the journey became more difficult. The expansion of the Seljuk Turks westwards meant that pilgrims using the land route from the West were no longer travelling through relatively peaceful, Christian-controlled lands after they crossed the Bosphorus into Asia. After the defeat at the battle of Manzikert in 1071, the Byzantine emperors progressively lost control of Anatolia. Further south the road was even more dangerous; in 1065 a large party of German pilgrims was attacked near Ramla by Arab bandits. Many were killed or wounded, while part of the group defended themselves for three days in a fortified building before they were rescued by the local Muslim governor.[1]

The first references to the beginnings of the Hospital of St John in Jerusalem date from around this period. This was not a hospital as we now understand it but more resembled a modern hospice. Although western European hospitals of this period nursed the sick and cared for the poor, medical procedures were primitive; for those with serious illnesses, such hospitals could hardly do more than ease the plight of the dying.

According to William, archbishop of Tyre (died c. 1184), some merchants from the Italian city of Amalfi asked the caliph of Egypt for a site within Jerusalem where their fellow countrypeople could stay. He gave them a site within the Christian quarter of Jerusalem, near where the Church of the Holy Sepulchre stands. Here they built a church of the Resurrection and a monastery dedicated to the Virgin Mary, known as St Mary of the Latins because it was founded and peopled by Latin (that is, Roman Catholic) Christians – in contrast to the native Syrian Orthodox Christians. A women's house dedicated to St Mary Magdelene was founded nearby. The monastery of the Latins constructed a hospital, or *xenodochium*, to support poor and sick pilgrims, and this was dedicated to St John the Almoner.[2]

William was writing around a century after events, between 1170 and 1184. His description of the early Hospital as relatively poor and humble and dedicated to the care of needy pilgrims was intended as a stark contrast with the rich, privileged and arrogant order of his own day. Modern historians have called

[1] E. Joranson, 'The Great German Pilgrimage of 1064–1065', in *The Crusades and Other Historical Essays Presented to Dana C. Munro*, ed. L. J. Paetow (New York, 1928; reprinted New York, 1968), pp. 3–43.

[2] William of Tyre, in *Willelmi Tyrensis Archiepiscopi Chronicon: Guillaume de Tyr, Chronique*, ed. R. B. C. Huygens, 2 vols, Corpus Christianorum Continuatio Medievalis 68–68A (Turnholt, 1986), 2, pp. 814–17; Bk 18, chs 4–5.

William's description of the Hospital's beginnings into question. Apart from William's assertion, there is no evidence that the foundation was ever dedicated to St John the Almoner, and the general consensus among scholars now is that the Hospital was dedicated to St John the Baptist from its first foundation. The cathedral at Amalfi was dedicated to the Virgin Mary and St John the Baptist; it would have been natural for the Amalfitans to have dedicated the hospice attached to the monastery of St Mary to St John the Baptist.

An anonymous Amalfi chronicler recounts how Archbishop John of Amalfi (c. 1070–1081/2) went on pilgrimage to Jerusalem, where he was welcomed by the Amalfitans who had a few years previously founded two hospitals (or hospices) for men and women respectively, in which they cared for the sick. The people running these hospitals followed a quasi-religious way of life; they were not fully professed religious, but they probably wore some sort of distinctive clothing, or habit, and took some sort of religious vow.

Religious institutions of this sort were becoming common in western Europe by the late eleventh century. The religious reform movement during this period stimulated the foundation of radical monastic movements, such as the Cistercians with their 'back to basics' agenda, and also a multiplicity of religious houses with different purposes and peopled by individuals of different levels of religious devotion. These included communities of hermits, groups of priests living in community, anchoresses living in community, and hospices caring for the sick and aged. The hospitals of Jerusalem fitted into this pattern of flexibility and adaptability in the religious life, where the emphasis was not only on spirituality but also on making a positive impact in the world through practical service for others.

The Hospital of St John, therefore, began in or shortly before the 1070s in Jerusalem. Its obscure origins must later have caused the Order problems in promoting its work among European donors. Unlike most religious orders, it could not even identify its original founder by name. This was a serious drawback when trying to persuade western Europeans to give money and land to the Hospital rather than to an order such as the Cistercians, whose origins were well known and whose earlier members were noted for their piety and sanctity. To meet this problem, the Hospital later claimed much grander and more distant origins for itself. By 1160 Gerhoh, provost of Reichersberg, was referring to the Order's claim to have existed since the time of the Apostles. By the 1180s, the Order's fictional history was even more impressive. According to the Anglo-Norman version of the Hospital's Rule, produced for the English province of the Order around 1185, the Hospital had been founded by Bishop Melchiazar and King Antiochus of Jerusalem, which would date the foundation to the late third or early second century before Christ. It was claimed that Judas Maccabaeus (died 161/160 BC) had been a patron of the Hospital, and that John the Baptist's parents had served the poor there. Christ Himself had visited the Hospital on many occasions, and had performed many miracles there. This was the house where He had appeared to His disciples after His resurrection; the early Church in Jerusalem had met here. St Stephen, the first Christian martyr, had been master of the Hospital.[3] Other material produced by the Hospital in the late twelfth and thirteenth centuries varied and embroidered these legends: the Hospital was made the foundation of the Apostles rather than of King Antiochus; the Virgin Mary lived in the Hospital for three years and from here she was taken bodily up to Heaven. Popes and kings repeated these legends when they wrote in support of the Order. Yet when Brother William of Santo Stefano (Guglielmo di Santo Stefano) set about writing a history of the Order in the late thirteenth century he rightly concluded that these accounts were myths, invented to encourage potential donors to give alms, or charitable donations, to the Order.[4]

Apart from these mythical and distant origins, the Order could point to the involvement of one saintly figure in its foundation. Gerard, the ruler of the Hospital at the time of the First Crusade (1095–99), was commemorated in the chronicle of William of Tyre as a venerable and pious man who cared for poor pilgrims and who was tortured by the Muslims because they thought that he had money hidden away. The fact that this event was overlooked by contemporary writers on the First Crusade may indicate that the story was a later invention, but on the other hand the sufferings of the ruler of what was then a relatively obscure pilgrim hospice could easily have been overlooked by contemporaries. The body of a 'Blessed Gerard' was preserved in a fine shrine in the chapel of the Hospital's house at Manosque in Provence in 1283, and it seems likely that this was the body of the Gerard who was master at the time of the First Crusade, and that his body had been taken to the West for safe keeping in response to the threat of Muslim attack on the last European strongholds in the crusader states. The later Hospitallers, then, regarded this man as the real founder of their Order, and promoted him as a saint, although he was not recognised as a saint by the Catholic Church.[5]

In 1113 in his bull granting papal protection and privileges to the Hospital, *Pie postulatio voluntatis*, Pope Paschal II (1099–1118) referred to Gerard as the 'institutor' of the Hospital, indicating that he was largely responsible for its existence as an independent institution. Exactly what this involved is not spelt out. In the wake of the successful First Crusade the Hospital of St John received many donations from the crusaders who settled in the newly conquered lands of the East as well as from donors in Europe who wanted to support the Hospital's

[3] *The Hospitallers' Riwle (Miracula et Regula Hospitalis Sancti Johannis Jersolimitani)*, ed. K. V. Sinclair, Anglo-Norman Texts 42 (Oxford, 1984), lines 1–368.

[4] Helen Nicholson, *Templars, Hospitallers and Teutonic Knights: Images of the Military Orders, 1128–1291* (Leicester and London, 1993), pp. 112–13; Karl Borchardt, 'Two Forged Thirteenth-Century Alms-Raising Letters used by the Hospitallers in Franconia', in *The Military Orders: Fighting for the Faith and Caring for the Sick*, ed. Malcolm Barber (Aldershot, 1994), pp. 52–6.

[5] Anthony Luttrell in *The Order's Early Legacy in Malta*, ed. John Azzopardi (Valletta, 1989), p. 45.

work and share in its spiritual benefits. This influx of wealth would have enabled it to become independent from the institutions which had previously supported it.

Before the capture of Jerusalem by the First Crusade, Gerard's hospice had been dependent on the monastery of St Mary of the Latins, and its members probably followed an adapted version of the Rule of St Benedict, which was the monastic rule followed by the monastery. At that time the patriarch of Jerusalem, the priests in charge of the Holy Sepulchre, and the ecclesiastical hierarchy all belonged to the Syrian Orthodox Church. After Jerusalem fell to the crusaders, a Latin Christian patriarch was established in the Holy Sepulchre, with canons (priests) following a religious communal lifestyle to serve the spiritual needs of the pilgrims, and a Latin Christian ecclesiastical hierarchy was put in place throughout the newly conquered territories. The focus of Latin Christian authority in Jerusalem therefore shifted; all Latin Christian institutions were now answerable to the Latin Patriarch, based in the Church of the Holy Sepulchre. It seems that the Hospital now came under the direct authority of the canons of the Church of the Holy Sepulchre.

The evidence for this change in the Hospital's position comes from the many charters to the early Hospital which give donations to 'the Holy Sepulchre and the Hospital of St John of Jerusalem', indicating that the two were linked, or even that they were one and the same. It would have been reasonable for the canons of the Holy Sepulchre to have taken over responsibility for oversight of the Hospital: their religious lifestyle, with its active work in the Christian community, was far more like that of the people serving in the Hospital than the work of the monks of St Mary of the Latins, who followed an enclosed lifestyle according to the Rule of St Benedict. The similarities between the earliest known Rule of the Hospital, ascribed to Master Raymond du Puy (1120–1158/60), and the Rule of St Augustine suggests that the Hospital's Rule was influenced by the canons of the Holy Sepulchre, who formally followed the Rule of St Augustine from 1114.

Yet the connection may not have been a formal one. In the first few years of the kingdom of Jerusalem, it would have been reasonable for the ecclesiastical authorities in the city of Jerusalem to have taken care of this pilgrim hospital, given the influx of pilgrims from the West following the recovery of the holy city for Christendom. As the kingdom became more established and institutions became more fixed, the Hospital began to move towards autonomy. The papal privilege of 1113 allowed the brothers and professed members of the Hospital to elect their own master, without reference to any other lay or ecclesiastical authority.

The papal privilege also took the Hospital under papal protection and confirmed possessions already granted to it. What is puzzling is that hospices listed in this privilege as belonging to the Hospital at Bari, Otranto, Taranto, Messina, Pisa, Asti and St Gilles (in the Languedoc, in the extreme south of France) cannot be identified before 1113, and may not have belonged to the

Hospital at this date.[6] It may be that these were hospices which the Hospital was hoping to take over, or that they had been given to the Holy Sepulchre and were being claimed by the Hospital. The fact that donors often gave their donations 'to God, the Holy Sepulchre, St John the Baptist and the Hospital of Jerusalem' meant that it was unclear whether the intended recipient was both the Holy Sepulchre and the Hospital of St John or the Hospital alone. To western Europeans, 'the Holy Sepulchre' was simply a symbol of Jerusalem and the Latin Christians in the Holy Land. Donors' confusion was compounded by the fact that the Hospital built some churches in the West with round naves as a visual reminder of the Order's connection with Jerusalem and the Holy Sepulchre.[7] As a result, the Hospital was able to claim and take over a number of churches in the West which had belonged to the canons of the Holy Sepulchre, and some donations which had nominally been given to the Holy Sepulchre.

By 1113 the Hospital of St John was also beginning to win financial independence from the ecclesiastical hierarchy in the kingdom of Jerusalem. In 1112 Patriarch Arnulf of Chocques (1112–18) had exempted the Hospital from paying tithes – the tenth of produce which was due from all Christians to the Church. Pope Paschal's privilege of 1113 allowed the Hospital to keep the tithes on produce from lands which the members of the Order cultivated themselves. This meant that income which would otherwise have been lost to the Order could be applied to the Order's vocation of serving the poor and sick. Over the succeeding decades, the papacy granted the Hospital a series of privileges which by 1154 had effectively freed it from the jurisdiction of the patriarch of Jerusalem and of archbishops and bishops throughout Christendom. These privileges gave the Order the freedom of action to continue its work unhampered by local regulations and levies, but led to numerous disputes with the ecclesiastical heirarchy.

Following *Pie postulatio voluntatis*, issued by Pope Paschal II in 1113 and confirmed by Pope Calixtus II (1119–24) in 1119, in 1135 Pope Innocent II (1130–43) issued the bull *Ad hoc nos disponente* which exempted the Hospital from being placed under interdict or excommunication by any bishop. This meant that the Hospital and its personnel were effectively exempted from the jurisdiction of bishops, as ecclesiastical sanctions could not be used against them. In addition, if a general interdict was laid over an area where the Hospital had a church, the Hospital could still celebrate services there, provided that the church bells were not rung and non-members of the Order were not admitted.

In 1137 Pope Innocent II issued the bull *Christianae fidei religio*, which gave the Hospital extensive privileges. If the Hospital was given deserted land it could

[6] Anthony Luttrell, 'The Earliest Hospitallers', in *Montjoie: Studies in Crusade History in Honour of Hans Eberhard Mayer*, ed. Benjamin Z. Kedar, Jonathan Riley-Smith and Rudolf Hiestand (Aldershot, 1997), pp. 37–54: here pp. 44–8.

[7] Michael Gervers, 'Rotundae Anglicanae', in *Actes du 22e Congrès International d'Histoire de l'Art, Budapest, 1969* (Budapest, 1972), 1, pp. 359–76; Robert Gilchrist, *Contemplation and Action: The Other Monasticism* (London, 1995), p. 94.

build villages, churches and cemeteries for the use of all those living there, not only the brothers of the Order. Elsewhere, the Hospital could build oratories, or private chapels, for the use of the brothers only. The Order was permitted to have a confraternity, an association of lay members who did not live in the Order's house but remained in their own home, but who had promised to join the Order if they joined a religious Order. They would make a small annual donation to the Order and in return were guaranteed church burial even if their own church was under interdict, provided that they themselves were not under personal interdict or excommunication. When the collectors of the confraternity payments came to a place which was under interdict, they were allowed to open the churches once a year and celebrate divine office for the purpose of collecting for the confraternity – although those under personal sentence of excommunication were not to be admitted. As before, this privilege enabled the Order to subvert episcopal jurisdiction by ameliorating the impact of a general interdict. Finally, Innocent stressed that because everything that the Hospital possessed was used to help pilgrims and the poor, the Order did not have to pay tithes on its own produce.

Between 1139 and 1143 Pope Innocent II issued *Quam amabilis Deo*, which was addressed to archbishops, bishops and other clergy on behalf of the Hospital of St John. He urged them to encourage their subjects to join the Hospital's confraternity. Everyone who joined the confraternity and made an annual donation would have one seventh of their penance remitted and could be buried in a church of the Order when they died, provided that they themselves were not under personal sentence of excommunication. Again, he stressed that the brothers' collectors of confraternity dues were allowed to open churches once a year, even in areas under interdict, in order to collect the confraternity. In addition, the pope stated that bishops could allow priests under their authority who wished to serve the Hospital to join the Order for a year or two. These priests should be allowed to continue to receive their own revenues while they were with the Hospital.

In 1154 Pope Anastasius IV (1153–54) reissued *Christianae fidei religio*, adding that bishops could not excommunicate the brothers nor lay their churches under interdict, as in *Ad hoc nos disponente*, and confirming that only the brothers had the right to elect their master. In addition, the Hospitallers could have priests and clerics in their Order if they were satisfied that they had been validly ordained. Their clerics would be exempt from the authority of the diocesan bishop and would only be subject to the pope. The Hospitallers could also take on laity to help serve the poor. No professed members of the Order might leave the Order without the permission of the brothers and master. Finally, the brothers were allowed to ask whichever bishop they preferred to consecrate their houses and clergy – not necessarily the appropriate diocesan.

Taken as a whole these privileges were impressive: they freed the Order from the authority of local diocesan bishops and put it under the authority of the pope alone. Some of these privileges – such as the Order having its own priests – may have simply been giving official recognition to what was already standard practice. None of them was unique. The Order of the Temple, formally founded in 1120 to defend pilgrims visiting the holy sites, had received similar privileges from Pope Innocent II in 1139 in the bull *Omne datum optimum*. Again, similar privileges were held by the Cistercian order. These were religious orders which had been taken under direct papal protection. Their direct link with the papacy was indicative of the papacy's increasing authority and control over the Church from the mid-eleventh century onwards. In theory, these Orders could have acted as the tools of the papacy, the agents of papal will. In fact, they operated as independent agents. The papacy did not bestow freedom from diocesan control in order to create tools for enforcing papal authority; this freedom was given to enable a religious institution to discharge its vocation more efficiently. For the Hospitallers, the Templars and the Cistercians, supranational religious orders with a central authority and a supranational organisational structure, local diocesan control was an impractical means of enforcing ecclesiastical authority. They could only be governed from above, on a supranational level. In the same way, in the thirteenth century, the supranational orders of friars were taken under direct papal control.

These exemptions from episcopal authority caused great resentment among the secular clergy. William of Tyre describes a bitter dispute between the Hospital and Patriarch Fulcher of Jerusalem in 1154–5 which led to the patriarch himself and most of the bishops of his province travelling to Italy to ask the pope to rescind the Hospitallers' exemptions. Pope Hadrian IV (1154–9) refused.[8]

In the first half of the twelfth century the Hospital was becoming an autonomous organisation, subject only to papal authority. At the same time, it was acquiring property on an international scale. After the fall of the city of Jerusalem to western European forces in July 1099 the Hospital quickly began to acquire independent means. The earliest known donation to the Hospital was by Godfrey de Bouillon, first Latin Christian lay ruler of Jerusalem (1099–1100), of a casal (or village) called 'Hessilia' and two ovens – a valuable source of income, as the Hospital's tenants would have had to pay to use these ovens for baking their bread. The text of this donation does not survive – indeed, it is possible that it was not recorded in writing. However, it was confirmed by Godfrey's successors, Kings Baldwin I (1100–18) in 1110 and Baldwin II of Jerusalem (1118–31) in 1129, and their confirmation charters do survive. King Baldwin I's confirmation charter of 1110 also refers to many other donations to the Hospital throughout the kingdom of Jerusalem: casals, serfs, lands and houses. By 1118 the Hospital had also acquired property in the county of Tripoli (Tarābulus) and the principality of Antioch (Antakya).

The Hospital was also acquiring property in the West, although not as early as was once thought. When Joseph Delaville le Roulx produced his collection of charters and documents relating to the Hospital of St John, published between

[8] William of Tyre, 2, pp. 812–20; bk 18, chs 3–7.

1894 and 1906, he dated a charter which refers to the Hospitallers' lands at Clerkenwell, north of London, to around 1100. If this dating were correct, the Hospital of St John could have been acquiring land in the West before the First Crusade; but scholars now believe that this charter belongs to the period 1144–8.

However, the Hospital was certainly receiving property in southern France and in the Iberian peninsula from early in the twelfth century. These were areas which either had long connections with pilgrimage to the Holy Land or which were themselves involved in a war for the defence or recovery of Christian territory from the Muslims. Between 1100 and 1110 one Sanches, count of Astarac, his son Bernard and several other lords gave to 'the Holy Sepulchre and the Hospital of Jerusalem' the land of Fonsorbes, with several other pieces of land, rights and revenues. In 1101 a large group of donors gave the territory of Puysubran, near Toulouse, to the Holy Sepulchre and the pilgrim brothers in Jerusalem; in practice this meant the Holy Sepulchre and the Hospital of St John. Anthony Luttrell, tracing the development of the Hospital's administrative centres in the south of France, deduced that there was already a house of the Hospital at Béziers, in the Languedoc, by 1108–9 and a 'master of the house of the Hospital' in the Albi area in 1108–10. There was a *xenodochium* of the Hospital at St Gilles by 1121: St Gilles later became the centre of the Hospital's organisation *citra mare*, 'on this side of the sea' – that is, in Europe.[9]

Roger I, count of Sicily (1062–1101), sent the Hospital a financial donation from Sicily before his death. Urraca, queen of Castile (1109–26), made donations to the Hospital from 1113 onwards. These were followed by a series of donations in Castile. In 1126 her son and successor, Alfonso VII (1126–57), gave the Hospital the town of Atapuerca, giving a list of motives for his donation which encapsulate the principal motivations for donations to the Hospital and to all religious orders at this period:

> for the redemption of my grandfather, Alfonso the lord emperor, and his wife Queen Constance, and for the souls of my father, viz. the count Lord Raymond, and my mother Queen Urraca, that the Lord Jesus Christ may give them eternal rest and in order that they may sit with Him with His elect in the celestial kingdom, and so that in the present time I may rule with good fortune and in the future time be presented with the same mercy before the face of God.[10]

He did not mention the care of pilgrims in Jerusalem; his concern was less with the actual vocation of the Order than the fact that its vocation won God's approval, so that those who supported its work would also win God's approval.

In 1122 Afonso I Henriques, king of Portugal (1114–85), in response to the requests of Albert, prior of the Hospitallers, and in commemoration of a victory he had won against the Moors, gave the Hospital some villages. Here we find the

[9] Luttrell, 'The Earliest Hospitallers', pp. 48–50.

[10] *Cartulaire général de l'ordre des hospitaliers de St Jean de Jérusalem (1100–1310)*, ed. Joseph Delaville le Roulx (Paris, 1894–1906), no. 78.

Hospital linked to the activity for which it would later become most famous: the war against the enemies of Christendom. As far as is known, the Hospitallers were not yet actively involved in physical warfare against Muslims in the East, but the fact that they cared for pilgrims to the holy places – which included pilgrims who went to fight the Muslims as well as those who simply visited the holy sites – made them part of the holy war effort. By supporting this order which was closely associated with the Holy Sepulchre, the centre of Christendom, Afonso declared his own interest in defending and recovering the lands of Christendom.

The first definite indications that the Hospital was becoming involved in military activity are found in Pope Innocent II's bull *Quam amabilis Deo,* issued between 1139 and 1143. The pope states that the Hospitallers retained servants, *servientes,* at their own expense for the express purpose of ensuring that pilgrims could advance more safely to the places made holy by the corporal presence of our Lord Jesus Christ. *Servientes* may mean simply 'servants', but it is also the term used to refer to non-knightly fighting men, in French *sergeants.* Innocent therefore apparently meant that the Hospitallers were hiring fighting men to escort pilgrims to and from the holy places.

This seems very likely when we consider that the Order of the Temple was founded in 1120 for this very purpose. Although the Order of the Temple grew rapidly after its official recognition at the Council of Troyes in January 1129, it would probably not have been able to supply sufficient troops to escort all the pilgrims who came to the Holy Land. It would have been an obvious development for the Hospitallers, who were already dedicated to the care of pilgrims once they had arrived in Jerusalem, to have expanded their operations to take care of them on the road also.

This interpretation of the pope's description of the Order's activities seems even more likely when other evidence from before 1139 is considered. The donations to the Order in the Iberian peninsula which have already been noted do not mean that the Hospital was already involved in military activity against the Muslims, but certainly if it were this would have been an obvious impetus for donations. In 1134 Alfonso I, king of Aragon and Navarre since 1104, died leaving his kingdoms to the orders of the Temple, the Hospital of St John and the Holy Sepulchre. Historians do not agree in their analysis of Alfonso's intentions. He may not have intended that these Orders should protect his kingdoms against the Moors, for the canons of the Holy Sepulchre were certainly not involved in hostilities against the enemies of Christendom. When the terms of the will were finally set aside and the three legatees were compensated, the Templars received castles and privileges in Aragon whereas the Hospital and the Holy Sepulchre did not; an indication that neither the Hospital nor the Holy Sepulchre wished to be involved in warfare in Aragon at this period. Nevertheless, the fact that the legacy was made suggests that Alfonso thought that all three of his legatees might be able to assist his kingdoms against the Moors.

A donation to the Hospital in 1126 by Barisan, constable of Jaffa in the kingdom of Jerusalem, was witnessed by several brothers of the Hospital, including Durand 'constable of the Hospital'. At this time, the constable was a major military official in western Europe, effectively the general-in-chief after the king, who led the royal army if the king was unable to lead it in person. However, as Durand appears last in the list of Hospitaller witnesses, it has been suggested that he could not have been a major official, but that either he was a minor administrative official or that he was one of the military personnel hired by the Hospital rather than a member of the Order himself. It seems incongruous that the Hospital's constable should have held a status so different from that in the West, but it must be admitted that we know of no other Hospitaller constables from the early years of the Order, which indicates that it was not a major office.

Stronger evidence of the military activities of the Hospital comes in the donation of the castle of Beit Jibrin to the Order in 1136 by King Fulk of Jerusalem (1131–43), 'by common advice', that is, on the advice of the great lords of the kingdom of Jerusalem. Fulk is not known to have made such donations to the Order of the Temple, although that Order had been specifically founded for military purposes. According to William of Tyre, the castle was built as part of a series of fortifications to surround the Muslim-held city of Ascalon, to reduce the danger to the kingdom from Muslim raids. The Hospital placed guards in it and as a result the Muslims' attacks in that area became much weaker. It could also be used as a base for raids against the Muslims. It does not seem likely that the king would have entrusted such a strategic castle to a religious Order which had no interest or expertise in military affairs. However, possibly Fulk did not originally intend the Hospital to guard the area but intended it to bring in settlers and colonise, thereby helping to defend this territory against Muslim attack.

In 1142–4 Raymond II, count of Tripoli (1137–52), entrusted to the Order of the Hospital a series of castles on the frontiers of the county of Tripoli, in order to defend his county against Muslim attack. These were Crac des Chevaliers, Castellum Bochee, Lacum, Felicium and Mardabech with rights over the towns of Baʿrīn and Rafanīyah. The last two had been captured by Zenghi of Mosul in 1137, and the Hospitallers would have to recapture them. Raymond did this by the consent and will of his barons and men. The Hospitallers would owe no feudal dues for these lands; they would take half the booty in any military campaign in which he was present, and if he was not present and there was no constable or marshal of his present (another indication of the status of the constable in secular households) they could take all the booty themselves. Finally, he would make no truce or peace treaty with the Muslims without the Hospitallers' consent.

In effect, the Hospital of St John had been given a small, virtually independent state within the county of Tripoli, whose defence was the Order's responsibility and which it could use as a base for raids against its Muslim neighbours. Raymond's donation had made the Hospital responsible for defending the city of Tripoli from the direction of the Muslim city of Hama. Clearly, by the date of

Plate 1. Crac des Chevaliers: the inner ward. Photo copyright: Denys Pringle

this donation the Hospital was well able to provide the military resources and expertise to do this.

Raymond's donation was not unique; other donations of land and fortresses on the frontiers of the crusader states followed. The Hospital received land in the far north, and properties in the south, on the east bank of the Jordan. It is clear that it was regarded as better able to utilise these territories than any other secular or religious lord, including the Order of the Temple. All this indicates that the Hospital was a military as well as a hospitaller institution by the early 1140s, and may have included military personnel by the mid-1120s.

James de Vitry, bishop of Acre from 1216 to 1228, wrote in his *Historia Orientalis*, or 'History of the East', that the Hospitallers took up arms in imitation of the Templars. To judge from the numerous anecdotes about the Templars that James included in his 'Sermons to a military order', he had close contacts with the Templars. This information about the militarisation of the Hospital may have come to him from Templars who resented the Hospitallers' military activity and regarded them as rivals. Modern scholarship is not inclined to regard the Templars of 1120–40 as rivals to the Hospitallers; the evidence indicates that before Hugh de Payns' publicising campaign in the West of 1127–29 the Templars received little attention from western donors, and they were not a large organisation even in the 1130s. It seems more likely that the Hospitallers took up military activities as a natural extension of their vocation of caring for pilgrims. As one major need of pilgrims in the Holy Land was for protection from Muslim bandits, any organisation which claimed to care for pilgrims needed to meet this need as well as their more mundane requirements for food and beds. Rather than caring for wounded and dying pilgrims after they had been attacked by bandits on the road, it seemed much more advantageous to protect them against being attacked in the first place. The militarisation of the Hospital did not reflect rivalry with the Templars; it reflected the desperate need of the kingdom of Jerusalem for military forces, which the Templars also tried to supply. Nevertheless, the forces of the military orders in the Holy Land were never large. It has been suggested that the Hospitallers and the Templars were each able to put a force of three hundred brothers into the field, plus mercenaries. Castle garrisons consisted mainly of mercenary troops with only a handful of brothers.

To the modern student, it may seem strange that a religious order dedicated to the care of the needy could take up weapons in order to kill and maim. Yet, even in the present day, organisations with a primarily peaceful purpose, such as the United Nations and NATO, have used military forces to keep the peace in troubled areas of the world. In the middle ages, although some warfare was regarded as harmful, it was believed that it could be not only justifiable but even necessary and charitable, and could win spiritual merit for those who fought and died in the cause. As Pope Innocent II wrote to the Templars in 1139 in his bull *Omne datum optimum*: 'You fulfill the Gospel saying, "Greater love has no man than this, that a man lay down his life for his friend"' (John 15 v. 13).

As this concept of spiritually meritorious warfare differs from modern concepts of warfare, it is worthwhile considering its origins and development.

In the New Testament, Jesus is recorded making various remarks that tell people not to use violence: 'Blessed are the peacemakers, for they shall be called the children of God' (Matt. 5 v. 9); 'Do not resist an evil person. If someone strikes you on the right cheek, turn to them the other also' (ibid. 6 v. 39); and 'Put your sword back in its place . . . for all who draw the sword will die by the sword' (ibid. 26 v. 52). At first sight, this indicates that Christians should not fight. In the Old Testament, the sixth Commandment seems to support this belief: 'You shall not kill' (Deut. 5 v. 17).

Yet not everything in the New Testament indicates that Christians should not fight. In Luke 3 v. 14, soldiers asked John the Baptist what they should do to achieve salvation. He did not tell them not to fight; instead, he told them not to extort money from civilians, and to be content with their pay. In Matt. 8 v. 10 and Luke 7 v. 9, Jesus declared that a centurion had more faith than anyone He had met, even in Israel. In Luke 22 v. 36, Jesus tells the Apostles to buy swords to protect themselves as they go out preaching. Acts 10 vv. 1–2 describe Cornelius, centurion of the Italian Cohort, who was a devout man who prayed constantly to God and gave alms liberally; he was the first Gentile to whom the Apostle Peter preached. None of these examples indicate that warriors are to be condemned simply because they fight. It is possible in Christian thinking not only for a warrior to be saved, but even for a warrior to be noted for piety.

The great Christian writer Augustine (died 430), bishop of Hippo Regius in North Africa (now Annaba or Bône in Tunisia), wrote a good deal on the problem of violence. In *The City of God* he condemned war, but saw that violence had to be met by violence in order to keep the peace. He expanded on this in his letters, writing that the Bible clearly shows that God does not disapprove of soldiers, and that it is possible to be a soldier and please God. Provided war is waged with the right intention, in order to gain peace, it is justifiable. Yet fighting is not the highest form of the religious life. The best way to gain God's approval is by withdrawing from the world and living a life of contemplation and prayer.[11]

Augustine's view of warfare was as a secular activity, under the legitimate authority of the secular prince. This was not a holy war in the sense that it was later understood. Under the Roman Empire, warfare remained the responsibility of the emperor. It was one of his duties as God's vicar on earth to defend the people whom God had entrusted to his care. This continued to be the view of educated Christian writers. Following the fragmentation of centralised secular authority in France in the tenth century, Church leaders looked to local lords to fulfill the function of defending the people. These lords, be they bishops or secular barons, employed warriors to keep the peace.

[11] *Augustine: Political Writings*, trans. M. W. Tkacz and D. Kries, intro. E. L. Fortin (Indianapolis, 1994), pp. 219–20, 221–9.

In the second half of the eleventh century, Pope Gregory VII (1073–85) and his supporters urged all warriors to fight in his defence against his enemy, King Henry IV of Germany (1056–1106). In serving the pope, warriors would be serving God, for the pope was the heir of St Peter, and he had jurisdiction over all things, spiritual and secular. This kind of service appears very like the service of Christian warriors under the emperor, when they were permitted to fight because the emperor was appointed by God. As Gregory claimed to be supreme even over the emperor, how much more should warriors fight for the pope, as God's representative on earth?

However, fighting for the pope was not the same as fighting for the emperor; it was not simply permitted violence, or violence as duty; it was violence that carried a reward. As Gregory wrote in January 1075, the pope 'promises eternal blessings, absolving them from all their sins'.[12] In this respect, fighting for the pope was a kind of holy war.

The roots of holy war lie in the Old Testament, where God is a warrior god, a god of battles, who fights for His people. Holy war, in the Christian context, is war which furthers God's purposes; God's war, in fact. It is assumed that those who fight directly for God receive an eternal reward. John Gilchrist showed that from the creation of the papal states in central Italy in the eighth century, the papacy depicted its wars against its enemies as holy war. Gregory VII's call to warriors to fight on his behalf continued this tradition.

In western Christian thinking, therefore, warfare was justified for secular rulers whom God had given the duty of defending their subjects, or for those who were fighting for such a ruler in defence of his subjects, to restore the peace. It was also justified when it was holy war, directly in defence of the Church. The first kind of violence was a sacred duty, and part of kingship, but carried no direct spiritual reward. The second kind of violence won an eternal reward, forgiveness of all sins.

The justification of certain kinds of warfare developed further with the concept of the crusade. Between 1106 and 1109, Guibert, abbot of Nogent (died c. 1125), wrote a book called *The Deeds of God through the Franks.* At the beginning of this work he considered when violence could be acceptable, and stated that until the present day almost all those who had taken up arms had done so for the wrong motives, to gain fame or money or land.

> They would be able to offer a morally acceptable excuse for fighting if they were taking up the cause of protecting liberty or defending the state; indeed, in the case of an invasion of barbarians or pagans, no knight could rightly be prevented from taking up arms. And if this was not the case, then they waged legitimate war simply when they were defending Holy Church.

[12] Ian Robinson, 'Pope Gregory VII and the soldiers of Christ', *History*, 58 (1973), 169–92: here 174.

Yet this was not enough.

> However, since everyone does not have this pious purpose, and instead everyone's hearts are full of the desire for material gain, in our time God has ordained holy wars, so that the knightly order and the wandering crowd – who had been engaged in mutual slaughter, like their ancient pagan forebears – could find a new way of earning salvation. Without having chosen a monastic life (as is the custom), and without any religious commitment, they gave up the world; they were free to continue their customary pursuits, but nevertheless, through their efforts, they gained some measure of God's grace.[13]

This new sort of holy war was the crusade. Yet the crusade was not simply another holy war, as Guibert implies; it had an added dimension. The speech of Pope Urban II (1088–99) when he called the First Crusade at the Council of Clermont in 1095 has not survived, but it is known that he promised that 'Whoever for devotion only, not to gain honour or money, goes to Jerusalem to liberate the city of God, may substitute this journey for all penance.'[14] This implied that the military expedition that he was proposing was a pilgrimage. Like pilgrims, those who decided to go on crusade took a vow to go and received a symbol in token of their vow – a cross. They also received the same privileges as pilgrims: amortisation of their debts, the protection of the Church over their families and possessions and a stay of payment on all taxes due.

Yet the crusade was also, as Guibert states, a holy war. As the war was intended to stop the Muslims of Palestine oppressing the native Christians, and to recover the lands where Christ had trodden which were regarded as Christ's inheritance, this was a holy war, fought on God's behalf. When Urban II had finished speaking, the crowd shouted: 'Deus lo volt!' – 'God wills it!' It is clear from the letters that some of the crusaders sent home during the expedition and from the account of the anonymous writer who wrote the earliest account of the crusade, the *Gesta Francorum*, that those on the crusade believed that they were fighting for God. Bohemond of Taranto (died 1111) is depicted saying to his constable: 'Know in truth that this is not a bodily but a spiritual battle.'[15] Pope Paschal II wrote to the crusaders after they had captured Jerusalem: 'Christ dwells in your hearts and through you is seen to have vanquished his enemies . . . through the divine mercy, we have seen the enemies of the Christian faith, oppressors of the Christian people, destroyed by your hand.'

In short, when the Hospitallers took up arms to protect pilgrims visiting the holy places against Muslim attack, they were acting fully in accordance with the Christian beliefs of their day. They were not themselves crusaders. The vows that they took were not crusaders' vows of pilgrimage, but lifelong religious vows of

[13] Guibert of Nogent, *The Deeds of God through the Franks: Gesta Dei per Francos*, trans. Robert Levine (Woodbridge, 1997), p. 28 (amended).

[14] Jonathan Riley-Smith, *The First Crusade and the Idea of Crusading* (London, 1986), p. 29.

[15] *Gesta Francorum et aliorum Hierosolimitanorum*, trans. Rosalind Hill (London, 1962), p. 37.

poverty, chastity and obedience. Other radical religious movements of the period allowed members to find salvation through physical work in God's name rather than contemplative prayer, and allowed those under religious vows to go about preaching rather than being enclosed in a monastery. The Hospitallers went further: they fought alongside crusaders for the same reasons as crusaders, to defend Christians and Christian territory. They and their contemporaries believed that this warfare won them God's favour, and an eternal reward in Heaven.

2

Holy War in the Latin East and on the European Frontiers, 1130–1291

BY THE 1130s the Hospital of St John in Jerusalem was becoming well known in western Europe for its care of poor pilgrims in Jerusalem. It had also been attracting gifts of land in Europe and in the East, and had been exempted by the papacy from episcopal and lay authority so that it could carry on its vocation more effectively. Its care for pilgrims led to its taking on military obligations, and this in turn meant that it became involved in military campaigns in the crusader states in the East and was made responsible for the fortification and defence of castles. This led to the Hospital acquiring an important political role in the crusader states, especially at periods when there was no strong centralised authority.

The Hospital of St John mainly came to the attention of western European writers during the course of its military involvement in the East. Only travellers who actually reached Jerusalem and saw the Hospital's care for pilgrims for themselves had much to say about its hospitaller activities. This chapter will consider the Hospital's military activity, while its care for pilgrims will be considered below, in chapter four.

The military involvement of the Hospital of St John in the East led to its being drawn into the defence of Christian frontiers elsewhere in Europe. Some of the early donations to the Order in the Iberian peninsula have already been touched upon in chapter one. The Hospital's military activity in the crusader states in the Latin East must be considered in the context of the history of the crusader states and of the crusades to the East.

□

Between 1100 and 1193 military events in the Latin East were dominated by the recovery of Muslim unity and the increase of Muslim aggression. After the success of the First Crusade in capturing Edessa (Urfa), Antioch, Tripoli and Jerusalem, the crusaders set up states centred on these cities: the principality of Antioch, the counties of Edessa and Tripoli and the kingdom of Jerusalem (figure 1). Modern

Fig. 1. Map of the Middle East showing sites connected with the Hospital of St John and major towns, 1099–1291.

historians refer to these states as 'the crusader states' for convenience, although the people living there were not crusaders. Throughout the twelfth and thirteenth centuries, military expeditions continued to come out from Europe to support these 'crusader states'. Warfare was not simply Christian against Muslim, but Muslim rulers also allying with the Christian newcomers against other Muslims. This was not all-out war so much as border raiding in search of booty and prisoners.

During their first three decades in the East, the Latin or Roman Catholic Christians were able to hold their own and increase their territory while the Muslims were divided. However, from the 1130s onwards the crusader states faced a series of Muslim leaders who united Middle Eastern Islam, or a substantial proportion of Islam, and depicted the war against the Christians as Jihad, holy war against non-believers. The first of these was Zenghi of Mosul (died 1146). In 1144 he captured Edessa. In response, Pope Eugenius III (1145–53) issued a bull, *Quantum praedecessores*, calling on the king and nobility of France to emulate their ancestors and travel to defend the holy places of Christendom. Two large expeditions went to the Holy Land, led by the kings of France and Germany. At the same time, the pope took a bold initiative in promoting holy war on all the frontiers of Christendom at once. Other expeditions went to fight Muslims in the Iberian peninsula or pagans in North Germany on the coast of the Baltic sea. Only the crusaders in the Iberian peninsula achieved anything: the expeditions to the Holy Land failed largely because of bad planning. They went by land, across Asia Minor, where their forces suffered such losses against the Turks that when they reached the Holy Land there were not enough fighting men left alive for a major campaign. The crusaders then proceeded to besiege the Muslim city of Damascus, but failed to capture it. The West was so disillusioned by the failure of the Second Crusade (1147–9) that for a whole generation no large military expeditions went to the East; there were only small expeditions of pilgrims whose primary purpose was to visit the holy places, but who might also join in military campaigns if they were needed.

Unlike the Templars, who played a significant role in the French advance through Asia Minor and a lesser role in the siege of Damascus, the contemporary sources did not record the Hospitallers playing a major military role in the Second Crusade. Like the Templars, the Order lent some money to King Louis VII of France while he was on crusade.[1] Money-lending was to become one of the valuable services which the military orders offered to monarchs.

The master of the Hospital, Raymond du Puy, was present at the military council at Acre ('Akko) in June 1148 which took the decision to attack Damascus, but no contemporaries mention the Order taking any part in the fighting which

[1] 'Lettres de Suger, abbé de Saint Denys', in *Recueil des Historiens des Gaules et de la France*, ed. Michel-Jean-Joseph Biral, new edn pub. under the direction of Léopold Delisle, vol. 15 (Paris, 1878), pp. 508–9, no. 68.

followed. In the same year the Hospitallers of Aragon were present at the siege of Tortosa on the River Ebro in the Iberian peninsula, but again there is no clear evidence that they took any part in the fighting, although some scholars consider that this would be the most obvious reason for their being present.

William of Tyre informs us that the master and some brothers of the Hospital were present at the siege of Ascalon in 1153 by King Baldwin III of Jerusalem (1152–63) with other leading clergy of the kingdom. The Hospitallers are not, however, depicted as being involved in the fighting; their role was purely advisory and in giving spiritual support to the army. However, William was not in the East at this time, and his account of the 1150s is based on official documents and the memories of those who were present or of their relations. It is therefore not possible to be absolutely certain that the Hospital had no involvement in military activity at Ascalon.

In any case, the Hospital had an important advisory role in the military affairs of the kingdom of Jerusalem by the 1150s. By the 1160s the Hospital was actively involved in military activity during King Amaury's invasions of Egypt. William of Tyre depicts the master of the Hospital, Gilbert d'Assailly (master 1162–70), as mainly responsible for persuading Amaury to break his 1167 truce with Egypt and launch an attack in autumn 1168. While other contemporary commentators do not comment on the matter, it was this campaign of 1168 which first brought the Hospitallers' military activity to the attention of a contemporary western European writer. Lambert Wattrelos included an account of the Hospitallers' involvement in his 'Annals of Cambrai'.

> The lord of the Hospital of Jerusalem travelled on the campaign with his own men. He was sharp and confident in his natural ability as a warrior, a strong and bold knight in battle. At last he came, with the Lord God's help, to a certain very strongly fortified city named Bilbais. The prince did not fear the strength or audacity of its inhabitants and boldly attacked the city with his men, broke the walls and brought it swiftly to the ground, killing those who came out to meet him. But some of the inhabitants escaped and told the other Turks about the destruction of the city, so that they were terrified. So the virtuous prince, with his men and God's help, obtained for himself victory over the city.[2]

Meanwhile, according to Lambert, King Amaury (1163–74) and the master of the Temple were each leading their own armies. This invasion did not conquer Egypt (which Amaury could not have held even had he conquered it) and prompted the invasion of Egypt by Shirkuh of Damascus in 1169. Skirkuh was followed as vizier of Egypt by his nephew Saladin. In 1174, following the death of Zenghi's son Nūr al-Dīn, Saladin took over power in Damascus. Amaury's Egyptian campaigns, urged on by the master of the Hospital, were disastrous for

[2] Lambert Wattrelos, 'Annales Cameracenses', *Monumenta Germaniae Historica Scriptores*, ed. G. H. Pertz *et al.*, 32 vols (Hanover, 1826–1934), 16, p. 529.

the kingdom of Jerusalem because they opened the way for the unification of the Muslim states of Damascus and Egypt under one ruler. While the Muslims were divided, the Latin Christians could play them off against each other; once they were united, the Latin Christians lacked the military strength to defeat them in the field.

The events of 1168 were also disastrous for the Hospital, for the Order was left bankrupt. Gilbert d'Assailly resigned. The pope, Alexander III (1159–81), rebuked the Order for taking up military action except in defence of Christendom; for, he wrote, the Hospital's vocation was one of hospitality, not arms. Gilbert's successors Castus de Muralo (1170–2) and Jobert or Josbert (1172–7) were not noted for their military activity, and it is noticeable that, when writing to the West, Jobert emphasised the Hospital's charitable work rather than its military responsibilities. He presumably felt that western Christendom should not be reminded of the Order's recent near-disaster. The Hospitallers, however, continued to play a military role in the kingdom, and in 1179 the master and some brothers were involved in the count of Tripoli's campaigns in the north.

In these early accounts of the Hospitallers' campaigns we see the Hospitallers already an organised force in the field, capable of acting alone (in frequent raids on the Muslims from its castles, or at Bilbais in Egypt) or as an integrated part of a larger force (as in the count of Tripoli's campaigns). They were respected by the Muslims as formidable military adversaries. Yet, unlike the rule of the Temple which had been given official Church approval in 1129, the early regulations of the Hospital give no details of military matters. It is not until the statutes of master Alphonso of Portugal, issued between 1203 and 1206, that regulations were made regarding the military officials of the Order: by this time the Order had a marshal – an official of the Order also mentioned in contemporary accounts of the Third Crusade, 1189–92 – a standard-bearer, turcopoles (native mercenaries), castellans (responsible for the administration and defence of castles), brother knights and brother sergeants. It is clear in these statutes that already by this period the rank of 'knight' was becoming coveted and particularly associated with those of higher social status, and that men should be of a certain age before being made knights. In general, knights were characterised as fighting on horseback with the lance or the sword, although in fact they did not always do this; and were expected to have equipment of a higher standard than other warriors, and to be highly skilled in the art of warfare through frequent training. In contrast, sergeants, whose name also meant 'servants', were generally regarded as being of lower social status and of lower military skill, with equipment of lower quality.

The lack of statutes does not indicate lack of military organisation. Accounts of the brothers' involvement in battle indicate that the Hospitallers were just as well-organised and disciplined in battle as the Templars, with similar organisation. A contemporary description of the Order in action on the plains of Arsūf on 7 September 1191 indicates that their army was made up of cavalry and infantry, relying on archers to harass the enemy, cavalry to divide the enemy ranks with a well-disciplined charge, and infantry to advance behind the cavalry to fight hand-to-hand.[3]

During the thirteenth century, statutes were issued at successive general chapters of the Order. These dealt with military matters on a piecemeal basis. In the statutes of 1262 it is stated that the marshal may entrust the standard of the Order to any brother whom he considers worthy to bear it, with the master's consent, and the procedure is set out for the Order to elect a lieutenant when the master has been captured in battle by the Saracens. These were matters which had certainly arisen before, and solutions must have been found as and when they arose. The statutes were simply a means of codifying what had already been decided and what had by this time probably become standard practice. The Order's practice of acting first and legislating later is epitomised by the fact that it was not until 1248 that the pope, Innocent IV (1243–54), approved a standard military dress for the Hospitallers to be worn in battle. Instead of a closed cape over their armour which restricted their movements, they should wear a red surcoat with the sign of the cross on it in white.[4] By this time the Order had been involved in military affairs for at least a century and the brothers must have found solutions to this problem before; however, the Order saw no need to have any regulations on the subject.

When Saladin finally invaded the kingdom of Jerusalem in spring 1187, the Hospital again played a significant role in military affairs. The master and some brothers fought in the battle at the Spring of the Cresson on 1 May 1187 when a small Latin Christian army attacked a much larger Muslim army and was massacred almost to the last man. Hospitallers were also involved in the battle of Hattin on 4 July 1187, at which the king of Jerusalem, Guy of Lusignan (1186–92), and the 'Lord's Cross', the most sacred relic in the kingdom of Jerusalem, were captured. Saladin had all the Templars and Hospitallers who were captured in this battle executed, because they were his most determined foes among the Christians.

During the Third Crusade (1189–92), the Hospitallers played a major military role for the first time in a crusade. As well as advising on strategy, they took part in attacks on the enemy, their ships assisted in the defence of Tyre (now Sūr) in the winter of 1187–8; their siege-machines played a role in the siege of Acre, 1189–91; their forces took it in turns with the Templars to take command of the rearguard or the vanguard on the march south from Acre to Jaffa in September 1191. On 7 September 1191, when the rearguard crusader army was attacked on the plains of Arsūf, the Hospitallers were in command of the rear and led the charge against Saladin's forces – too enthusiastically, in fact, as commentators complained that

[3] Ambroise, *The Crusade of Richard Lionheart*, trans. John L. La Monte and Merton Jerome Hubert (New York, 1976), lines 6122–630; *Chronicle of the Third Crusade: a Translation of the Itinerarium Peregrinorum et Gesta Regis Ricardi*, trans. Helen Nicholson (Aldershot, 1997), pp. 246–53.

[4] *Cartulaire général de l'ordre des hospitaliers de St Jean de Jérusalem (1100–1310)*, ed. Joseph Delaville le Roulx (Paris, 1894–1906), no. 78, no. 2479.

the marshal of the Hospital had been one of those who charged too soon and ruined the crusaders' chances of destroying the Muslim ranks. This was not the only time that the Hospitallers were accused of breaking ranks: in a battle at Bait Nūbā on 12 June 1192 a Hospitaller knight was rebuked for infringing the rule of the Order by breaking rank and charging alone against the enemy. He only escaped receiving the discipline of the Order because leading nobles among the crusaders pleaded with the master of the Order, Garnier de Nablūs (1190–92), to excuse him on the grounds of his great skill and courage as a knight.

The Hospitallers' castles were also significant during the period of Saladin's initial successes in conquering the kingdom of Jerusalem. Their castle of Marqab in the county of Tripoli was so difficult to assault that Saladin did not even attempt to attack it. The castle of Belvoir (Kaukab) in the Jordan valley held out against Saladin's siege from July 1187 to 5 January 1189. Between 1168 and 1187 Belvoir had been rebuilt by the Order to a concentric design, and is regarded by modern historians as the first consistent concentric castle. The concentric design with enclosure within enclosure fitted the Order's requirements as a religious Order, cut off from secular society, but more importantly it also provided effective defence against new and improved Muslim siege techniques. During the siege of 1187–9, the Hospitallers did much to reinforce their image in the eyes of the Muslims as doughty and fearless warriors. 'Imād al-Dīn al-Isfahānī, Saladin's secretary, described the Hospitaller's fortress of Belvoir/Kaukab as 'an inaccessible citadel, an inaccessible refuge, an unattainable summit, an unstrikeable flint, an inviolable woman, a maiden who could not be asked in marriage, an uncovetable fortress'. In January 1188 Saladin sent his general Sayf al-Dīn Mahmūd to command the siege. 'Imād al-Dīn describes what followed:

> The surveillance of the fortress went on for a long time, and precautions were maintained for so long that Mahmūd felt that the besieged were becoming weaker and that he was safe against them. He believed that they were in the depths of despair, he was tranquillized by their inaction; he regarded them with a negligent eye, imagining that their eyes had become dulled; he abandoned himself to events, he dealt carelessly with what was difficult, lacked firmness and decision, underestimated his adversaries, and imputed their inaction to weakness. He was installed in the castle called 'Afrabalā, near to Kaukab, completely at ease, resembling at one and the same time the bitter and the sweet. His religious faith was strong: he was always at his devotions, holding vigil and praying for most of the night; he had made his lodging into a mosque; his companions surrounded it and guarded it in the strength and power of Allah.
>
> On the last night of the month of shawwāl, a night fertile with terrors, dark, obscure, shadowy, pitch-black, deep, cold, making one shiver, all light gone, a night abundant in rain which fell in torrents – impenetrable cloud, black everywhere, with an icy wind – one could not tell the earth from the sky; the shadows flowed together. At

> dawn, the defenders of Kaukab made a sortie and advanced on Mahmūd. The latter was resting after having kept vigil all night; his people were asleep, his sentinels were dozing, his troops were inert, aspirations calmed, desires resting; non-existence and existence had drawn close to each other. The noble Mahmūd and his drowsy companions came to themselves only when the Franks had entered and placed their knees on their chests. They were then incapable of defending themselves, they could not resist; supreme blessing came to them, for martyrdom took them by surprise. The emir defended himself until he died, surrounded by his enemies; Allah's order is a judgement fixed in advance.
>
> The Franks carried off to their citadel all the arms, equipment and horses which they could find.

This daring sortie was not sufficient to save the castle. In late 1188 an attempt by the Hospitallers to relieve the castle met with disaster when they were intercepted by the Muslims. Saladin displayed his courtesy in sparing the lives of the leaders of the relief force. The castle finally succumbed to assault and surrendered on 5 January 1189. Nevertheless, the Hospitallers' defence had reinforced the Muslims' opinion of them as formidable opponents.[5]

The Hospitallers' prominent military role during the Third Crusade established the Hospital in the minds of western European commentators as a military order. From this period onwards, the Hospitallers were usually named alongside the Templars in western accounts of military activity in the Holy Land. Regrettably for the Order, the military significance of the brothers in the East meant that they also received blame when the crusader states received military reversals. The Hospitallers were able to deflect this sort of criticism somewhat by drawing attention to their charitable work for pilgrims, but as Guiot de Provins, French trouvère turned Cluniac monk, wrote in the first decade of the thirteenth century: 'They have changed their business too much; I did not see any hospitality in them. They are not acting reasonably when they have forgotten their name.'[6]

□

From the death of Saladin in 1193 until 1260, the Muslims were divided and the Latin Christian states recovered. At first Aleppo, Damascus, and Egypt were ruled by different members of Saladin's family who were constantly at war with each other – so the Christians played them off against each other. In 1250 there was a change of government in Egypt when the Mamluks seized power, but Aleppo and Damascus were still ruled by the Ayyubids, the descendants of

[5] 'Imād al-Dīn al-Isfahānī, *Conquête de la Syrie et de la Palestine par Saladin (al-Fath al-qussî fi l-fath al-qudsî)*, trans. Henri Massé (Paris, 1972), pp. 81–2, 125–6.

[6] Guiot de Provins, 'Le Bible', in *Les Œuvres de Guiot de Provins, Poète Lyrique et Satirique*, ed. John Orr (Manchester, 1915), lines 1800–5.

Saladin's father Ayyūb, so that the Christians could still play the rival dynasties off against each other.

The years 1193 to 1260 saw a pattern of truces lasting for between five and ten years, followed by a crusading expedition when the truce expired, followed by another truce. The Latin Christians in the Middle East made some gains, but also suffered some very serious reverses during this period. The most notable was on 23 August 1244 when Jerusalem was finally lost to the Khwarismian Turks, led by the Uzbek warlord Jalal al-Dīn Menguberdi. The Khwarismians, displaced from their homelands near the Aral Sea several years earlier by the Mongols, had been drawn into the area by as-Salih Ayyūb, sultan of Egypt, who wished to employ them against Aleppo and Damascus. The loss of Jerusalem was followed by a heavy defeat of the combined Latin Christian–Damascene forces at La Forbie, near Gaza, against the combined forces of the Khwarismians and Egyptians on 17 October 1244. Yet overall the crusader states held on well. The area was still rich, because it was a staging post for Asian–European trade.

During this period the Hospitallers' military role in crusades continued to be significant, but in addition, due to political upheavals in the kingdom of Jerusalem, the Order became increasingly importance in the political arena. Following the fall of Jerusalem to Saladin in October 1187 the Hospital of St John had been forced to move its administrative centre and hospital; after the recapture of Acre in July 1191 the Order set up its base there, on the north side of the old city, building a fine hospital and extensive buildings around a large central courtyard. At Acre, the Order continued to play an important role in accommodating poor and sick pilgrims on their arrival in the Holy Land, in addition to its military and political involvement.

The Order of the Temple was also based at Acre from 1191, its headquarters being situated on the south-west of the city, on the sea wall. During the siege of Acre other religious orders were founded which later developed into military orders. The Hospital of St Thomas of Canterbury, an English Order, was never particularly significant on the international stage, but a field hospital set up by German pilgrims was transformed in 1198 into a military order with a rule which combined elements from the Order of the Temple and the Order of the Hospital. The Teutonic Order, although never as prominent as the Temple and the Hospital in the Latin East, was to become a major power in north-eastern Europe; and like the Hospital of St John it survives to the present day.

No contemporary writer mentions the Hospitallers playing an active military role in the Fourth Crusade, but Hospitallers were clearly present in at least a supportive spiritual capacity. In June 1205, after the capture of Constantinople by the crusade, the death of the first Latin emperor Baldwin of Flanders and the crowning of a second, his brother Henry, the emperor Henry wrote to Pope Innocent III (1198–1216) explaining that the Templars and Hospitallers in his council agreed that the conquest of Constantinople by Latin Christians would produce unity in Christendom and help the war effort against the Muslims in the

Plate 2. The courtyard of the Hospital's compound at Acre. Photographer: Howard Smithline. Courtesy Israel Antiquities Authority.

Holy Land.[7] The military orders of the Temple, the Hospital of St John and the Teutonic Order were given land within the conquered territory (called 'Romania'), as were other clergy and bishops. In 1210 the Hospitallers also seized the castle of Gardiki in the Pindos mountains from the Latin bishop to whom it had been granted in the wake of the conquest, and refused to return it despite the bishop's appeal to Pope Innocent III. In general, however, it appears that the military orders and the Latin clergy preferred not to become involved in military activity in 'Romania'; at least, there is no record of their having done so. Although the bishops, clergy and military orders were not obliged to perform garrison duty, they were expected to provide military aid to the lay princes, as if they were secular knights. The fact that land was being taken back from the Templars indicates that they were not always prepared to do this.

The Hospitallers' military role during the Fifth Crusade (1217–21) is much better chronicled. The Hospitallers gave military advice and took part in military expeditions and the fortification of a castle. They used their ships to attack

[7] Innocent III, 'Registers', *Patrologiae Cursus Completus, Series Latina*, ed. J. P. Migne, 217 vols and 4 vols of indices (Paris, 1834–64), 215, col. 708, year 8, no. 131.

Damietta (Dumyat) from the river with a siege ladder – with fatal results when their siege ladder broke. They had a stonethrower (a *perrière*), and a trebuchet, which were set up on the riverbank opposite Damietta to bombard the city walls. With the Templars, they covered the Christians' final retreat.[8] Despite their activity, however, both they and the Templars were the subject of hostile rumours during the siege of Damietta, to the effect that they were deliberately impeding the siege. Pope Honorius III (1216–27) wrote in their defence, stressing the Orders' immense expenses during the siege, without which the army would not have been able to remain at Damietta. He wrote:

> Our beloved sons the brothers of the Hospital and the knighthood of the Temple have been outstanding among all the Christians in the world, standing as defenders of the orthodox Christian faith, their hearts inflamed with the fire of the Holy Spirit, because they continually fight the Lord's battles to receive the martyr's crown; and because they also become for Christ's sake the servants of the poor, pressing on with the service of hospitality and unwearyingly exercising works of piety.[9]

The Hospitallers again came under criticism alongside the Templars during the Egyptian campaign of King Louis IX of France (1249–50). If the Latin Christians could conquer Egypt they could then hold the Holy Land securely. In February 1250 Louis's forces, having captured Damietta, advanced on Mansurah. The count of Artois was leading a detachment, with Templars and Hospitallers and some English knights under William Longespee. The count wished to attack Mansurah; the military orders and William advised against it. According to the English contemporary chronicler Matthew Paris (died 1259), who seems to have been informed of events by someone close to William, the count then accused William of cowardice and the military orders of treachery towards Christendom.

> Oh ancient treachery of the Temple! Oh old sedition of the Hospitallers! Oh fraud long-concealed, now you burst out openly into our midst. This is what we have predicted and foreseen for a long time, and it was truly predicted, that this whole eastern land would have been captured long ago if our forces had not been impeded by the fraud of the Temple and the Hospital and of others who claim to be religious . . . For the Templars fear and the Hospitallers and their accomplices are afraid that if the land is subdued to the Christian faith their dominion, which they feed with ample revenues, will expire.

[8] Oliver Scholasticus, 'Historia Damiatina', in *Die Schriften des Kölner Domscholasters, späteren Bischofs von Paderborn und Kardinalbischofs von S. Sabina*, ed. H. Hoogeweg (Tübingen, 1894), pp. 166–8, 176, 179–80, 199–200, 214–17, 271–3; 'Fragmentum de captione Damiatae', in *Quinti Belli Sacri Scriptores Minores*, ed. Reinhold Röhricht, Société de l'Orient Latin (Geneva, 1879), pp. 167–202: here pp. 177, 187–9.

[9] *Cartulaire*, no. 1633.

The Templars and Hospitallers, horrified by these accusations, replied together:

> For what purpose, O noble count, did we receive the religious habit? Surely not to overturn the Church of Christ and to lose our souls through plotting treachery? Far be it from us, far be it from us, no, far be it from every Christian![10]

Despite the reasonings of William Longespee, the military orders then ordered the attack, if only to defend their honour against the count of Artois's accusations. The result was the utter defeat of the Christians. The count and William Longespee were killed, with almost all the brothers of the military orders; only three Templars and four Hospitallers escaped.

Matthew Paris's account was obviously written for full dramatic effect, but the essentials are agreed by other contemporary sources. The continual activity of the military orders in the crusades won them admiration from Christian and Muslim alike, but, because they were widely regarded as unbeatable, when the Christians did suffer defeat or failed to make progress the obvious group to blame was the military orders. The Orders, however, did not help their own situation by becoming embroiled in the political disputes in the crusader states during the thirteenth century, which sometimes led to them being at war with each other.

In particular, the Hospitallers and Templars became involved on opposite sides of the succession crisis in the principality of Antioch in the first decade of the thirteenth century. Following the death of Prince Bohemond III in 1201, the Templars supported the claim of Bohemond III's second son, Bohemond of Tripoli, while the Hospitallers supported Raymond-Rupen, Bohemond III's grandson by his eldest son Raymond. Raymond had married Alice, niece of King Leon of Cilician Armenia, but had died in 1197. Cilician Armenia was an independent Christian state in southern Asia Minor; its people were Armenian Christians, not Roman Catholics like the western Europeans. Its prince, Leon, had won recognition as king from the chancellor of the Roman emperor Henry VI and the papal legate in 1198, and was now planning to unite Cilician Armenia and the principality of Antioch under the person of Raymond-Rupen, who was his own heir. Raymond-Rupen had been recognised as heir to Antioch by the papal legate, but in 1201 he was not yet five years old, and therefore an Armenian regency would be necessary. However, the population of the city of Antioch was not prepared to submit to Armenian domination, and supported the claim of Bohemond of Tripoli to be prince.

By the beginning of the thirteenth century the Hospitallers had extensive landholdings in the county of Tripoli and in the principality of Antioch, in which they held virtually independent status. They had held some land in Cilician Armenia since the mid-twelfth century. The Order was clearly anxious

[10] Matthew Paris, *Chronica Majora*, ed. H. R. Luard, 7 vols Rolls Series 57 (London, 1872–85), 5, pp. 149–50.

to extend its landholdings and influence in northern Syria. In the first disturbances after the death of Bohemond III, the Hospitallers seem to have supported Bohemond of Tripoli as his heir. However, by 1205 they were beginning to show sympathy for the claim of Raymond-Rupen, and in 1208–9 they assisted Leon of Armenia against Bohemond of Tripoli's Muslim allies. Certainly Raymond-Rupen had the better claim to Antioch in terms of strict primogeniture (inheritance of the eldest son), but this was not yet established as the invariable rule of inheritance in Europe, where in England, for example, in 1199 the youngest son of King Henry II of England (John) inherited the throne instead of the grandson of Henry II by John's elder brother Geoffrey (Arthur of Brittany). The inheritance of a child could be disastrous in a war-torn area such as the principality of Antioch. Possibly legal considerations swung the Hospitallers to support the Armenian cause; but political and territorial considerations were probably more important.

Raymond-Rupen granted the Hospitallers various territories in the principality of Antioch in 1207. In 1210 Leon of Armenia gave them territories and privileges in south-western Armenia which gave them freedom in making war and peace on the Muslims, and allowed them to keep all booty. Leon seems to have intended the Hospitallers' territories to form a frontier zone to the west of his kingdom, like their quasi-independent marches in the county of Tripoli and the principality of Antioch.

Supported by the Hospitallers – who even lent him money for the marriage of his daughter Rita to King John of Jerusalem early in 1214 – Leon went from strength to strength. In 1216 Raymond-Rupen won control of the principality of Antioch. However, his success was short-lived. He quarrelled with Leon and alienated many of his supporters. In 1219 Bohemond of Tripoli recovered Antioch by conspiracy. Following Leon's death in the same year, the Hospitallers supported Raymond-Rupen's attempt to claim the Cilician throne, but he was defeated, captured, and died in prison. The Hospitallers continued to curry favour with the ruling party in Armenia at the expense of their relations with the princes of Antioch, which remained poor.

The Hospitallers' involvement in the political crisis in the north of the crusader states demonstrated how territorial and political interests could conflict with the interests of Christendom as a whole. In their support of the military efforts of Leon and Raymond-Rupen against Bohemond of Tripoli, the Hospitallers were using resources which had been given to them for the defence of Christendom and the care of the poor. The Hospitallers could have argued that it was in the best interests of Christendom to bolster the power of Cilician Armenia rather than to support the Latin Christian Bohemond. Yet many Latin Christians in the principality of Antioch – including the Templars – did not agree with them, and the Hospitallers' continued disputes with the princes of Antioch undermined the military strength of the principality.

The Hospital also became involved in the succession problems in the kingdom of Jerusalem during this period (see figure 2). In 1225 Isabel, daughter of Marie de Montferrat and John de Brienne, queen and king of the kingdom of Jerusalem, married the emperor Frederick II of Hohenstaufen (1197–1250). Frederick took over the title and role of king of Jerusalem. He did not go to the kingdom of Jerusalem himself until 1228, by which time Isabel was dead, and his authority was only that of regent for their baby son Conrad. He was under sentence of excommunication, as Pope Gregory IX (1227–41) had excommunicated him for failing to set out on crusade by the date on which he had vowed to do so. The people of the kingdom of Jerusalem were in a difficult position; on the one hand they should honour and respect Frederick as emperor and as regent for their king, and on the other they could not associate with him as an excommunicate. The Teutonic Order co-operated with Frederick and attempted to assist him; the Orders of the Temple and Hospital tried to assist his military effort while not associating with him as a man. Frederick's treaty with the Egyptian sultan al-Kāmil in February 1229 recovered Jerusalem peacefully, but was unacceptable to the Christians of the kingdom of Jerusalem because they were not permitted to refortify the city, or to assist the county of Tripoli and principality of Antioch if they were attacked by the Muslims. Frederick made a pilgrimage to Jerusalem, where he held a ceremonial crown-wearing in the Church of the Holy Sepulchre. The Hospital and Temple promised their help in refortifying the city, but Frederick had no such plans. He returned to Acre, from where contemporaries reported that he tried to take the Templars' fortress of Castle Pilgrim by force. He failed, and left the country.

Despite the problems of the emperor's crusade, the Templars and Hospitallers tried to adhere to the truce. The fact that the emperor had also confiscated their property in Sicily under his mortmain regulations led the pope, Gregory IX, to attempt a *quid pro quo*: the Orders would do all they could to protect Christendom and uphold the truce, but Frederick must return their Sicilian properties, which were essential to them. In fact there is no positive evidence that Frederick ever returned the properties of the Hospital and Temple in Sicily, but by 1239 diplomatic relations between the Hospital and Frederick had been restored. During the crusades of Theobald, count of Champagne and king of Navarre, and Earl Richard of Cornwall, 1239–42, the Hospitallers supported the emperor's policy of making peace with Egypt and maintaining war against Damascus. The Templars, the Italian communes and many of the barons of the kingdom of Jerusalem supported the opposite policy. In 1242 the two sides came to blows.

In 1242 Conrad (died 1254), son of Isabel II of Jerusalem, wrote to the people in the East that he was now fourteen and therefore of age. As he had no intention of coming in person to govern his kingdom, he wished to appoint his own regent, Richard Filangieri. However, according to the customs of the kingdom of Jerusalem, the regent should have been his nearest relative in the kingdom: Alice of Champagne, queen of Cyprus and her husband Ralph de Coeuvres. The powerful Ibelin family expected to act on their behalf in return for their support.

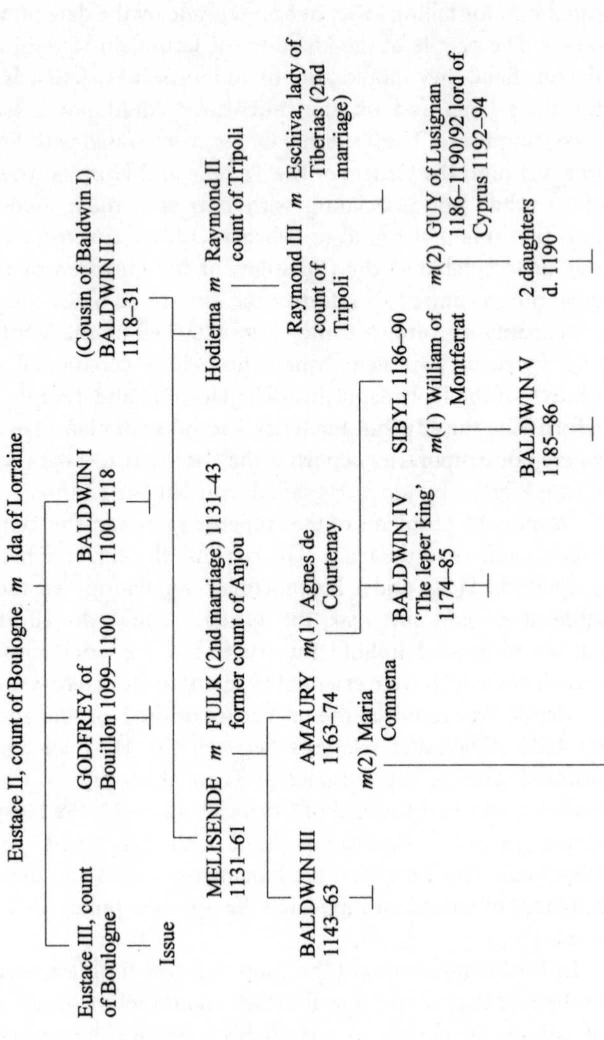

Eustace II, count of Boulogne m Ida of Lorraine
Eustace III, count of Boulogne
Issue
GODFREY of Bouillon 1099–1100
BALDWIN I 1100–1118
(Cousin of Baldwin I) BALDWIN II 1118–31
MELISENDE 1131–61
m
FULK (2nd marriage) 1131–43 former count of Anjou
Hodierna m Raymond II count of Tripoli
Raymond III count of Tripoli
m
Eschiva, lady of Tiberias (2nd marriage)
BALDWIN III 1143–63
AMAURY 1163–74
m(1) Agnes de Courtenay
m(2) Maria Comnena
BALDWIN IV 'The leper king' 1174–85
SIBYL 1186–90
m(1) William of Montferrat
m(2) GUY of Lusignan 1186–1190/92 lord of Cyprus 1192–94
BALDWIN V 1185–86
2 daughters d. 1190

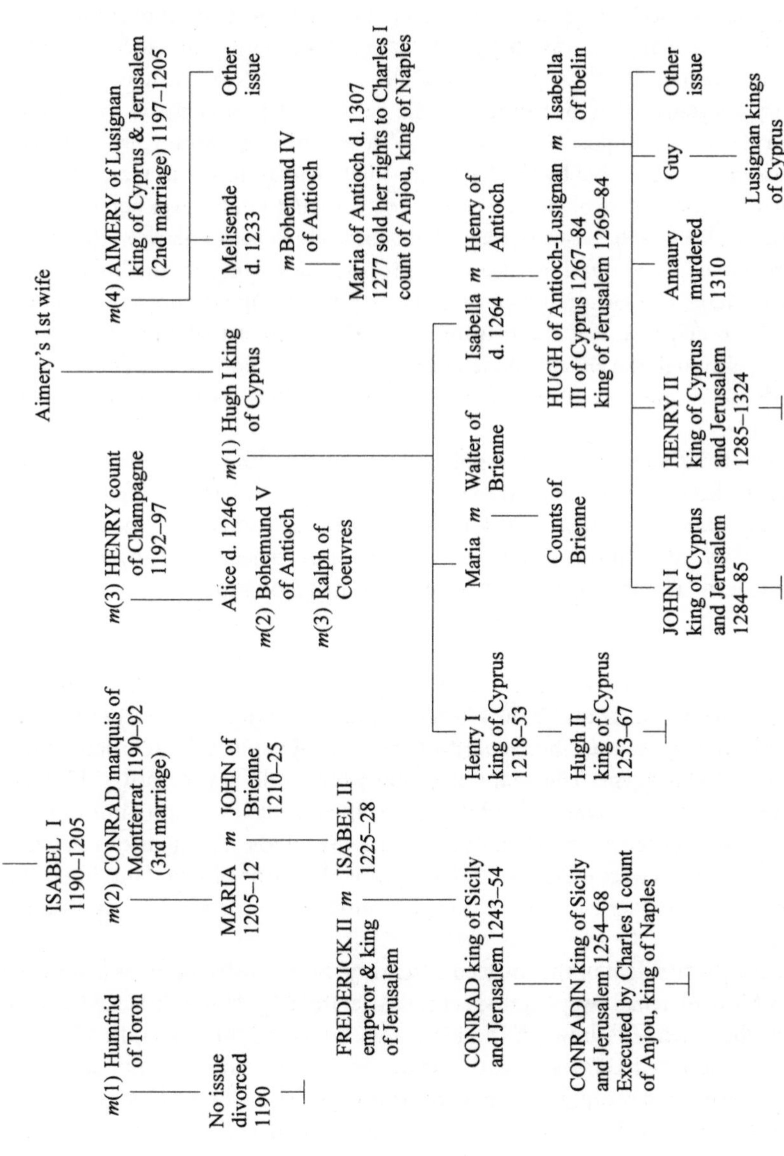

Fig. 2. Family tree of the rulers of Jerusalem, 1099–1291.

Richard Filangieri came from Tyre to Acre in spring 1242 and took refuge in the Hospital of St John, from which he attempted to launch a *coup d'état.* This failed, and the Hospital was besieged by the supporters of Alice and the Ibelins. Richard had to retreat, and the Ibelins took over control of Tyre. This coup by the anti-imperial faction led to a change in foreign policy; the policy of support for Egypt, backed by the Hospital, was changed to support for Damascus. Al-Salih, sultan of Egypt, reacted defensively and called on a troop of Khwarismian Turks for military assistance. The outcome was the capture of Jerusalem by the Khwarismian Turks in August 1244, and the defeat of the Latin Christians and Damascenes at La Forbie by the Egyptian–Khwarismian forces in October 1244.

The Hospital was involved in a completely different kind of war between 1256 and 1258. This was the so-called war of St Sabas, which began between the Italian communes of Genoa and Venice over property belonging to the abbey of St Sabas in Acre. The Hospital supported Genoa; the Templars supported Venice. There is no evidence that the two military orders were actually involved in the fighting, although the episode added to their reputation for rivalry. The Genoese were defeated and driven out of Acre; the Hospitallers were again left on the losing side.

The Hospital's involvement in political upheavals of this kind led to criticism in western Europe, but it is hard to see how it could have been avoided. The lack of strong central authority in the kingdom of Jerusalem after 1225 meant that all those parties with military power had to share in the defence and government of the kingdom. The military orders were foremost among these.

□

Between 1260 and 1291 the situation in the Middle East was characterised by renewed Muslim unity under the Mamluks and Christian retreat. In 1250 a coup in Egypt by the Mamluk bodyguard of the Ayyubid sultan, Turanshah, ended Ayyubid rule in Egypt. The Mamluks, who would rule Egypt until 1517, were elite Turkish slaves, trained as soldiers from their youth, with no family ties to cause the sort of feuds which had divided the Ayyubids. The divisions between the Muslim states were ended in 1260 following the battle of 'Ayn Jālūt in Galilee in 1260. The crusader states were then surrounded by a determined and united enemy.

During the first half of the thirteenth century the Mongols, nomads from what is now Mongolia, had swept across central Asia. In 1240–41 they attacked eastern Europe, but then withdrew. In the 1250s they advanced into Syria. In 1259 and 1260 they captured Damascus and Aleppo, while the prince of Antioch had to come to terms and recognise Mongol overlordship. The Mongols had never been defeated in the field, and it seemed that the crusader states and Egypt were doomed. In 1260 the Mamluk sultan of Egypt, Kitbuqa, marched north to meet the Mongol army. He asked the Latin Christians for assistance; but they preferred a stance of 'benevolent neutrality' and awaited results, expecting the Mamluks to be decimated as so many armies had been before. But Kitbuqa was triumphant; he defeated the Mongols at ʿAyn Jālūt in Galilee. This victory saved both the crusader states and Egypt from the Mongols, but also enabled the Mamluks to take over Aleppo and Damascus, which had previously resisted them. The crusader states were now surrounded, and over the next three decades the Mamluk generals drove the Latin Christians out of Syria and Palestine.

The kingdom of Jerusalem, recently divided by fierce political disputes over the inheritance to the kingdom and still without a king present in the realm, was ill-equipped to meet this new danger. An additional problem was the failing wealth of the kingdom. Fighting between the Italian communes of Genoa and Venice disrupted trade. In addition, the Mongol invasions had disrupted the traditional trans-Asian trade routes, which had hitherto passed through Syria and Palestine. During the 1240s and 1250s these trade routes moved further north, out of the war zone, and by the 1260s they were passing through the Black Sea, while the ports of Syria and Palestine declined in importance.

The Mamluk sultan Rukn al-Dīn Baibars Bunduqdārī launched his great offensive against the crusader states in January 1265. He captured Caesarea, Haifa, Toron and the Hospitaller castle of Arsūf, which the Order had acquired from its lord only a few years before. His successes prompted an outcry of despair from the Templar poet Ricaut Bonomel in his poem *I're dolors*:

> At the first assault, they conquered Caesarea
> And the strong castle of Arsuf was taken by force.
> Alas! Lord God, and what was their fate,
> All those knights, all those sergeants, all those townsfolk
>   Who were within the walls of Arsuf?
>   Alas! The kingdom of Syria
> Has lost so much, if one may speak the truth
> It will never recover again.[11]

He fiercely criticised papal policy, which had led popes to promote crusades against the Hohenstaufen in Sicily, while leaving the Holy Land to be overrun by the Muslims.

The following year it was the turn of the Templars. Baibars attacked Cilician Armenia in the north, and captured the Templar castle of Safed in Galilee, as well as taking Ramla and Lydda. In 1268 Jaffa and Antioch fell to Baibars, as well as the Templar castle of Beaufort. In the same year Hugh Revel, the master of the Hospital (1258–77), wrote to Ferrand des Barres, prior of St Gilles and the leading official of the Order in Europe, that he should not be surprised if he was forced to trouble him with repeated requests for financial aid.

> The tiny number of Christians who are on this side of the sea are unable to resist the indescribable power of the Saracens. Even the city

[11] Old Provençal text and French translation in Antoine de Bastard, 'La colère et la douleur d'un templier en Terre Sainte, *I're dolors s'es dins mon cor asseza*', *Revue des Langues Romaines*, 81 (1974), 333–73. English translation by the author.

> of Acre cannot be fortified as it ought to be by all the Christians everywhere on this side of the sea. In any case, the Christians are so stupified at the immense damage which they have received and which they are receiving every day, that they can provide no remedy of defence. Look how this year the town and castle of Jaffa were captured in one hour, and the castle of Caesarea which was so strong could not sustain the sultan's attack for two days, and Safed, about which the Templars boasted so much, could not defend itself for more than sixteen days. The castle of Beaufort, which was so strong, and which was believed able to hold out for a year, was captured within four days; similarly, the noble city of Antioch was captured on the fourth assault. . . . However, the place which put up the most resistence to the sultan's attack was Arsuf, which sustained an attack for forty days, although it was reckoned to be rather weak.[12]

In 1271 the Hospitallers' castle of Crac des Chevaliers in the county of Tripoli fell to Baibars, as did the Templars' castle of Chastel Blanc. Baibars died in 1277, but his successors carried on his offensive. In 1284 the Hospitallers' castle of Marqab, which even Saladin had not attempted to attack, came under siege from Sultan Qalawūn. The Muslim historian Abū' l-Fidā described the course of the siege:

> The sultan al-Malek el-Mansūr Qalawūn came at the head of the army of Egypt and laid siege to Marqab. This place was of an elevation and strength such that none of the sultan's predecessors had dreamt of attacking it. When the army had begun its attacks against Marqab and placed several catapults in battery, large and small, the miners began to sap the walls. The besieged, seeing their ramparts cut into, asked to capitulate, and the sultan, who wished to take the place in a good condition, came to an agreement with them. Yes, if Marqab had been taken by storm and its walls had been damaged, there would have been a lot of trouble to restore them. The Franks had permission to leave with all that they could carry, not including their arms. The sultan's flags were then hung on the walls of Marqab. This happened on Friday 15 May 1284, at the eighth hour. On this memorable day were avenged the evils caused by the house of the Hospitallers, and the brightness of day replaced the shadows. On the sultan's order, the people of Marqab were escorted to the place of safety that they had chosen.[13]

Improvement in Muslim siege techniques since the late twelfth century made it possible for Qalawūn to achieve what his predecessors had not even dreamt of. He was assisted by the weakness of his enemies; not only were the crusader states suffering financial hardship due to the decline in trade, but the dispute over the succession to the throne of the kingdom of Jerusalem continued. After the death

[12] *Cartulaire*, 4, no. 3308.

[13] Abū' l-Fidā, 'Annals', in *Recueil des Historiens des Croisades: Historiens Orientaux*, 5 vols (Paris, 1872–1906), 1, p. 158, with French translation.

of Conradin in 1268 the crown was disputed between King Hugh III of Cyprus (1267–84) and Maria of Antioch. Legally, Maria had the better claim, but Hugh had more resources. In 1277, however, Maria sold her claim to Charles I of Anjou (younger brother of Louis IX of France) king of Naples and Sicily, and relative of William of Beaujeu, master of the Temple from 1273. Charles sent his representative to Acre to rule in his name. Hugh of Cyprus found that he was unable to enforce his authority in Acre and returned to Cyprus. The kingdom was divided between supporters of Charles (including the Templars) and supporters of Hugh of Cyprus (including the Hospitallers).

The situation was not resolved until after Charles of Anjou's death in 1285. Even the master of the Temple then agreed to recognise the king of Cyprus as king of Jerusalem, and in 1286 Henry II of Cyprus (1285–1324) was crowned in Acre as Henry I of Jerusalem. By this time there was little territory remaining to the Latin Christians in the Middle East. Tripoli fell to Sultan Qalawūn in 1289. Qalawūn's death in 1290 brought only a brief breathing space; on 6 April 1291 his successor al-Ashraf Khalil attacked Acre.

The siege lasted over a month. The Muslims began their final assault on 18 May. Contemporary writers described the final battle in the city streets. The military orders were generally praised: the Teutonic Order fought to the last man, the Templar master William de Beaujeu was killed in action. Several commentators on the last battle judged that his death was the final blow which sealed the fate of the crusader kingdom of Jerusalem; if only he had not died, the city could still have been saved. Those of the population of the city who could escape fled to the port to seek ships. The military orders assisted with the evacuation. The master of the Hospital, John de Villiers, wrote from his sickbed in Cyprus to William de Villaret, prior of St Gilles, describing the last dreadful hours:

> They [the Muslims] entered the city on all sides early in the morning and in very great force. We and our convent resisted them at St Anthony's Gate, where there were so many Saracens that one could not count them. Nevertheless we drove them back three times as far as the Cursed Tower. And in that action and others where the brothers of our convent fought in defence of the city and their lives and country, we lost little by little all the convent of our Order, which is so much to be praised and which is close to Holy Church, and which then met its end. Among them our dear friend Brother Matthew de Clermont our Marshal lay dead. He was noble and doughty and wise in arms. May God be gracious to him! On that same day the Master of the Temple also died of a mortal wound from a javelin. God have mercy on his soul!
>
> I myself on that same day was stricken nearly to death by a lance between the shoulders, a wound which has made the writing of this letter a very difficult task. Meanwhile a great crowd of Saracens were entering the city on all sides, by land and by sea, moving along the

Plate 3. The castle of Marqab. Photo copyright: Denys Pringle.

> walls, which were all pierced and broken, until they came to our shelters. Our sergeants, lads and mercenaries and the crusaders and others gave up all hope and fled towards the ships, throwing down their arms and armour. We and our brothers, the greatest number of whom were wounded to death or gravely injured, resisted them as long as we could, God knows. And as some of us were lying as if we were half-dead and collapsing before our enemies, our sergeants and our household boys came and carried me, mortally wounded, and our other brothers away at great danger to themselves. And thus I and some of our brothers escaped, as it pleased God, most of whom were wounded and battered without hope of cure, and we were taken to the island of Cyprus. On the day that this letter was written we were still there, in great sadness of heart, prisoners of overwhelming sorrow.[14]

Some commentators criticised the master and brothers of the Hospital for escaping, believing that they should have laid down their lives for the Christian cause. Hence John de Villiers was anxious to stress that he had intended to die in

[14] *Cartulaire*, 4, no. 4157; translated by Edwin James King, *The Knights Hospitallers in the Holy Land* (London, 1931), pp. 301–2 (amended).

Plate 4. Marqab: the chapel. Photo copyright: Denys Pringle.

the last stand, and would have done so if God had not intervened by allowing his servants to carry his dying body to safety. Brother Matthew de Claremont the marshal was praised by all for his self-sacrifice and courage in the last battle; he had died surrounded by the enemy, crushed by sheer weight of numbers, as a true knight of Christ.

This marked the final fall of Syria and Palestine to the Muslims. The remaining Latin Christian fortresses surrendered over the next few months. The last outpost, the Templars' garrison on the island of Arwad (also known as Arados or Ruad, off the coast from Tortosa/Tartūs), was captured by the Mamluk sultan in 1302 or 1303. The Teutonic Order moved its headquarters to Venice, half-way between its centres of operation in north-eastern Europe and the Middle East; the Templars and Hospitallers set up their headquarters on Cyprus. Western Europe put forward various crusading plans. The pope called provincial church synods for early 1292 to discuss how the Holy Land could be recovered: one of the points for debate was whether the military orders should be united into one Order. No one called for the abolition of the military orders, but their future was unclear.

Like the Teutonic Order, the Templars and Hospital also had military commitments elsewhere, especially in the Iberian peninsula, which meant that they were still valuable to Christendom even though they had obviously failed in their first task of defending the holy places and pilgrims to the holy places. In 1149 the Order had been given the important fortress of Amposta by Ramón Berenguer IV, ruler of Aragon and count of Barcelona (1137–62), 'for the propagation of the Christian faith and religion and to crush and confound the Moorish people'. In 1194 Sancho I of Portugal (1185–1211) gave the prior of the Hospital in Portugal land on the River Tagus where a castle could be built. In 1157 Ramón Berenguer IV gave them – 'for the propagation of the holy faith and religion of Christianity' – various territories, some still to be conquered, and promised them one tenth of lands which he conquered without foreign aid; although his successors did not keep to this undertaking, nor give the Order all that he had promised. Similar gifts were given to the Order of the Temple. Clearly the rulers of the Iberian peninsula saw the military orders as valuable in their territorial-religious wars against the Muslims. In particular, the Hospital became very close to the royal house of Aragon: Sancha, queen of Alfonso II of Aragon, founded a house for Hospitaller sisters and brothers at Sigena in 1187, which received its own rule. Peter II, king of Aragon (1196–1213), chose to be buried there.[15] His son James I (1213–76) wrote of the prior of Amposta, Hugh of Forcalquier:

> I had made this Lord Hugh of Forcalquier Master of the Hospital in my dominions, after asking leave of the Grand Master beyond the seas. He was a man whom I loved much, and he loved me.[16]

James' esteem for Hugh of Forcalquier was such that he forgave Hugh for arriving too late for the conquest of Majorca, and gave the Hospital a share of the newly conquered land as if the brothers had been present in his forces.

Although the military orders' forces in the Iberian peninsula were not large and kings were able to prosecute their wars without them, they were clearly significant. The Orders were worth controlling. Their attraction was that they were not involved in the political disputes of the peninsula, and they did not owe loyalty to any secular ruler. In practice, in the Iberian peninsula this meant that they owed loyalty only to the relevant monarch. They gave sensible and well-informed military advice; they could usually be relied upon to turn up with their forces on the day and place given. They were always ready to go into the field, and would not break off a campaign to go home and get in the harvest, for example. However, the kings of the Iberian peninsula were anxious that the military orders should remain under their control; they did not want them to become too powerful.

Unlike the Teutonic Order and even, briefly, the Templars, the Hospital did not become involved in the crusading campaigns in north-eastern Europe. They had been endowed with property in eastern Europe since the mid-twelfth century, but this was to assist their activities in the Holy Land and/or to

[15] *Cartulaire*, no. 987.

[16] *The Chronicle of James I of Aragon*, trans. John Forster (London, 1883), ch. 95, p. 183.

Plate 5. The Hospitallers' castle of Espluga Calva, Lleida (Lérida), Spain. Photo copyright: Juan Fuguet Sans.

encourage colonisation rather than to defend the country against non-Christians. The Hospital did provide forces in Poland and Hungary to fight the invading Mongols in 1241, but this was in their capacity as landholders, as it was the obligation of all landholders to help to defend the kingdom.

In 1247 King Béla IV of Hungary (1235–70) came to an agreement with Rembald, grand commander of the Hospital of Jerusalem. He gave the Hospital extensive territories in Little Wallachia, which the Hospital undertook to colonise. The Hospital would provide a hundred armed brothers to fight invading pagans, including Bulgars, or fifty brothers to defend royal castles against invading Christians, or sixty to fight the Mongols. The Hospital was not given independent status, as in the county of Tripoli, but its role in the defence of the frontiers of Hungary would be significant. However, there is no evidence that this agreement was ever put into effect.[17]

It is likely that the Hospitallers' military obligations in the Holy Land by 1247 made it impossible for them to provide the armed forces which Béla required. Likewise, the kings of Aragon were complaining by the late thirteenth century

[17] *Cartulaire*, no. 2445.

that the military orders were not providing sufficient troops. The Order's financial problems in the East, described by the Master Hugh Revel in his letter of 1268 to Ferrand des Barres, were exacerbated by military commitments elsewhere. It was partly for this reason that the Hospitallers did not get involved in the wars in Europe against heretics, and tried not to get involved in wars against other Christians. As Hugh Revel explained in his letter, when Brother Philip d'Egly of the Hospital led Hospitallers against the supporters of the Hohenstaufen in Sicily, the Sicilians attacked the Hospitallers' houses and cut down their orchards and vineyards. The Order simply could not afford to commit itself to warfare outside its own particular vocation.

3

The Hospitallers on Rhodes, 1306–1522

AFTER THE loss of Acre, the Hospitallers and Templars set up their headquarters on the island of Cyprus. They did not intend to remain there, but hoped to return to the Holy Land as soon as possible. Cyprus was conveniently situated for use as a bridgehead for attacks on the Syrian and Palestinian coastline, and could serve as a mustering point for a new crusade.

The loss of the kingdom of Jerusalem cannot have been a great surprise to anyone. Since the 1240s charters written in the kingdom had included terms to cover the eventuality of the territorial losses to the Muslims, and it is clear that the Hospitallers had been moving valuable materials such as charters and relics to Cyprus and the West in the 1280s. Nevertheless, the final loss of Acre was a serious psychological blow, as well as costing the lives of many Christians and much financial loss in terms of buildings and equipment.

The military orders could not now afford to appear idle. As defenders of the Holy Land, they were first in line to be blamed for its loss. Contemporaries were particularly critical of the rivalry between the military orders, which was believed to have undermined the defence of Acre. Pope Nicholas IV alluded to these criticisms when he instructed the provincial Church councils which were to meet in February 1292 to discuss whether the military orders should be united as part of the strategy for the recovery of the Holy Land. Unsurprisingly, every provincial council declared that they should. The provincial council of Canterbury, for example, declared that the joint properties of the Templars and Hospitallers 'which were originally conferred on them by the generosity of kings and princes and others in pious devotion for the defence of the Holy Land' should be able to support thousands of strong men as a permanent garrison in the Holy Land. As they had failed to do this, the true value of their revenues should be assessed, the number of warriors who could be supported from this calculated, and they should be forced to maintain that number of warriors in the Holy Land forever. Such declarations reflected a belief in the West, also expressed at the second Council of Lyons in 1274, that the military orders were inefficient in their use of their resources.

Pope Nicholas IV, however, died in March 1292, before the conciliar decisions reached him. The plans to unify the military orders did not proceed; but the question remained open. The Majorcan mystic and writer Ramon Llull wrote in his novel *Blanquerna*, composed in the 1280s, that the pope should unify the Templars and Hospitallers to create one military order which could convert the Muslims by arms and by debate. He developed this proposal further in his treatise *Liber de Fine*, in which he set out a detailed plan for the recovery of the Holy Land. The new united military order should be called 'the Order of the Holy Spirit' and its master would become king of Jerusalem when the land was recovered. In this he was echoing the situation in Prussia, where the Teutonic Order ruled the country which it had conquered for Christ. After 1309, it would also be the situation on Rhodes under the Hospitallers.

Other authors of crusading plans also urged the unification of the military orders into one force. In June 1306, Pope Clement V (1305–14) asked the masters of the Hospital and Temple to produce a plan for a crusade and to comment on the proposal to unify the two Orders. The master of the Temple, James de Molay, hotly opposed the union of the two Orders, which he said operated more efficiently and more effectively on behalf of Christendom as two Orders rather than as one. The comments of the master of the Hospital, Fulk de Villaret, on the question of unification have not survived, but in his crusade proposal he assumed that the military orders of the Hospital, Temple and the Teutonic Order would continue to operate as independent entities.

Aside from such plans, the popes encouraged the military orders to remain active in the East – but now at sea, rather than on land. In January 1292 Nicholas IV authorised the masters of the Temple and Hospital to use their ships to assist the Armenians. He had already ordered them to build up a fleet, and had given money to the Hospitallers to assist them in this. The Hospitallers had been allied with the rulers of Armenia since the early thirteenth century, and had sent aid in the past; this was not, then, a new policy, but a development of old policies. It is clear that the military orders had had ships commanded by members of the Orders for at least the past century, not only for carrying money, warriors, horses and equipment to the East but also for transporting pilgrims. There is some indication of Templar ships being used for military purposes before 1291. It was only after the loss of Acre, however, that the military orders' naval forces began to become significant. The office of admiral is first found mentioned in the Hospital's records in 1299.

In 1294 the master of the Temple, James de Molay, travelled to the West to see the pope, Boniface VIII, and discuss the possibilities of a new crusade, but the Hospitallers were not involved. They had their own problems in the East. John de Villiers, the master who had evacuated Acre, died some time between 20 October 1293 and 30 September 1294. His successor was Odo de Pins, whose administration aroused so much resentment within the Order that in 1295 a group of senior Hospitallers presented the pope with a plan for reforming the Order. This proposed that one brother from each major regional division of the Order (called *langues*, that is, 'tongues', because they were based on linguistic differences) should be appointed as a 'diffinitor', making seven 'diffinitors' in all. The master would act as 'diffinitor' for his own tongue. These seven would then govern the Order, decisions being made on the basis of a majority vote. In theory, the master was already bound to take into account the opinions of the convent when making decisions, but this reform would ensure that their opinions actually counted. The pope did not enforce this reform, and Odo de Pins died shortly afterwards – apparently of old age.

His successor, William de Villaret, was soon causing anxiety for a different reason; he appeared intent on transferring the central government of the Order to the West. He remained in the West, held a general chapter at Marseilles in 1297, and continued in the West until in 1300 he proposed to hold another general chapter at Avignon. The convent, or central headquarters of the Order, which was still on Cyprus, protested vigorously. The brothers objected that statute and custom held that general chapters should be held in the East. The master's continued refusal to come out to the East implied that the purpose of the Order had been turned away from the Holy Land, towards a more general religious purpose. In 1300 the general chapter passed a statute stating that so long as the Order was based in Cyprus, general chapters should be held in Limassol, its Cypriot base. William de Villaret was eventually persuaded to go out to the East, confirming the Order's continued dedication to the recovery of the Holy Land.

Meanwhile, a hope of assistance in the recovery of the Holy Land had appeared in the person of the Mongol Ilkhan of Persia. The Mongols had initially been regarded with dread on their eruption into eastern Europe in 1241, but by 1280 they were regarded as potential converts to Christianity and allies against the Muslims. In late 1299 the Ilkhan Ghazan, who was in fact a recent Muslim convert, wrote to King Henry II of Cyprus and the masters of the Hospital and Temple asking for their aid in his current campaign against the Mamluks in Palestine. The Ilkhan succeeded in overrunning Palestine, but by the time that the Christian forces arrived he had withdrawn to Persia. His forces remained in the Holy Land until May 1300, when they were driven out by the Mamluks. The Christians, led by the king of Cyprus and the masters of the Military Orders, hoped to join the Ilkhan's forces later in the year, but the Ilkhan did not arrive until February 1301, by which time the Christian forces had raided the Syrian coast and withdrawn. The Templars retained a base on Arwad island off Tortosa until October 1302 or 1303 when the island was recaptured by the Mamluks.

The Hospitallers were also involved in the defence of Cilician Armenia against the Mamluks. The master William de Villaret led two large expeditions there between 1300 and 1305. Apart from the Order's long connections with the kingdom, it could be used as a base from which to launch attacks into Syria. Yet it was also vulnerable to attack on its frontiers from Mamluks or Mongols. Cyprus was more secure, but the Order was unable to mobilise resources there to support the large forces necessary for advances into the Holy Land. King Henry II was suspicious of the power and influence of the military orders, and restricted their operations on the island. The Orders also became involved in the political upheavals of the kingdom. In 1306 King Henry's brother Amaury seized power with the support of the Templars, although not of the Hospitallers, who endeavoured to remain as neutral mediators. Clearly the political instability of Cyprus made it unsuitable as a long-term military base.

The Hospital also faced problems in the West. Although it had papal support, war between England and France, and the restrictions placed on the Hospital by King James II of Aragon, hindered the transfer of resources from its western estates. The convent and chapter of the Order had confirmed their dedication to the defence of Christendom in the East, but the Hospital now needed to take steps to put this into action. Only through being seen to be active could the Order convince Christians in western Europe that it was still effective in holy war and would make good use of donations and resources in Christ's cause. This would necessarily involve finding a new base from which to operate, where the Order would have some freedom of action away from secular politics.

The island of Rhodes lies some 250 miles or 400 km west and a little to the north of Cyprus. It is a fertile island and is strategically placed as a base for military action against the coast of Asia Minor or naval control of the Aegean Sea. In the early fourteenth century the Byzantines, Venetians, Genoese and Turks had interests in it. Technically in the late thirteenth century Rhodes was a possession of the Byzantine emperor, but in the face of Turkish raiding and Venetian aggression the emperor Michael VIII had in around 1278 appointed the Genoese corsair Giovanni dello Cavo as governor of Rhodes. Cavo had been an admiral of the imperial fleet since 1275, and was hence well-known and trusted by the emperor. Yet he was unable to hold off the Turcoman pirates, and was forced to cede eastern Rhodes to them. Cavo soon vanished from the scene. By 1304 the emperor had given influence on the island to another Genoese corsair, Andrea Moresco, and his brother Ludovico, although it is not clear exactly what authority they exercised.

In 1305 Fulk de Villaret succeeded his late uncle William de Villaret as master of the Hospital. His crusading scheme, mentioned above, was presented to Pope Clement V in the following year, demonstrating his dedication to the recovery of the holy places. In 1306 he was approached by Vignolo dei Vignoli, uncle of Andrea and Ludovico Moresco, and a landowner on Rhodes. Vignolo wanted the aid of the Hospital to gain control of Rhodes or of part of Rhodes for himself. On 27 May 1306 Vignolo and Fulk made a pact by which the Hospital would rule the islands of Rhodes, Kos and Leros, while Vignolo would retain his manor at Lardos on Rhodes and another manor, and would have extensive rights over all the islands except Rhodes. Other incomes acquired would be divided, one third to Vignolo and two thirds to the Hospital. It is unclear whether Vignolo intended to keep to this treaty once Rhodes had been conquered, or whether he planned to take Rhodes for himself. Yet the initial attack in June 1306, which included only two galleys and four other craft provided by the Hospitallers, was not able to conquer Rhodes immediately.

While the attackers settled down to besiege the town of Rhodes, Fulk de Villaret set off for Europe in late 1306 or spring 1307, where he hoped to get support for his Rhodian campaign from Pope Clement V in the form of a crusade. In March 1307 Fulk sent envoys to the Byzantine emperor Andronicus II requesting that he grant Rhodes to him in fief in return for his homage and military service, but was refused. Andronicus sent an expedition in April 1307 to raise the siege of Rhodes town, but the Byzantines themselves suffered heavy losses. In June the pope excommunicated Andronicus, and in September granted Rhodes to the Order on the basis that it had been captured from Byzantine schismatics and Turkish infidels. The pope also made a monetary contribution to the costs of conquest. A second Byzantine relief expedition in summer 1308 also failed to raise the siege of Rhodes town, and the town eventually surrendered to the Hospital, probably on 15 August 1309. The Order went on to annex the rest of the Dodecanese islands.

Meanwhile, Fulk de Villaret's crusade was being prepared in the West. Villaret had hoped for a major expedition or *passagium generale*, but because of lack of support from western European monarchs this was reduced to a small preparatory expedition or *passagium particulare* which was to strengthen Latin Christian defences in the East in preparation for the larger campaign which would follow. In the event the larger campaign never materialised, and the small expedition, which set out in spring 1310, was used by Fulk to consolidate the Hospitallers' conquest of Rhodes. The Genoese claims to the island were set aside, although the manor of Lardos remained in the hands of Vignolo and his family.

While the Hospitallers were showing themselves to be active and effective in holy war, the Templars were undergoing investigation on various charges of misconduct and heresy. The charges were clearly trumped-up, but the Templars' failure to raise a new crusade in the West had left them politically vulnerable to attack. On 22 March 1312 at the Council of Vienne, the Order of the Temple was dissolved by the pope on the grounds that although the charges against it were unproven the Order had been brought into too much disrepute to continue. On 2 May 1312 in the bull *Ad providam* the pope granted the Hospital all the properties of the dissolved Order of the Temple, except those in the Iberian peninsula.

It is unclear why the pope favoured the Hospital in this way while at the same time dissolving the Order of the Temple and investigating the Teutonic Order in Livonia for heresy and witchcraft. It is clear that western rulers and clergy were critical of the Hospital. King Philip IV of France had refused to support the Hospital's crusade because he claimed that French brothers in the Order were not given sufficient influence. King James II of Aragon was very anxious about the great power the Hospital would gain in Aragon if it acquired the Templars' castles there; he wanted the Hospitallers' assistance for his campaigns in Granada; and he accused the Hospitallers of attacking the Byzantine Christians when they should be attacking Muslims. The French clergy demanded that the Hospitallers' ecclesiastical privileges be withdrawn and that the Order be reformed root and branch before it received any of the Templars' property. The representatives at the Council of Vienne accused the Hospitallers of evils and vices and of spending their wealth on fair halls and palaces instead of on the war against the infidel. Complaints against the Hospital were not new: accusations of pride and greed had been voiced from the second half of the twelfth century. The pope, however, later stated that he had given the Hospitallers the Templars' property because the Hospitallers seemed to be the best military order to carry on holy war in the East. By transferring the Templars' property to the Hospital, he was in effect achieving the unification of the two Orders, as had been suggested by Pope Nicholas IV and the provincial councils of 1292. In August 1312 King Philip IV of France agreed to the Hospitallers receiving the Templars' lands; perhaps he hoped that the Hospitallers would assist his brother Charles of Valois in his projected crusade against Constantinople. In any case Philip and the pope agreed that the transfer of the Templars' property to the Hospitallers was conditional upon the reform of the Order, and the Hospital was to pay Philip compensation for his expenses in the trial of the Templars. In fact, the Order was not reformed, and it is unlikely that all the money was ever paid.

Despite papal support and enormous expense, met by heavy borrowing from the Italian banking houses, the Hospitallers never received all the Templars' lands to which they were entitled. In England and Germany in particular, many were taken back by the descendants of the original donors, possibly to be donated to different religious orders, while others were sequestered by rulers and granted out to their favourites. Even when the lands were handed over, the Hospital also inherited debts and obligations attached to them, which involved it in further expense. In addition, the Order had incurred great costs in the conquest of Rhodes, and further expenses were incurred in the early years of its occupation in defending it against the Greeks and the Turks. The Order's difficulties were further compounded by, firstly, increasing demands on the national loyalties of brothers in the western provinces, as kings increasingly took them from their international duties to serve as generals and as advisers; and secondly by its own internal problems, which resulted in increasing interference in the Order's affairs by the papacy.

The Order's relations with European monarchs will be discussed in chapter five, but its internal problems should be discussed at this point. In 1317, the brothers at Rhodes attempted to assassinate the master, Fulk de Villaret. He escaped to the fortress at Lindos, where the brothers besieged him. They then deposed him and elected Brother Maurice de Pagnac to replace him. Pope John XXII (1316–34) summoned the two masters to Avignon, where he confirmed Villaret as master, apparently on the understanding that Villaret would resign. Villaret did resign, and the pope made him prior of Capua for life (although in the event he did not remain there, first transfering to Rome and then becoming a simple brother with an annual pension). The pope then appointed Brother Hélion de Villeneuve, prior of Provence, as the new master.[1]

Although the pope insisted that he had acted without prejudice to the rights of the Hospital, a precedent had been set for papal interference in the Order's affairs. The most infamous case of this occurred in September 1377, when Pope Gregory XI (1370–78) appointed his general Juan Fernández de Heredia, castellan of Amposta and therefore the Hospital's leading official in Aragon, as grand master of the Hospital (1377–96). On the convent's protests, the pope promised again that this appointment would not prejudice the Order's rights to elect its own master. Yet the fact was that the Order had become closely tied to papal policy, and hence was restricted in its actions. For instance, Pope Benedict XII (1334–42) would not allow the Hospitallers to launch a major expedition because this would mean their withdrawing their deposits from the Florentine banking houses that were also the papal bankers, which would lead to the collapse of those banking houses and papal bankruptcy. Some of the greatest problems for the Hospital occurred between 1378 to 1417, when the Great Schism divided Latin Christendom between two or more popes. The grand master and convent of the Hospital remained obedient to the pope in Avignon, but the fact that some tongues of the Order (such as the English tongue) belonged to kingdoms which were obedient to the pope in Rome could in theory have caused internal problems in the Order, although the evidence indicates that these were not severe. More damaging was the privilege assumed by the indigent schismatic papacy of granting out the Order's benefices to papal protégées – a convenient way for popes who lacked resources to reward their supporters. Innocent VII (pope at Rome, 1404–6) conferred on Nicholas Orsini, prior of Venice, a series of vacant commanderies dependant on the priory of Venice – without reference to the grand master and convent, who were obedient to the Avignon pope; Benedict XIII (pope at Avignon, 1394–1423) assumed the right of directly appointing commanders and priors of the Order in Spain, Catalonia and France; in 1411 John XXIII (pope at Pisa, 1410–15) conferred commanderies and priories in the priory of Venice as he pleased, and in 1412 conferred the grand commandery of Cyprus on an illegitimate son of King Janus of Cyprus (1398–1432). The brothers protested vehemently, stating that their properties had been given to them by the faithful for the work of hospitality and to fight the infidel, not to reward courtiers; if justice was not done, they would return to their commanderies and no longer defend Rhodes. Pope John cancelled his bestowal of the grand commandery, but the Hospital had to reimburse the king of Cyprus for the 6000 florins he had paid the pope for the gift.[2]

[1] Anthony Luttrell, 'Notes on Foulques de Villaret, Master of the Hospital, 1305–1319', in *Guillaume de Villaret 1er Recteur du Comtat Venaissin 1274, Grand Maître de l'Ordre des Hospitaliers de Saint-Jean de Jérusalem, Chypre 1296* (Paris, 1985), 73–90; reprinted in his *The Hospitallers of Rhodes and their Mediterranean World* (Aldershot, 1992), ch. 4.

[2] Joseph Delaville le Roulx, *Les Hospitaliers à Rhodes (1310–1421)* (Paris, 1913, reprinted London, 1974), pp. 323–5.

Partly as a result of these problems, the Order's military policy on Rhodes was never as strongly focussed or as effective as it had been in the Holy Land. The Hospitallers became involved in various naval leagues, in the occupation of Smyrna (Izmir), and the building of fortifications on the coast of Asia Minor; for a while they had plans to acquire property in 'Romania', the Frankish states in Greece and the Aegean, and they played a role in the various crusading expeditions which came out into the Balkans. But they had no clear-cut, overriding, long-term plan which could inspire western Christendom, and they followed the lead of crusading leaders and of popes rather than taking the initiative themselves. Many contemporaries accused them of not doing enough for Christendom, such as Geoffrey of Paris in his *Le Dit des Paternostres* of around 1320, Marino Sanudo Torsello in his crusading treatise *Liber Secretorum Fidelium Crucis* written for Pope John XXII in 1321, the monk John Dupin in his *Les Melancholies,* written between 1323 and 1340, and Emmanuele Piloti in his crusading treatise written and revised between 1420 and 1441. In fairness to the Hospitallers, however, it is clear that crusading itself lacked direction in the fourteenth century. Following the loss of the Holy Land, it took several decades for western European crusading to reorientate from the desire to recover Jerusalem to the need to defend Greek Constantinople, 'Romania' and the Balkans from the Ottoman Turks. The Hospitallers had to adapt from being primarily a land-based fighting force to being primarily a naval force. Their obvious allies in their naval campaigns were the Italian naval cities of Venice and Genoa, but these cities were often at war with each other and both wished to trade with the Muslims as well as expanding their own political influence in the East. They also allied with the Muslims against the Hospital. Meanwhile, in the West, France and England were engaged in a long conflict now known as the 'Hundred Years War', which both sides promoted as a holy national war. This formed a distraction for warriors seeking honour and glory in warfare, for while the crusade was more glorious than war in western Europe, warriors were less likely to travel to the East to fight the Muslims when they were needed by their king at home.

The Order's forces on Rhodes were never large. Anthony Luttrell has calculated that there were never more than 250 or 300 brothers in the East after 1306 (knights and sergeants), although the Order also employed mercenaries and the local people on Rhodes were used as militias when the island came under attack. In 1522 there were apparently only 290 knight-brothers involved in the defence of the island, with donats or associate members of the Order, brother sergeants, town militia and mercenaries making up a total of perhaps 7,500. The Order could usually muster only three or four galleys for naval campaigns. It was therefore limited in its military action: it provided a highly skilled, professional support force, but could hardly initiate and carry through large campaigns alone. Most of the brothers of the Order remained on the Order's estates in Europe, although many of these estates were not administered by the brothers themselves but were entrusted to managers or leased out. Other brothers were in royal or papal service, and tended to put the interests of their western employer above those of their Order. The western resources of the Order were not always efficiently administered and collected, and the portion of income due to be paid to the convent on Rhodes as 'responsion' was not always paid. In addition, western rulers made increasing financial demands on the Order.

The expenses of maintaining the Order had risen considerably since the twelfth century, while income did not rise in comparison. The fourteenth century saw a decline in the climate of Europe, which became cooler and wetter. Agricultural yields therefore fell. The economic and commercial expansion which had characterised the twelfth and thirteenth centuries, with new land being brought under the plough, rapid town growth and the expansion of trade, now slowed. The Hospitallers had previously benefited from many pious donations, large and small, given in alms by the faithful for the good of their souls; but by the mid-thirteenth century donations to all religious orders had declined. As political stability increased, the social need for such donations was reduced; and patterns of piety had also shifted from the institutional to the personal. Pious donors were now less likely to give to a large, institutionalised order, and more likely to give to a local hospice where the local poor and sick were cared for, or to endow a chantry chapel for the benefit of their own soul alone. Added to these changes, legislation enacted by kings across Europe during the thirteenth century forbad donations in 'mortmain' – that is, to a religious corporation – without royal licence. This was to prevent lands which owed dues to the king from passing into the hands of institutions which did not pay these dues, thereby causing royal revenues to be lost. All these changes reduced the income enjoyed by all religious orders by the early fourteenth century.

At the same time, the Hospital's expenses had risen. The Hospital was a military order, and its leading members (although only a small proportion of the whole) were knights. By the early fourteenth century, western European knighthood was becoming a social caste, bestowing high social status on those who held it, but available only to those of wealth and nobility. This was a far cry from the twelfth century, when many knights were simply mounted warriors who need not have great social status. By the early fourteenth century the knight was a member of the nobility, even if only the lower nobility, and required high quality armour, weapons and horses. He would expect the Order to provide a suitable level of income to maintain his status. Brothers were not supposed to hold the command (and receive the income) of more than one commandery or priory, but this regulation was clearly flouted. In 1371 Pope Gregory XI allowed brothers to occupy two or three commanderies providing that they were all part of the same provincial priory (administrative division) and the total of their responsions – the portion of income due to the convent on Rhodes each year – was under 200 florins. He stated that he did this because of mortality through plague, losses and upheaval in war which had reduced the income from commanderies so far that one commandery no longer produced sufficient income to support a commander or keep up hospitality.[3] Certainly the plague, and the Anglo-French and Anglo-Scottish wars (for instance), had reduced the income from certain commanderies, but the expenses of maintaining a commander had also risen.

Not only had individual expenses increased, but also the cost of warfare itself. The fourteenth century saw significant advances in weaponry and armour. Plate armour began to make its appearance early in the century, on shoulders, elbows and knees; by the middle of the century cloth-covered armour, small plates of armour enclosed in a padded jacket, had become the standard garment of the footsoldier. Plate armour and cloth-covered armour were far more effective against a lance-thrust than chain mail, but also required more skill and higher-quality steel in manufacture. In the 1320s the first guns are recorded in Europe. While initially they may have added little to artillery in physical impact on the enemy, the noise and smoke that they produced certainly had an effect on morale. As cannon and hand-held guns improved during the course of the century, they became more powerful and effective than the traditional stone-throwers and bows, prompting changes in defensive architecture. Yet they were also far more expensive to manufacture and operate. The Hospital's military expenses therefore increased while its income declined. The result was that the Order resorted to borrowing, and then incurred the additional problem of servicing its debts.

The papacy was well aware of the Order's problems, and attempted to support the Order through them – not always in a productive manner. In 1343 Clement VI (1342–52) wrote to the Order instructing it to reform itself and show greater commitment to holy war against the Muslims; if it did not do so, he would take back the Templars' lands and use them to found a new military order. He accused the brothers of misusing their money on fine living, ignoring the fact that his predecessor Benedict XII had refused to allow the Hospitallers to use their funds in Florentine banks for a crusade, and that the Hospitallers had lost those deposits when the Florentine banks became bankrupt in the 1340s, so that they now lacked the money to launch a crusade. In 1355 Pope Innocent VI (1352–62) repeated Clement's instructions and threats more strongly: rather than living comfortably on Rhodes, the Hospitallers should move to the mainland of Asia Minor where they could get to grips with the Turks. He hinted that the brothers were being accused of sexual depravity, and compared them unfavourably with the Teutonic Order which had been founded long after the Hospital but was now surpassing it in wealth and in success. In 1373 Pope Gregory XI initiated an inquest of the Hospital's possessions and income, to establish the extent of the Order's actual resources and how much it could put into military action. The results indicated that the situation of the Order was every bit as bad as the Order had claimed: apart from the poor economic state of

[3] Delaville le Roulx, *Hospitaliers à Rhodes*, p. 163, note 7; Valetta, National Library of Malta, Archives of Malta, 12, no. 20.

the Order's estates, most of the brothers in the West were middle-aged priests, not fighting men who could be sent out to wage war on the Muslims. The pope nevertheless continued to urge the Order to greater efforts. In fairness to the pope, he was aware of the urgency of the situation in the East, where the Ottomans were advancing into Europe, and saw that the Hospital was in the best position to provide effective military force to oppose them – if only it could muster sufficient forces.

Popes could also, however, give much-needed help to the Order in its financial difficulties. In 1433, Pope Eugenius IV (1431–47) asked the Emperor Sigismund (1433–7) to ensure that the Order's officials in the western Empire paid the money that they owed to the convent on Rhodes. In the 1440s he supported the convent's decision to ask for increased payments from their European estates, in the face of the Mamluk threat, and commanded all clergy to help the Order's officials in assessing and collecting the money. In 1467 and 1471 Pope Paul II (1464–71) ordered moratoriums on the interest due on the Order's debts. It was one thing for the pope to order, and another thing to enforce that order; but the good intention was there.

□

With all these problems in mind, the Hospital's military achievements on Rhodes appear more impressive. The Order maintained military activity against, and diplomatic activity with, the Muslims; although the military activity was often at the level of raiding rather than strategic campaigning. The initial conquest of Rhodes was supported by an agreement with local Turks to attack the emir of Menteshe, whose emirate lay opposite Rhodes. The Hospitallers captured a number of Turkish castles on the mainland in 1310–11, and the island of Kos; Kos was lost in 1319, but recovered in around 1336. Turkish demands for tribute in 1318 were met by a naval campaign which wreaked such havoc on the Turks that no further demands were made. In the following years the Hospitallers enjoyed a number of naval victories over the Turks. There were also alliances with, and conflict against, the Orthodox Christian Greeks, who – like the Hospitallers – had Turkish allies. The activities of the Hospitallers against the Turks would, on occasion, indirectly weaken the Christian Greeks by damaging their allies.

The first significant joint crusading activity in the eastern Mediterranean involving the Hospitallers after their capture of Rhodes was the naval league. These leagues were religious enterprises, made up of ships and warriors provided by the Venetians, Genoese, Hospitallers and other Christians, with the aim of fighting the Turks of Asia Minor. The first productive league of this sort was formed in 1333/4: Lesbos (Mitylene) was captured from the Greeks. Another Venetian–Hospitaller league was planned in 1335 and 1336 but was barred by Pope Benedict XII, who refused to allow the Hospitallers to use the money they had on deposit with his Florentine bankers.

In 1344, urged on by the enthusiastic Pope Clement VI, a naval league comprising mainly of Venetian, Cypriot and Hospitaller vessels launched a campaign against the Turks, capturing the important port of Smyrna. The port was retained despite the break-up of the league and the failure of the crusade which followed. The Hospitallers played a major role in the administration of Smyrna. In 1374 Pope Gregory XI entrusted the Hospitallers with sole responsibility for its defence, as other custodians had proven unreliable. It came under Ottoman attack in 1389 and Turks from Smyrna attacked the Hospitallers' islands in the 1390s, but the Hospital held the port of Smyrna until it was captured by Timur the Lame (Tamerlane/Tamberlaine: died 1405), in 1402.

Further plans for a new naval league in the Aegean in 1350 were halted by the outbreak of war between Venice and Genoa. In the 1360s the Hospitallers became involved in Cypriot crusading campaigns in the far eastern Mediterranean. A hundred Hospitallers, four galleys and other vessels accompanied King Peter I of Cyprus (1359–69) in 1365 in his campaign to capture Alexandria, and the Order sent galleys and other vessels to help King Peter's campaigns in 1367. The grand master, Raymond Bérenger, attempted to settle the disputes between the Genoese and Peter II of Cyprus (1369–82) in 1373. When talks broke down and the Genoese attacked Cyprus, the Hospitallers avoided military involvement but tried to mediate. This political crisis was at least partly to blame for the Hospitallers' failure to send a force to help defend Cilician Armenia in 1375 when the kingdom was finally conquered by the Mamluks, but they did give assistance to the messenger sent to Cairo to negotiate with the Mamluk sultan for the release of King Leon VI of Armenia (1374–5), and they welcomed the king on Rhodes when he returned from imprisonment.

The Hospitallers' lack of action in Armenia was also due to increasing commitments in Greece ('Romania') and the Balkans, in response to the growing threat from the Ottoman Turks. The Muslim Ottoman Turks were initially invited into Thrace in 1345 as Byzantine mercenaries; from here they demanded and then captured further territory. In 1354, in alliance with the Genoese, they captured and refortified Gallipoli. The result was that Constantinople was effectively cut off from the West. It was clear that the Ottomans were a serious threat to Christendom.

In 1359 Pope Innocent VI ordered crusade preaching and sent the bishop of Coron, Peter Thomas, as his legate to the eastern Mediterranean. Peter Thomas inspected the fortifications at Smyrna and organised a naval force of Venetians and Hospitallers to proceed to the Dardenelles, where with Byzantine assistance they attacked the Turks' tower at Lampsakos. The tower was captured, but had to be abandoned when the Turks counter-attacked; the Hospitallers covered the crusaders' retreat, as they had done traditionally in the crusades in the Holy Land. After the recapture of Thessalonica and Gallipoli from the Turks, Gregory XI proposed that the Hospitallers be made responsible for their defence, as at Smyrna. This did not come about, but the Hospital did begin to take on other military responsibilities in 'Romania'.

Achaea (also known as the Morea or Peloponnese) had been conquered by western Europeans after 1204, as a result of the Fourth Crusade. By the 1370s the western European lordship was under heavy pressure from Turkish pirates, although it was supported by the Greeks and the Venetians. The overlord, Queen Joanna I of Naples (1343–82), leased it to the Hospitallers for five years from 1376 in return for an annual rent. The Order's commander in the Morea hired two mercenary companies to defend the lordship, but when their contract ended in 1379 the mercenaries set out to carve out territories for themselves.

Pope Gregory XI also pressed the Order to send an expedition to 'Romania'.[4] In late 1377 newly appointed grand master Juan Fernández de Heredia left Naples for the Morea to lead such an expedition. The expedition went north into the territory of Epirus, recapturing Lepanto, which had been recently captured by the Christian Albanians, who were in alliance with the Ottoman Turks. Having secured Lepanto, Heredia marched on Arta, residence of the Albanian prince; but in summer 1378 the army was ambushed and Heredia was captured by the Albanians, who sold him to the Ottomans. He was released within a year on the security of hostages; the Order held an assembly at Valenciennes in February 1380 to discuss how to raise the money for his ransom and to secure the release of the hostages.

The Order still hoped for great things in the Morea, and reinforcements were sent from Rhodes, but the death of Pope Gregory XI in March 1378 and the subsequent election of two popes, Urban VI (1378–89) and Clement VII (1378–94) – beginning the Great Schism – ended hopes of a crusade. Although the Hospitallers' lease of the Morea had not yet expired, the Order withdrew in 1381. The two mercenary companies they had employed continued to wreak havoc in the Morea.

The Order's hopes for expansion into 'Romania' had suffered a severe setback, but were not finished. The Order continued trying to acquire authority in the area, and in 1397 the Despot Theodore gave the Hospital the castle of Corinth, then in 1399–1400 sold the whole Byzantine Despotate of the Morea (that is, the south-eastern Peloponnese) to the Order, and fled into exile in Venice to escape the Turkish advance. His Greek ex-subjects revolted, but were unable to evict the Hospitallers. The Hospitaller presence does seem to have given the Turks pause. In his 1402 peace treaty with the Despot Theodore, Sultan Bayezid I (1389–1403) insisted on the Hospitallers leaving the Morea; but the Hospitallers hung on until 1404. By 1405 they were planning to fortify the island of Tenedos at the mouth of the Dardenelles, a plan ended by Venetian opposition.

In 1422 the Hospitallers declined an invitation from Latins and Greeks in the Peloponnese to become involved in that region again. Yet the Order apparently still had ambitions of finding another base nearer to the centre of the war against the Ottomans. In 1423 it offered to exchange Rhodes for the Venetians' island of Euboea (Negroponte, now Evvoia or Evia), but this came to nothing. In the event, as Latin settlements in the eastern Mediterranean fell

[4] On this, see Delaville le Roulx, *Hospitaliers à Rhodes*, pp. 202–6.

to the Turks, Rhodes was becoming more central, not only militarily but also commercially.

As well as their involvement in Greece, the Hospitallers had also been involved in the Balkans against the Ottomans. By the 1390s the Ottomans, under Bayezid I, were in control of western Anatolia; Bulgaria was conquered in 1393, Thessaly in 1393–4. Prompted by appeals for aid from King Sigismund of Hungary (1387–1437: later emperor of the West), the western European nobility formed a crusade. This was decisively defeated by Bayezid at Nicopolis on the Danube in 1396. The Hospitallers were involved in the campaign, contributing galleys to the naval league which was formed prior to the crusade by the Venetians, the Greek emperor and the Christian princes of Chios and Lesbos (Mitylene). This fleet, consisting of 44 ships and under Venetian command, sailed past Constantinople and across the mouth of the Danube, but not, apparently, up the river. However, some Hospitallers reached the main crusading army, although historians are not in agreement as to their identities or their role in the battle. Philibert de Naillac, grand-master elect (1396–1421), assisted King Sigismund to escape down the Danube after the battle.[5] The Hospitallers assisted in the ransoming of the French nobles captured at Nicopolis. They also provided two galleys for a naval force raised by Marshal Boucicaut, one of those who had been captured and ransomed, which in 1399 attacked the Turks in the area of the Bosporus. In 1403 the Hospitallers also took part in Boucicaut's attacks on the coast of Asia Minor and Syria, for which Rhodes was used as a base.

In July 1402 the victory of Timur the Lame at Ankara halted the Ottoman advance in Europe. Timur, a nomadic conqueror from Central Asia who had set up his capital at Samarkand, had led his forces east in 1399 to punish the Mamluks and Ottomans for encroaching on his territories. He had sacked Aleppo, Baghdad and Damascus before turning his attention to the Ottomans. The Hospitallers strengthened Smyrna's defences and encouraged Turkish opposition to Timur, but Smyrna fell and was dismantled. The Ottoman sultan Bayezid I died in Timur's prison. Fear of Timur united Christians and Muslims in a common cause, and the Greeks and Latin Christians made an alliance with Bayezid's son Suleiman against Timur if he should invade Europe. According to this, the Hospitallers would receive Salona, north of Athens. However, Timur withdrew in 1403.

Having lost Smyrna, the Hospitallers resorted to diplomacy to gain ground. Following their involvement in Boucicaut's raids, they negotiated a treaty with the young Mamluk sultan Faraj which presented them as protectors of all pilgrims and maintainers of the holy places: allowing them to maintain hospitals at Jerusalem and Ramla for pilgrims to Jerusalem, to make repairs to the Holy Sepulchre and other holy places, to maintain a consul at Damietta and to pass through the sultan's lands without paying tribute (among other terms). In the event, after the withdrawal of Boucicaut the sultan refused to ratify the treaty and

[5] Ibid., pp. 235–7.

the Franciscan friars continued to play the leading role in care of pilgrims in Jerusalem. At the same time, the Hospitallers were negotiating with the various Turkish princes of Asia Minor, playing one off against the other. In the course of these negotiations they acquired land at Bodrum from Mehmed, son of Bayezid I and brother of Suleiman, and in 1407/8 began to build a castle here, utilising stones from the ruined Mausoleum of Halicarnassos, one of the seven ancient wonders of the world.

Bodrum was obviously a replacement for Smyrna, although its site was less strategic. Nevertheless it enabled the Hospital to claim that it still had a foothold in Asia Minor and that it was still actively campaigning against the Turks at a time when it was actually involved in little military activity. The castle could be conveniently supplied from Kos, held by the Hospital, while being difficult to reach from the mainland. The Hospital supported the building of the fortress with a vigorous publicity campaign in the West to raise funds. Yet at this period the Hospital as an Order seemed anxious to avoid direct confrontation with the Turks in the field. Its alliances with Turkish leaders made action problematic: the Order preferred to play the Turks off against each other, rather than resort to military action.

In preference to direct action by the Order, individual brothers were arming their own ships to attack Muslim ships that were the enemies of the Hospital, sharing out the booty between themselves. They had to obtain a licence from the Order to carry on these naval attacks against infidels: the licences included the right to attack infidels with whom the Hospital had truces, provided that the attack occurred outside the area of the truce. This licensed piracy, the *corso*, remained a major feature of the Hospital's war against the infidel for the rest of its military existence.

The balance of power ended in 1421 with the death of the leading players: the grand master Philibert de Naillac, the Ottoman sultan Mehmed (1413–21) and the emir Ilyas of Menteshe. The new Ottoman sultan Murad II (1421–51) went on to the offensive, subduing the quasi-independent Turkish emirates which bordered the Aegean, and threatening the Hospital. He also waged war on Venice, besieged Constantinople and captured Thessalonica (1430), but then went to campaign in the Balkans. Meanwhile, the Mamluk sultan Barsbay invaded Cyprus in 1426, sacked the Hospitaller commandery at Kolossi and captured King Janus. The Order contributed towards his ransom. The Hospital made a truce with the Mamluks in 1428, and relations returned to peace for a time; but the Order was anxious, and made active preparations to withstand a Mamluk attack on Rhodes. It was clear to the Order that its survival depended largely on the rivalry between the Mamluks and the Ottomans, and its own ability to play one side off against the other. Its houses in Europe also had financial problems: the Anglo-French wars had damaged its properties and revenues in France, while the Hussite wars in Bohemia had inflicted severe damage on the priory of Poland.

The Hospital appealed to European rulers for assistance, and Philip the Good, duke of Burgundy, responded. Philip was the son of John the Fearless, duke of Burgundy, who had been a leader of the Nicopolis crusade, during which he had been captured and ransomed. Himself born in the year of Nicopolis, Philip had been brought up in the crusading tradition and had long taken an active interest in the Holy Land and in crusading. In 1438 he began to put together a fleet, possibly intended for the Portuguese crusade against Tangier, to aid Constantinople. But after the events of 1440, it was sent to protect Rhodes.

In 1440 a fleet of eighteen Mamluk galleys was dispatched from Egypt by Sultan Jakmak (or Chakmak) az-Zāhir. As the fleet approached Rhodes, the Order's fleet went out to meet it: the Order's fleet consisted of seven or eight galleys, four other ships and six lesser vessels. In the battle which followed the Muslims used cannon and Greek fire and then moved off towards the Turkish coast. The Hospitallers attacked again, drawing off only at nightfall. The Muslims attacked Kos and departed with many Christian prisoners.

In May 1441 the duke of Burgundy's fleet, under the command of Geoffrey de Thoisy, was seen off at Sluis by the duke. It sailed to Rhodes, where it was based throughout 1442, harassing Muslim shipping and coastal settlements. It then returned to Villefranche, near Nice, to refit. By spring 1444 it was again in action off the African coast, among the Greek islands, and defending Rhodes.

In 1444 a second Mamluk fleet reached Rhodes and besieged the town of Rhodes for forty days until it was beaten off by the Hospitallers with the help of the Burgundian fleet and some Catalan and other ships. On this occasion the Hospitallers had four great ships and eight galleys. The Mamluks may have had Genoese assistance. One of the Catalans present, Francesc Ferrer, wrote a verse report of the siege, *Romanç de la Armada del Soldà contra Rodes*. According to this the Mamluk fleet arrived on the 10 August and landed in the north-west of the island at 'Malpas' (a common term for a narrow, dangerous road through difficult country). The Muslims set up camp near the fortress and attacked the grand master's bulwark. They concentrated on the weakest part of the walls, St Antony's gate (to the west of the fortress) and on the St Nicholas tower, which guarded the Mandraki harbour to the north of the town. Meanwhile the elderly, the women and the children in the town ran to the churches and prayed to the Blessed Virgin Mary for help. A sortie by the French and Catalans drove the Mamluks out of the port, to the joy of the defenders. However, the enemy regrouped and returned. The great assault came on 10 September. The author describes the battle between the Catalans and the Mamluks at the bulwark of the Virgin Mary. The Mamluks were defeated, and they withdrew.

After the Mamluk withdrawal, the Burgundian fleet sailed up to Constantinople and the Black Sea to attack the Ottomans, while the Hospitallers negotiated with the Mamluk sultan. Peace had been made by early 1446, but the Hospital did not trust the Mamluk sultan to keep it and also feared Ottoman attack. The general chapter of 1445 raised the responsions due from the European commanderies in order to meet the costs of defending Rhodes; but the commanders in the West appealed to the pope against the general chapter.

The situation in the East became critical with the capture of Constantinople by the Ottoman sultan Mehmed II (1451–81) in May 1453. The sultan's interests, however, were focussed on the Balkans. Rather than attack Rhodes, he demanded tribute from the Order, which the brothers refused to pay. The sultan retaliated with naval raids on Rhodes and the surrounding islands in 1455–7. In 1455 he sacked the islands of Symi, Nisyros and Kos, and the town of Archangelos on Rhodes; in 1456 he captured Chios. However, he did not attempt to hold the islands and withdrew. In 1462 the Hospital agreed to pay an annual 'gift' to the sultan in place of tribute.

Two years later the sultan was again demanding tribute. Clearly a major attack could not be long in coming. Lesbos fell to the Ottomans in 1462; the Venetian possession of Euboea fell in 1470 – the Hospitallers sent two galleys to assist in the defence of the latter. The grand masters concentrated their efforts on fortifying Rhodes town and harbour, reinforcing the fortresses in the countryside and on the neighbouring islands, and issued decrees for the defence of the town and villages.

□

The fortifications of Rhodes town date back to the Hellenistic period. They consist of walls with fortified gates, and a deep dry ditch that surrounds the town on three sides – the fourth side being protected by the sea. The modern visitor may see the excavated remains of the original Hellenistic fortifications overlaid by later Byzantine fortifications, surmounted by the medieval fortifications of the Order of St John. The grand master's palace, in the north-western corner of the old town, was originally the citadel of the town, built by the Byzantines in the seventh century. It was built into the Collachium, the northern area of the old town which formed a sort of inner fortress within the fortified town. The walls of the citadel and Collachium were repaired and rebuilt by Grand Master Hélion de Villeneuve (1319–46), whose coat-of-arms was built into the wall; Ludolph von Sudheim, who visited Rhodes during his grand-magistracy, referred to the extensive building operations on the walls at this time. The brothers had based themselves within the Collachium, building their Hospital there and their administrative buildings. The local inhabitants were moved out of this area into the main body of the town. This, too, was fortified, although not as strongly.

One source refers to Grand Master Déodat de Gozon (1346–53) repairing the Hellenistic harbour mole and building a sea wall. Construction work continued under grand masters Heredia and Philibert de Naillac. In particular, Philibert de Naillac constructed a magnificent tower at the north-western side of the entrance to the harbour, from which a chain extended across the harbour mouth to a tower on the opposite side. When an enemy fleet approached, this chain could be raised to block entrance to the harbour. The tower was destroyed in an earthquake in the nineteenth century, but the position of the chain may still be seen.

So far as is known, the brothers used local craftsmen and master-masons for

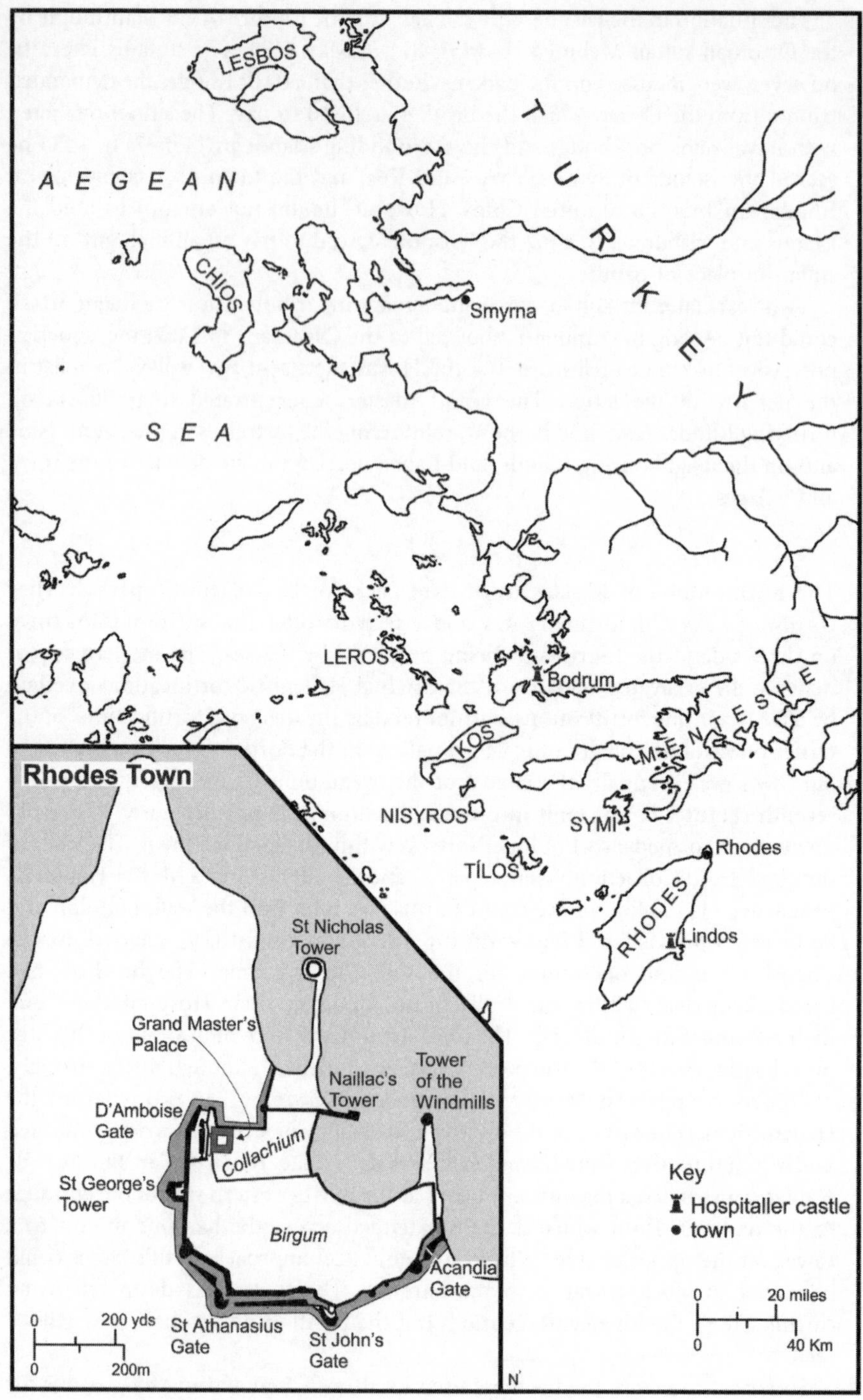

Fig. 3. Map of Rhodes and its environs during Hospitaller rule

their building works, but after the siege of 1480 they also brought in engineers from Europe, who were familiar with the latest techniques of defence. Improvements and developments in the fortifications were constant throughout the brothers' occupation of Rhodes, but after 1450 they became more intensive. In 1464–67, Grand Master Pedro Raimondo Zacosta (1461–67) reconstructed the St Nicholas tower at the north-east side of the entrance of Mandraki harbour, to the north of the old town. This tower, controlling the entrance to the main harbour of Rhodes, had been a focus of attack in 1444 and was to play a decisive role again in the siege of 1480. Around the same period the tower of the Windmills (or 'of France') was built opposite Naillac's tower at the north-east tip of the main harbour. The responsibility for the defence of the walls of Rhodes was assigned to the individual 'tongues' of the Order. Measures were also taken to protect the countryside. In 1474 Grand Master Giovanni Batista degli Orsini (1467–76) and in 1479 Grand Master Pierre d'Aubusson (1476–1503) issued decrees designating the fortresses where the inhabitants of the countryside were to take refuge during an enemy attack.

Western Europe was far from indifferent to the plight of Christendom in the East. The fall of Constantinople had prompted many promises of assistance, although translating these into action proved more problematic. The crusade planned by Pope Pius II (1458–64) was halted by the pope's death, but a naval league, initiated by Pope Paul II (1464–71) and supported by Pope Sixtus IV (1471–84), set off in 1471–2 combining the forces of Venice, the pope, Aragon, Naples and the Hospital – the last contributed two galleys. The league attacked and sacked Smyrna, and raided along the south coast of Asia Minor. It also negotiated an alliance with Uzun Hasan, the Turkoman ruler of eastern Anatolia, against the Ottoman Turks. Yet nothing came of this, as Uzun Hasan was defeated in battle in August 1473.

The Hospital also renegotiated its treaty with the Mamluk sultan: the brothers were allowed to travel freely to the Holy Sepulchre and to the monastery of St Catherine in Sinai, but apparently they no longer maintained a hospice in Jerusalem for pilgrims. A commercial treaty was made with the ruler of Tunisia. Prince Jem, one of the sons of Mehmed II and governor of Caria in Menteshe, opened negotiations with the Hospital, and a commercial truce was concluded relating to the waters between Rhodes and the Turkish coast. This could not, however, prevent attack from the Ottoman sultan himself.

Naval raiding began in the winter of 1479–80. In May 1480 an Ottoman fleet landed forces, commanded by Mesih Pasha. Although this was a large army, it represented only a small portion of the sultan's forces, as the sultan was also involved in military operations in the Otranto region of Italy, at Belgrade, on the Lower Danube and on the Persian frontier. The Turks had a force of perhaps ten to fifteen thousand men and brought heavy artillery of cannon and bombards which hurled stones and iron shot. In contrast, there were perhaps 250 warriors of the Hospital in Rhodes, with a militia of around 2,000 from the town and mercenaries, perhaps 3,500 defenders in all. The Turks' initial attack was made on the St Nicholas tower: if this could be captured, it would allow the Turks to bombard the old town from its weakest side, the sea, as well as cutting off the two harbours and thereby prevent the town from being relieved from the sea. The attack lasted through June and July. The Turks also attacked the wall on the south-east side of the town, which was vulnerable because the land on the outer side of the dry ditch is higher than the wall.

Although Turkish bombardments demolished the western side of the St Nicholas tower, Grand Master Aubusson ordered that the defence continue. A night attack was driven back by the brothers' cannon. The Pasha then concentrated his attack on the south of the town. Attempts to persuade the town to surrender with guarantees of retaining lives and property were firmly rejected. On 28 July an assault was made on the south-east side of the town: the Turks succeeded in entering the town, but the grand master led a counter-assault, cut off and killed the Turkish force which had entered the town, and drove the Turks back. The assault was repulsed. John Kay's translation of Guillaume Caoursin's account of the siege states that the Turks fell back when they saw in the sky a vision of the Blessed Virgin Mary, St John the Baptist and a company of martyrs from the Order coming to assist the Christians. In the following century a Turkish historian wrote that the Turks had withdrawn because Mesih Pasha had forbidden plundering and commanded them to preserve the town intact for the sultan; deprived of their reward for their fighting, the Turkish troops had given up. Whether the Turkish morale broke, or whether the desperate determination of the Hospitallers – led by the grand master – and town militia was alone sufficient to drive them back, the Turkish attack failed. The Turkish army withdrew from Rhodes at the beginning of August 1480.

The Hospital publicised in Europe what was depicted as a miraculous victory. Pope Sixtus IV sent his congratulations and authorised the brothers to sell indulgences in Europe to those who contributed towards the rebuilding of their fortifications. The Latin account of the siege by Guillaume Caoursin, vice chancellor of the Order, was printed and between 1481 and 1489 editions were published throughout western Europe, as well as translations into English (by John Kay) and French. This raised the Order's prestige in Europe and encouraged donations; but nevertheless it was left very vulnerable to another attack. The defensibility of the town was further undermined by a succession of earthquakes in 1481. If Mehmed II had attacked in 1481 he would probably have captured Rhodes, but his death, followed by the war between his sons Bayezid II and Jem, prevented immediate assault. Instead, Bayezid made a truce with the Hospital in late 1481, while Jem turned to the Hospitallers for assistance. He arrived in Rhodes in late July 1482 and made a perpetual treaty of peace with Grand Master Aubusson. He then sailed to the West to seek assistance for a war against his brother. The Hospital was authorised to negotiate on his behalf with Bayezid, and a peace treaty was made between the sultan and the Order in December 1482. According to this, the Hospital would keep Jem in the West and prevent western European sovereigns from using him against Bayezid. To demonstrate his debt to the Order in this matter, Bayezid promised an annual payment for Jem's expenses, and sent the Hospital the relic of the right hand of St John the Baptist, patron of the Order. The hand, enclosed in a reliquary, remained one of the Order's most precious relics. During the Second World War it was sent to the Balkans for safety and its location was lost, but has recently been rediscovered in Montenegro.

The affair of Prince Jem thus ensured the Order's safety for as long as he lived – until 1495 – although it did also prompt some criticism of the Order for not doing enough to help him recover his throne. Not only did the Order have a favourable treaty with the Ottoman sultan but it was also able to renew its treaty with the Mamluk sultan Ka'itbey in 1484. Grand Master Aubusson set about restoring and rebuilding the fortifications of Rhodes in order to meet the next Turkish attack, in line with the latest developments in military architecture. The fortifications as we now see them are the result of this rebuilding of the last forty years of the Hospitallers' occupation of the town. The coats-of-arms adorning the walls mark which grand master was responsible for each section of building work.

The walls were greatly thickened and extended and reconstructed at two levels: a lower outer level and a higher inner level. An enemy attempting to scale the walls with a ladder must first mount to the exposed outer level, where they could be raked by gun and cannon fire, before being able to mount an assault on the upper ramparts. The massive St George tower was constructed, commanding the dry ditch on the west side of the town; this was capable of holding out against the enemy even when the town itself had fallen. Outworks at the base of the town wall housed cannon to control the base of the ditch, while cannon were also mounted on the inner walls to cover the lower rampart, the terre-pleins and the far side of the ditch. In an attempt to compensate for the high terrain outside the town, long terre-pleins were built to protect exposed parts of the wall on the south and south east side, where the Turks had concentrated their attack in 1480; these are long fortifications running parallel with the town wall and as high as the town walls. Their walls enclose a hollow space which is filled with earth to form a huge rampart. They have crenellations on the outer side but are open on the inner side, so that an enemy capturing them could be fired on from the inner walls. Between the terre-pleins and the town wall runs a long, narrow inner dry ditch or 'boulevard', open at one end to the main ditch but closed at the other. This would restrict and mislead the enemy who penetrated it; exposed to cannon fire from above and each end, the enemy who attempted to run down the inner ditch would find it concluded at a dead end, with no way out but back into the cannon fire. The town gates were rebuilt, notably the St Anthony gate, where massive outworks and a new gate were constructed by Grand Master Emery d'Amboise (1503–1512) in front of the vulnerable old gate which had been the centre of attack in 1444. The land gates of the town are narrow, barely wide enough for a cart to pass through, with (for instance) a sharp turning to the left,

Plate 6. The late fifteenth- and early sixteenth-century fortifications of Rhodes town: the south side of the city, looking east towards St John's Gate. To the left are the town walls; to the right a massive terre-plein runs parallel to the walls. In 1522 the English tongue was responsible for the defence of this section of the fortifications. Photo copyright: Nigel Nicholson.

to the right and again to the left immediately inside the outer wall. It would be impossible for an attacking enemy to launch a charge through such a gate. The gates were protected by drawbridges and holes from which missiles could be dropped from above.

The expected attack on the death of Jem did not materialise; Sultan Bayezid (1481–1512) was occupied in fighting the Venetians with the support of Naples and Milan, capturing Lepanto in 1499. In 1501 a new naval league was formed, sponsored by Pope Alexander VI (1492–1503). The members were Venice, France, Spain (recently unified under Ferdinand of Aragon and Isabella of Castile, and fresh from the conquest of Muslim Granada, 1492), Portugal, the pope and the Hospital, which provided three galleys, a great ship and a bark, under the command of the admiral of the Order. This set out in 1502 and attacked the Ionian islands, capturing Santa Maura (Leucas). Grand Master Ambusson also sent out a galley which captured many Turkish pirates.

In December 1502 Venice made peace with the Ottoman sultan. For the rest of the decade, the sultan was occupied by rebellion in eastern Anatolia and the political struggle between his five sons. The Hospitallers did not yet fear a major assault from the Ottomans, although piracy and raiding continued. The Mamluks of Egypt were now a declining threat. In 1507 the Hospitallers captured near Kos seven Egyptian ships which were coming to attack Rhodes; they also harried Egyptian commercial shipping. In 1510 the Order's fleet, under the command of Philippe de Villiers de l'Isle Adam and with Andrea do Amaral in command of the galleys, ambushed an Egyptian fleet on its way to the Gulf of Alexandretta (Iskenderun) to load Turkish timber, and defeated it, capturing eleven cargo ships and four battle galleys. This raid was marked by a fierce difference in opinion over strategy between the two commanders, which Amaral won. The Mamluks lacked the naval power to respond with a counter-raid. During the next decade the Hospitallers and Mamluks became allies against the Ottomans.

In 1512 the Ottoman sultan Bayezid II died, imprisoned by his son Selim I (1512–1520). Selim was a warlike and resolute sultan. He conquered eastern Anatolia in 1515–17, defeated the Mamluk sultan Kansawh al-Ghawri in battle at Marj Dabiq, north of Aleppo, in August 1516, occupied Syria and Palestine and then went on to conquer Egypt in January 1517. In these campaigns his naval force was of great help to him, ensuring his supply lines hundreds of miles from his base. The Hospitallers – who had supported Selim's enemies, sent artillery to the Mamluk sultan and still held Prince Jem's son Murad, a potential rival to Selim – were now in the front line, faced with an enemy who controlled the eastern Mediterranean Sea and who had every reason to see them as a menace to be stamped out. Selim's death in 1520 could not save the Order. Selim's young son Suleiman, now known as 'the Magnificent' (1520–66), captured Belgrade in 1521. In December 1521 he made a treaty with Venice, to ensure Venetian neutrality in his forthcoming campaign. In spring 1522 he made careful preparations for his attack on Rhodes, which he would lead in person.

As the Hospitallers lost the ensuing siege, and the European sources for the siege emanate directly or indirectly from the Hospitallers, it is difficult to be certain of the details of the siege itself. It appears that the Hospital was hopelessly outnumbered, with around 7,500 persons defending the town against a Turkish force of 200,000 on four hundred ships, and a good deal of heavy artillery. The siege began on 28 July. As in 1480, each of the 'tongues' was responsible for the defence of a section of the wall, although the respective sections of wall were not quite the same as in 1480, reflecting changes in resources of the different tongues. Rather than attacking from the sea, which had wasted their efforts in 1480, the Turks concentrated on the land defences on the south and south-west, which had been vulnerable in 1480 and despite extensive rebuilding were still the most vulnerable part of the town. The Turks mined the bastions and walls, the Hospitallers counter-mined; but despite constant assaults, the Turks were unable to take the town by storm.

The siege continued through August and September. In October a report arrived that help was coming from Naples and Messina, but this did not materialise; while ships which set out from England, Spain and France never reached Rhodes because of bad weather conditions. As it became clear that the enemy intended to stay the winter if necessary (unlike the siege of 1480, which had departed as the winter weather began), morale in the town began to flag. The grand chancellor of the Order, Andrea do Amaral of the tongue of Portugal and Castile, was accused of sending information to the enemy and was tried and hanged. He refused to confess even under torture and it is likely that he was used as a scapegoat. He had been an unsuccessful candidate for the grand magistracy in 1521, when Philippe Villiers de l'Isle-Adam (1521–34) was elected. He was known to be critical of the grand master's defence of the town. His dispute of 1510 with Villiers de l'Isle Adam over strategy hints that the two had long been rivals in the Order. While Bosio is fierce in his condemnation of Amaral, Abbot Vertot – at a safer distance of two centuries – believed that he had been unjustly condemned.[6]

At the end of October the winter rains began, but the siege continued. Suleiman offered peace terms. Grand Master Villiers de l'Isle-Adam refused them. He hoped that help would come from the Pope, Hadrian VI (1522–3) and the emperor Charles V (1519–56), if they succeeded in defeating King Francis I of France (1515–47) in Italy. The sultan then made his proposals to the people of the town, who sent representatives with Archbishop Clement of Rhodes to the grand master and convent to ask them to treat for peace. According to the customs of war, if the town surrendered peacefully the people would be allowed to retain their lives, and might also be allowed to take some of their property with them, whereas if the town fell by storm everyone would be slaughtered. The

[6] Abbé René d'Aubert de Vertot, *Histoire des Chevaliers Hospitaliers de S. Jean de Jerusalem, appellez depuis Chevaliers de Rhodes, et aujourd'hui Chevaliers de Malthe*, 5 vols (Paris, 1726), 3, pp. 252–6, 272–4, 355–62.

grand master called a council of the Order, which voted to treat. While negotiations continued, the assault began again, and on 17 December the bastion of Spain, on the south west side of the town, fell to the Turks. While this was a short section of the defences which could have been recovered, without hope of relief and with resources dwindling the grand master made the decision to save the lives of his brothers and the people rather than to continue what appeared to be a hopeless defence. On 18 December he surrendered the town to the sultan.

The grand master and brothers of the Hospital of St John left Rhodes on 1 January 1523. With them went many Rhodian citizens; but Sultan Jem's son Murad and his family, who had been living in exile on Rhodes, were detained and executed by Suleiman. The brothers took with them their archives and their relics and other treasure. The castle of Kos and the castle of Bodrum were still holding out, but surrendered soon after the evacuation of Rhodes. The brothers went to Crete and thence to Sicily, then on to consult with Pope Hadrian over the future of the Order. There were hopes that the people of Rhodes would rebel and enable the Order to return to the island, but this plot was repressed by the Turks. Instead, after protracted negotiations, in spring 1530 the emperor Charles V ceded the islands of Malta, Gozo and Comino to Grand Master Villiers de l'Isle-Adam, and the Order took up residence on the islands in October. The brothers' mission was to defend the Maltese archipelago and the city of Tripoli on the North African coast (captured by a Spanish crusade in 1510) against the infidel. Geographically they were now far removed from Jerusalem, but their vocation was the same as ever: to defend Christendom against the aggression of Islam. It was still hoped that the conquest of North Africa could lead at last to the recovery of Jerusalem by another route; and with Suleiman repulsed from the gates of Vienna only in the previous year, the forces of Islam were currently a greater direct threat to Europe than at any time since the eighth century.

4

The Hospitallers' Organisation and Religious Life

THE Hospital of St John of Jerusalem is a supranational religious order with a rule which was to be followed by all fully professed members. It appears, however, that in its first centuries of existence it was not as centralised as other supranational religious orders such as the Cistercians or the Templars. In 1216 Pope Honorius III (1216–27) complained that different Hospitallers were bound by different vows, and that Hospitaller observance varied from one area to another. In another letter of 1216 he forbad the brothers to make vows or to keep observances except those laid down by the general chapter of the Order. They should all be 'of one heart and soul in the Lord'. As the thirteenth century progressed the general chapter issued increasing numbers of statutes in an attempt to regulate practice throughout the Order.

It is necessary to remember that although the Hospital's written records indicate certain systems of organisation and certain regulations, in fact the practice may have been a long way from what was laid down. With a multiplicity of houses of different sizes across Europe and in the Middle East, it was not surprising that practices varied, or that the members of houses might feel more loyalty to the secular ruler of the country in which they lived than to the convent of the Order far away in Jerusalem, Acre, Cyprus, Rhodes or Malta. It was a continual problem for the Order to keep all its members focussed on its vocation and moving, so to speak, in the same direction.

The organisation of the Order developed during the twelfth century. The central administration was based in Jerusalem, at the central infirmary of the Order; and it would remain the case throughout the Order's history that wherever the Order's headquarters was it would have its main infirmary. The two went together, so that the primary visible function of the Order was always the care of the sick. The Order was governed by a master (by the early fourteenth century known as the grand master), elected by the central convent, which was located wherever the Order's centre of administration was located – Jerusalem, Acre, Cyprus, Rhodes, Malta. The central Convent consisted of the great officers of the Order, the companions of the master, senior brothers who had been in the Order for over twenty years, and the conventual brothers, which included the brothers-at-arms, and may have included the priest-brothers and serving brothers, although this is not certain. The convent acted in chapter: the chapter was an assembly of members of the Order which acted as a lord's court did in the secular world, judging cases and conducting administrative business. A general chapter of the Order, comprising the senior officials of the Order across the whole of its territories, all the brothers in the East, the master and the convent, met (usually at the central convent) at regular intervals, although – unlike the Cistercian Order – not as often as annually. Between 1324 and 1344 there were seven general chapters; between 1383 and 1420, due to the Great Schism, there were only four general chapters, three held by grand masters of the Avignon obedience in 1383, 1410 and 1420, and one held by the grand master of the Roman obedience, in 1384. After 1421 general chapters were held more frequently, with at least twenty-two held before 1522. This followed a regulation by Grand Master Philibert de Naillac that general chapters should be held every five years, although in fact they were sometimes held in consecutive years, and sometimes six or seven years apart. During the seventeenth century the trend towards the suspension of parliaments in Europe may have influenced the Order, as no general chapter was called between 1631 and 1776.

□

While the master in theory had supreme authority over the Order as an abbot did in a traditional monastery, the convent also had rights. Both had their own seal. The master was bound by the customs and statutes of the Order, and he should consult the convent and the general chapter. While Pope Alexander III found it necessary to spell this out in 1172, it was standard practice among rulers in general that they must observe custom and should consult with their leading officials, and this procedure must have always been the custom within the Order. Alexander did, however, specify certain matters on which the master must take advice, such as the acquisition and fortification of frontier castles.

During the twelfth and thirteenth centuries the general trend in secular government was for increasing specialisation in administration, increasing power for the monarch and resulting pressure from those who had traditionally advised the monarch for their customary rights of influence over government to be safeguarded. This trend can be seen to result in Magna Carta (1215 and reissues) in England, and in the Golden Bull of 1222 in Hungary. Within the Order of the Hospital, it can be seen in various statutes and records of *usances*, or customs, which state that the convent or certain committees of brothers should make certain decisions, rather than the master. In the *usances* it was stated that when the general chapter made appointments to offices, these were to be decided by a committee which did not include the master. The first *usance* recorded states that the master's orders were only to be obeyed if they complied with the usages and customs of the Order. These measures indicate that the brothers were anxious to ensure that the master did not gain too much individual power within the Order.

Nevertheless, this did not prevent masters throughout the middle ages from exercising considerable power and acting outside the customs of the Order if they chose. It has been noted in chapter three that in 1295 the brothers complained to Pope Boniface VIII about the arbitrary actions of Master Odo de Pins, and that in 1317 the brothers on Rhodes attempted to murder Master Fulk de Villaret and then besieged him in Lindos castle, apparently because he had been acting beyond his rights. Master Jean l'Evêque de la Cassière (1572–81) was deposed in 1581 because the brothers resented his moral reforms – removing all the brothers' lady friends out of the city to the villages – while at the same time regarding him as militarily incapable and too old to govern the Order effectively. Deposition was a desperate last resort; in general the brothers did not need to go so far. In February 1379 the general chapter at Rhodes voted to curb the grand master's powers, following the imposition of Pope Gregory XI of his friend Brother Juan Fernández de Heredia, castellan of Amposta, as grand master. Heredia's career at Amposta had seen him enriching himself, his relatives and his illegitimate children at the Order's expense, gaining power over the priories of Aragon (the castellany of Amposta), Catalonia and Provence, and refusing to pay the due responsions to Rhodes. Clearly the brothers at the general chapter feared that Heredia would use the magisterial office to enrich himself and weaken the Order. Statutes were passed stating that the grand master was to associate the convent in all his decisions, the convent was to control appointments to offices and grants of land and the convent would appoint commissioners to oversee the grand master's expenditures.[1]

By the end of the twelfth century the master had become a major political figure in the Latin East, and as such his office developed along the same lines as that of an abbot in a traditional monastery, or of a secular prince. He had his own seal, his own household and his own sources of income, which were used to deal with magisterial business without having to call upon the Order's resources; this was intended to protect the Order's finances from extravagant masters. These incomes could also be used to assist the Order if necessary. As the pressures on the Order grew and its debts increased, the brothers turned to the grand master for help. In 1429, in the face of financial crisis within the Order, Grand Master Antoni Fluviá (1421–37) took over the government of the Hospital's common treasury for three years. This policy was continued by his successors, until 1471 when the bulk of the Order's debts had been paid. Clearly,

[1] Abbé René d'Aubert de Vertot, *Histoire des Chevaliers Hospitaliers de S. Jean de Jerusalem, appellez depuis Chevaliers de Rhodes, et aujourd'hui Chevaliers de Malthe*, 5 vols (Paris, 1726), 3, pp. 154–7; Victor Mallia-Milanes, *Venice and Hospitaller Malta, 1530–1798: Aspects of a Relationship* (Marsa, 1992), pp. 37–45; Anthony Luttrell, 'Intrigue, Schism and Violence among the Hospitallers of Rhodes: 1377–1384', *Speculum*, 41 (1966), 30–48, here 32–3; reprinted in his *Hospitallers in Cyprus, Rhodes, Greece and the West (1291–1440)* (London, 1978), ch. 23.

however, the Order's own officials still could not cope with the financial pressures on the Order, and in 1478 the grand master, Pierre d'Aubusson, was pressed to take over the administration of the treasury. Jürgen Sarnowsky notes that by the start of the sixteenth century 'it had almost become custom for the Master also to be head of the treasury', and the practice continued for the remainder of the Order's sojourn on Rhodes. Hence, while the brothers of earlier centuries had been anxious to curb the master's expanding authority where it threatened the interests of the brothers, as the Order came under greater financial pressure the brothers saw that it was in their interests to have a strong central administration led by a single individual. As masters were usually quite elderly by the time they were elected, they were unlikely to use their wide powers to make any sweeping reforms in the Order.

General chapters judged officials of the Order who had committed faults, discussed matters of importance for the Order and issued statutes; but these statutes appear to be the recording of custom rather than new legislation. The term 'general chapter' first appears in 1176 and 1182. The feature of the general chapter was that it included not only the master and convent but also leading officials from the West. Officials from the West are known to have attended chapters in the East from 1170 onwards, but the procedures for summoning and holding a general chapter were not laid down until the general chapter of 1206. These indicate that each general chapter began by hearing Mass of the Holy Spirit. Then the master opened proceedings. The officials of the Order reported on their offices, surrendered their seals as a token of giving up their offices, and rendered their accounts (which were read aloud, and therefore heard – *auditum*: hence audited). Any complaints were heard and judgement was given. The master then appointed a committee of leading brothers from the provinces of the Order and other brothers. This committee legislated for the Order as necessary, heard reports from overseas, and appointed new officials. The committee, rather than the complete assembly, performed the actual business of the general chapter. Its decisions were read to the whole assembly, the master commended them to the general chapter, and the meeting ended with a prayer by the conventual prior.

Although statutes survive from earlier general chapters, the first general chapter for which a complete record survives is the 1330 general chapter of Montpellier.[2] This begins by listing fourteen names of conventual officials and overseas officials present at the chapter, who formed the committee carrying out the business of the general chapter: the prior of the church of Rhodes, two procurators of the convent of Rhodes, the priors of France, Champagne, Aquitaine, Auvergne, Toulouse, Navarre, Portugal, Pisa, Capua, Venice and the Castellany of Amposta (Aragon). It then sets out the names of the high officials, who are confirmed in their posts for the next ten years: the prior of the

[2] Published by Charles Tipton, 'The 1330 Chapter General of the Knights Hospitallers at Montpellier', *Traditio*, 24 (1330), 293–308.

church of Rhodes, the grand commander, the hospitaller, the marshal, the admiral, the turcopolier, the draper, the treasurer; then the priors of France, Champagne, Aquitaine, Auvergne, St Gilles (including Toulouse and Provence), Navarre, Portugal, Rome with Pisa, Capua, Baroli, England, Ireland, Germany with Bohemia, Denmark with Norway, Messina, Lombardy; finally the preceptor of Holy Trinity Venusi, the preceptor of St Euphemia, and the preceptor of St Stephen of Monopoli. The responsions and dues to be paid by the various provinces to the convent on Rhodes are set out: these consist of special dues payable by each province to enable the Order to discharge its heavy burden of debt, and the regular responsions. Statutes are set down, the commands of the general chapter are recorded, and the names of the brothers 'retained' by the master for his personal service. These would be brothers of experience and status in their province. In 1330 the grand master retained Philip de Thame and Robert Court in England; Philip de Thame went on to become prior of England in January 1335. The first part of the record of the Montpellier chapter is in Latin: the second part, from the statutes onwards, is in French.

Over the years the procedures for holding general chapters were set out in more detail. For instance, according to the regulations of 1489 each tongue was to have two representatives, *capitulares*, on the committee which dealt with chapter business; a glance at the list for 1330 will show that this was not the case then, when there were no *capitulares* from the English or German tongues. Appeals against the decisions of the *capitulares* were not allowed. The chapter was limited to fifteen days. In 1501 it was laid down that brothers personally involved in issues to be discussed during the general chapter should not be included among the *capitulares*.[3]

The Hospital's procedures for its general chapters were not likely to lead to great innovations within the Order. Those eligible to be included among the *capitulares* were the provincial officials, who would have already been in the Order for many years before receiving office: the statutes of the general chapter of 1344 laid down that no brother could be prior before he had been in the Order for twenty years and in that province for five years, while no brother could be made a commander until he had been in the Order for five years.[4] These were men familiar with the customs of the Order and unlikely to challenge its structures.

Each province of the Order also held a regular chapter of all officials of the Order, which was supposed to meet annually. Each house held a regular weekly chapter on Sundays, which dealt with the business of the house and was presided over by the most senior brother present. At the central convent, the master

[3] Jürgen Sarnowsky, 'The Oligarchy at Work. The Chapters General of the Hospitallers in the XVth Century (1421–1522)', in *Autour de la Première Croisade. Actes du Colloque de la Society for the Study of the Crusades and the Latin East (Clermont-Ferrand, 22–25 juin 1995)*, ed. Michel Balard (Paris, 1996), pp. 267–76: here, pp. 270–2.

[4] Valletta, National Library of Malta, A.O.M. 280, fol. 47.

should preside over the weekly chapter; in his absence, his lieutenant or the grand commander presided.

By the later thirteenth century the Hospital was informally divided for purposes of the general chapter proceedings and for the organisation of the central convent into *langues*. The division into tongues had certainly appeared by 1295, and may have been in operation in the East by 1283. The 'tongues' which developed initially were Provence (the Languedoc), Auvergne (central eastern modern France) France, Spain (which included the whole of the Iberian peninsula), Italy, England and Germany. The German tongue vanished at some point between 1330 and 1344: in the general chapter of 1330 it appears as a tongue, but in 1344 as merely a province. There then were only six tongues until the German tongue was officially revived in 1422.[5]

The tongues of Provence, Auvergne and France spoke dialects of French. These three tongues dominated the Order. The other nations resented this situation, and eventually the general chapter of 1461, under Grand Master Zacosta, decided to divide the tongue of Spain into two, Aragon and Portugal-Castile – thus partially recognising the linguistic and political differences within the Iberian peninsula. This division continued even after the unification of the kingdoms of Aragon and Castile under Ferdinand (1475–1516) and Isabella (1474–1504). After the dissolution of the English, Irish and Scottish priories in the sixteenth century, at general chapters two brothers were chosen for the occasion from the members of the other tongues to act as representatives of the English tongue.

On Rhodes, each of the tongues had its own 'inn' (French: *auberge*) which acted as a central assembly hall and administrative centre for the brothers on Rhodes belonging to that tongue. The brothers themselves did not usually live in the inns. The tongues continued on Malta; it is not clear whether the tongues had also maintained their own inns in the Hospitallers' complex in Acre.

Immediately below the master in order of seniority were the 'conventual bailiffs', the chief officials of the Order, so called because they were expected to reside within the central convent. While these might hold the same titles as officers in other military orders, they did not necessarily hold the same responsibilities. In 1330 these were the prior of the church of Rhodes or conventual prior, the grand preceptor or grand commander (the Latin form is *preceptor*, the French *commandeur*), the hospitaller, the marshal, the admiral, the turcopolier, the draper and the treasurer. The office of admiral first appears in the Order's records in 1299, when the office was held by Fulk de Villaret; the office became a conventual *bailie* (bailiwick, or responsibility) in 1300. The other offices had existed from early in the Order's history. Originally these officials were chosen by the general chapter according to merit, but during the first half of

[5] Anthony Luttrell, 'Papauté et Hôpital: l'enquête de 1373', in *L'Enquête Pontificale de 1373 sur L'Ordre des Hospitaliers de Saint-Jean de Jérusalem*, ed. Jean Glénisson, vol. 1, *L'Enquête dans le Prieuré de France*, ed. Anne-Marie Legras (Paris, 1987), pp. 3–42: here p. 3, note 2.

Plate 7. The interior of the *auberge* or 'inn' of the tongue of France, Rhodes town. Photo copyright: Nigel Nicholson.

the fourteenth century it became the custom that each office was given to one specific tongue.

The conventual prior was responsible for the Order's churches and what they contained, and the priests of the Order. He was in effect bishop for all the Order's priests, although he was not a bishop and he had no spiritual authority outside the Order. Within the central convent he held spiritual responsibility for the brothers, and was responsible for the care of the conventual church of St John. As holder of a spiritual office, he was not assigned to a tongue. He was not chosen by the general chapter but by the chaplains of the Order. *Ex officio* he was a member of the general chapter, and the conventual prior was always one of the capitulares. The conventual prior had a long-running dispute with the grand master over their respective jurisdiction: in 1648 the prior wanted to call an assembly of brother chaplains which would legislate for the chaplains separately from the rest of the Order, while the prior also claimed sole rights for spiritual care of the Order's sisters. The Grand Master Jean Paul de Lascaris Castellar (1636–57) would not allow the assembly to be called, and claimed the right to approve the sisters' confessors. The dispute was settled in 1699 by Pope Innocent XII (1691–1700), apparently to the satisfaction of both parties.[6]

The grand commander was the master's second-in-command who acted on his behalf when he was absent from the convent. He was also generally responsible for the administration of the Order in the East. By the late thirteenth century he had his own seal. The non-fighting serving brothers (French: *sergeants*) were answerable to him, while the fighting serving brothers and brother knights were answerable to the marshal. The grand commander was also responsible for leading the Order in the field if the master was absent. From the first half of the fourteenth century the grand commander was chosen from the tongue of Provence.

The hospitaller was in charge of the infirmary, later known as the *sacra infirmaria*, the holy infirmary, the centre of the Hospital's vocation, and had oversight over the Hospital's other charitable activities. By the late thirteenth century he had his own seal. The various officials concerned with the holy infirmary, the infirmary for sick brothers and almsgiving were under his authority. From 1340, the hospitaller was a brother from the tongue of France.

The marshal was the chief military officer within the Order. His responsibilities were first set out and defined in the general chapter of 1206, although the Hospital had had a marshal since at least 1168. He was in command of the Hospitallers in the field, although the master (or his lieutenant the grand commander) was in supreme command, and he had his own seal. His department included the arsenal – responsible for weapons and armour – and the stables, responsible for the horses, essential for the mounted warfare which was the hallmark of the warrior elite in the middle ages. He was allowed to make extensive demands on the treasury in order to meet necessary military needs. All

[6] Vertot, *Histoire*, 5, pp. 211, 288.

brothers-at-arms, that is, knights and fighting sergeants, were under his command. He was the superior officer of the castellans of the Order's castles in the East, the gonfanier or standard-bearer, the master of the squires (French: *escuiers*; assistants to knights and often warriors of age and experience), and the turcopolier. By 1350 it was the custom that the marshal should be a brother from the tongue of Auvergne.

The admiral was in charge of the Order's warships – mainly galleys – and the hiring of additional warships if needed. In the case of a naval expedition, the admiral commanded the fleet while the marshal (if he were present) was in charge of the soldiers on them. By 1350 it was the custom that the admiral should be a brother from the tongue of Italy.

The turcopolier was commander of the native mercenary troops, turcopoles or turcoples, which made up a significant part of the military orders' armies in the East, but were not formally brothers of the Order. They would have been light horsemen, using a bow rather than a heavy lance. The office of turcopolier was raised to the rank of a conventual *bailie* in 1303, reflecting the increasing significance of the turcopole troops. From the first half of the fourteenth century the turcopolier was always from the tongue of England (which included Ireland, Scotland and Wales). On Rhodes and Malta he was in charge of the coastal defences. In 1582, following the dissolution of the priories of England and Ireland in 1540 and the priory of Scotland in 1563/4, the office of turcopolier was amalgamated into the office of grand master, and its duties were discharged in part by the grand master's seneschal.

As well as mercenaries drawn from its eastern territories, the Order also employed European mercenaries on a regular basis. These mercenaries were professional troops, highly skilled and well-equipped, who were more valuable in the field than a feudal host. Their only disadvantage was that they had to be paid, and when conditions were dangerous they (quite reasonably) demanded a higher rate of pay.

The draper was responsible for the issue of clothing and fabric, such as bedding, to the brothers. He could also issue alms to the poor from the clothing of dead brothers. During the thirteenth century the Office acquired a seal. By 1350 the draper was always selected from the tongue of Spain, later Aragon. In the early modern period his title was changed to 'grand conservator'.

The treasurer was one of the earliest offices to appear in the Hospital. Initially the treasurer used the master's seal, but by the late thirteenth century the office had its own seal. The treasurer was also responsible for the conventual seal. He was responsible for receiving the dues or responsions sent from the Order's houses in the West, and alms given to the Order, and for issuing cash as needed. He was also responsible for the safe care of the brothers' property, such as copies of the rule and the decrees of general chapters. The treasury of the Hospital also came to perform some general money-management functions, acting as a depository for valuables belonging to third parties and transferring money from one country to another for kings and merchants, but it was never as prominent in this role as was the Order of the Temple. During the first half of the fourteenth century it became the custom that the treasurer was always drawn from the tongue of Germany.

The German tongue was demoted to a province between 1330 and 1344, and the office of treasurer was subordinated to the grand commander.[7] In 1428, following the reinstatement of the German tongue in 1422, a new office was created for the tongue of Germany: the 'Grand Bailiff'. He was responsible for oversight of the priories and commanderies in Germany and for oversight of the Order's new castle of Bodrum. After the loss of Rhodes, he was given similar responsibilities on Malta: oversight of the fortifications of the Order's capital and of the fortress on Gozo.[8]

From 1461 a new office was created, the grand chancellor, which was given to the new tongue of Portugal and Castile. The grand chancellor was in command of the grand master's chancery.

Various subordinate officers were answerable to these senior officers; these might change and develop in time as the Order's role changed and developed.

The Order's properties in the East and the West were administered by various officials of the rank of capitular bailiff. They were not expected to be resident at the convent but were supposed to remain in their bailiwick and administer it. In the West, these officials included the priors of the western provinces (administrative regions); and in the East, castellans, who were responsible for the Order's castles and their surrounding territories, and commanders of estates whose title was drawn from the major city in that area, such as the commander of Tyre, or the commander of Acre. Many of these eastern bailiwicks were large, with their own hierarchy of subofficials and their own treasury, and their titles survived the loss of the Holy Land: even in the eighteenth century, there was still a prominent official in the Order with the title 'Bailiff of Acre'. Although the kingdom of Cilician Armenia had been lost to the Muslims in 1375, the office of bailiff of Armenia was not abolished until 1600.[9] In contrast to the important eastern bailiwicks, many of the commanderies in the West were quite small, with very few brothers and nothing as structured as an organised treasury, and their officers were of lower status.

The Order's property in the West is referred to in its archives generated in the East as *Dela mer* or *Outremer* – overseas – in contrast to property in the East, *citramer*. From the thirteenth century the Hospital had an official, or officials, entitled 'grand commander overseas' who was responsible for overseeing the European houses; later the same official was also called 'visitor'. Part of his function was to ensure that standards of religious life were upheld, but he was

[7] The reason for the disappearance of the German tongue is not clear. The Hospital was flourishing in Germany: see, for instance, Karl Borchardt, 'The Hospitallers, Bohemia and the Empire, 1250–1330', in *Mendicants, Military Orders and Regionalism in Medieval Europe*, ed. Jürgen Sarnowsky (Aldershot, 1999), pp. 201–31.

[8] On the Grand Bailiff see Vertot, *Histoire*, 2, pp. 431–2, and 5, p. 358.

[9] Vertot, *Histoire*, 5, p. 311 (referring to the year 1716), p. 167.

also responsible for ensuring that the western provinces did not lose their link with the East and remembered that their reason for existence was to supply and support the Order in the East.

The provincial priories in the West varied in size and developed over time. The nomenclature of the Hospitallers' European officers can be confusing. The title 'prior' was used for the official in charge of a province (called a 'priory') – such as the priory of England or the priory of France; and also for the official in charge of a single house and its attached estates. The officer in charge of a single house could also be called a commander (or a preceptor, to use the Latin term), or a master, or a procurator. The Hospital had a priory of St Gilles by around 1120: the Order owned property at St Gilles, in what is now southern France, and the official in command there was also responsible for the oversight of the Order's properties in western Europe. The English priory, to which all the houses in England and Wales were subject, became independent from St Gilles in around 1185.[10] It was based at Clerkenwell to the north of the city of London. By the early fourteenth century there were more than twenty provincial priories in the Hospital.

Each provincial priory represented a coherent geographical-political area. The prior was responsible for collecting together the responsions, dues owed to the central convent. In theory, since the papal bull *Pie postulatio voluntatis* of 1113, each commandery owed a third of its income to the central convent, but in practice this varied. The commander must transmit or carry his dues to the provincial priory. From there they were sent to the central convent, carried either by brothers of the Order or paid agents; the Hospitallers' western accounts of the 1370s show responsions being received by the procurator-general or receiver-general at Avignon, whence they were transferred to the treasurer on Rhodes. Priories which got into financial difficulties had to give account to the convent: in 1338 Philip de Thame, prior of England, sent a detailed report of the state of the English priory – its properties, incomes and expenses – to Grand Master Hélion de Villeneuve in order to explain why the English priory was unable to pay its responsions and was heavily in debt.

At times of military need in the East, especially after a serious defeat such as Hattin in 1187, the convent in the East would send letters to the provincial priors in the West asking for aid in money and men. In the West, it would be essential to exploit the Order's estates as effectively as possible and grasp every opportunity of raising funds in order to send as much money as possible to the East. As a result, the Hospital and the other supranational military orders earned a reputation in the West for being greedy. As one of the seven deadly sins, religious orders had to avoid the sin of avarice, but the Hospitallers' military commitments made this unavoidable.

The provincial prior also called regular chapter meetings of the commanders

[10] *The Hospitallers' Riwle (Miracula et Regula Hospitalis Sancti Johannis Jerosolymitani)*, ed. K. V. Sinclair, Anglo-Norman Text Society, 42 (Oxford, 1984), p. xlviii.

(or preceptors, priors and prioresses) within the provincial priory – at best annually, although probably less often. The prior was also bound to visit the commanderies and priories within his priory on a regular basis – for instance, annually – to ensure that they were being administered efficiently and that the members of the Order were following the communal life according to the Rule. In turn, the priors themselves had to report to the convent in the East on a regular basis. One of the complaints against Grand Master William de Villaret in 1299 was that although he was supposed to have reported to the convent six times during his thirty years as prior of St Gilles, he had only gone twice to the East. In 1301 the general chapter issued a decree that two or more priors must be recalled to the East each year, those who had been away from the East for longest being recalled first. When he reached the East and had rendered his account, a prior might be relieved of his office (and possibly given another elsewhere) or confirmed in it. In June 1343 King Edward III of England (1327–77) wrote to the grand master that if the Order wanted to retain his favour it must not demote Philip de Thame from his position as prior of England when he arrived in the East. In the event, Philip de Thame remained prior until 1353. In practice, although provincial priors were appointed by the general chapter, the king of the area of their province could exert considerable influence over who was chosen.

The posts of conventual bailiff, capitular bailiff and provincial prior were only open to knights. By the early modern period these offices carried the honour of 'Grand Cross', whereas lesser offices, such as commanders, held only the 'Little Cross'. There were also bailiffs of honour, who had received the Grand Cross as a mark of esteem but who had no authority in the Order.

The commanderies (or preceptories, from the Latin term for them) consisted typically of a house resembling a secular manor house with hall, chapel, kitchen and dormitory and surrounded by farm buildings. There would not normally be a hospice, although there might be; the house would not normally include a cloister, although houses of clergy (priories) and women's houses did. This house was responsible for collecting donations to the Order and receiving recruits from the locality. It was the centre of an estate or a group of estates, which it administered. It might also have churches to which the Order had the right to present the priest and from which it could collect the ecclesiastical dues. It might also be entitled to collect other tithes and ecclesiastical dues which had been bestowed on the Order in that area. The property administered from an individual commandery could be widely scattered. Michael Gervers's studies of the Hospital's possessions in Essex, where the Order held many small areas of land, indicate that here the Order leased out its lands and collected rents. It probably used non-brothers as administrators of its estates, and employed rent-collectors from outside the Order. In Italy, in contrast, the Hospitallers worked their own estates.

A commander was also responsible for all the duties of a lord of the manor within the commandery, and must hold court for the Order's tenants and do justice. The Hospitallers in England had been given by King Henry II (1154–89) in 1155 all liberties 'in soc and sac and toll and team and infangenthef' – in other words, considerable jurisdictional freedom – and exempted from many royal dues and exactions by the king, except only justice of life and limb. From at least the donation of King John (1199–1216) in 1199, one of the Hospital's men in each town, borough and village in the royal estates was exempted from taxes and the payment of aids to the king.[11] In short, the Order was exempted from much of royal jurisdiction, but was still responsible for jurisdiction over its own tenants.

Commanders and priors were generally chosen by the provincial prior, although by the second half of the fourteenth century grand masters bestowed commanderies on deserving brothers without reference to the prior. The exception was prioresses, who were chosen by the sisters of the relevant house, and approved by the provincial prior. If a house of brothers was attached to the house of sisters, then a separate commander would usually be appointed for the brothers by the prior. The exception to this practice was the great royal Aragonese house at Sigena, where the brothers were subject to the prioress. Prioresses attended provincial chapters, and were responsible for the administration of the estates of their house and the payment of dues to the provincial prior in the same way as commanders; but they could not be promoted to administer provinces. Hospitaller women's houses were more like traditional nunneries, enclosed houses of prayer and charity, than Hospitaller commanderies, which were not enclosed and whose function was primarily for fundraising and recruitment.

Local commanders, priors and prioresses were not independent entities. Their actions were regulated by the general chapter, which issued statutes limiting their rights to admit brothers and sisters. They could not alienate land or build without permission from the provincial prior. In practice, however, the localities could operate with little reference to the East. Close relationships – both of blood and friendship – with local authorities would be more important to the average commander or prioress than the opinion of the provincial prior, let alone the general chapter far away in Jerusalem, Rhodes or Malta.

The commandery was the basic unit of conventual life within the Order. All members of the Order were assigned to a place in a commandery when they joined the Order (a *stagia*), and the official in charge of this commandery was responsible for their maintenance and training in the Order. By the late middle ages, however, commanders were not usually resident – preferring to draw the income from the commandery and to live elsewhere, for instance at a royal court, at the papal court or on Rhodes – and brothers of the Order usually no longer actually lived within their commandery.

Even in the earlier centuries of the Order, when most of the commanderies still functioned as centres of religious life, the personnel belonging to a commandery or priory could be of widely differing status. All full members of

[11] *Cartulaire*, nos 238, 1088 (and 1089–93).

the Order took the three monastic vows on admittance to the Order: personal poverty, chastity and obedience to the master of the Order. Unlike most traditional monastic orders, however, the majority of the members of the Hospital were laity; they were not in priestly orders. The priest-brothers, permitted to the Order since at least 1154 in the papal bull *Christianae fidae religio*, made up only a small proportion of the members. The function of the priest-brothers was to provide spiritual services to the Order. Priests could enter the Order already ordained, or become ordained after joining the Order. Priests could elect to join the Order for a fixed term. Some Hospitaller priests in the East became bishops of territories associated with the Order. Hospitaller clergy did not often achieve high office, although Pope Clement VII (1523–34) had been a Hospitaller. Little is known of the everyday lives of the priest-brothers of the Order in the medieval period, apart from the Order's regulations; but a late seventeenth-century document by a priest-brother of the Order giving advice to chaplains on board the Order's ships gives a valuable insight into demands on a brother chaplain in the early modern period.[12]

The most high-profile members of the Order were the knight-brothers. The statutes of the Order first distinguished between brother knights and brother sergeants in the statutes of Master Alphonso of Portugal of 1203–6. This was a distinction which had long existed in the Order of the Temple, but which was initially of less importance in the Hospital as it had not been founded as a military Order. In the early thirteenth century a knight was already a person of some status: he was a warrior who typically fought on horseback (warhorses were expensive) with a lance (requiring long hours of practice to be used efficiently) or a sword (requiring great expense to purchase it). His armour was typically to be of chainmail, covering the whole body, with a full-face helmet. The fact that not all knights met these conditions did not prevent their being knights. By the early thirteenth century, the 'knightly class' was acquiring its own traditions and myths which defined it and set out its ideals: the stories of Charlemagne and Arthur. Ceremonies of bestowing knighthood, although often very simple, were becoming widely used: for instance, John of Salisbury, writing his *Policraticus* in 1159, expected that every new knight's sword would be laid on the altar of a church before being given to him (Bk 6, ch.10). Knights did not have to be the sons or relatives of knights; they might have won their right to knighthood on the battlefield. For the modern historian it is sometimes difficult to define what constituted a knight at the beginning of the thirteenth century, and certainly this seems to have varied from one area to another; but contemporaries do not seem to have been in any doubt. They knew what a knight was, and who was a knight and who was only a squire or a sergeant – warriors who had not been knighted.

By the mid-thirteenth century knighthood was becoming a caste in France and

[12] David Allen, '"A parish at sea": Spiritual Concerns aboard the Order of Saint John's Galleys in the Seventeenth and Eighteenth Centuries', in *The Military Orders: Fighting for the Faith and Caring for the Sick*, ed. Malcolm Barber (Aldershot, 1994), pp. 113–20.

in England. The social and political obligations of knighthood and the costs of maintaining knighthood discouraged many families from taking it up; the status of knighthood rose correspondingly for those who did. Knights were on the way to becoming members of the nobility, albeit of the lower nobility. In the Hospital, those who applied to join the Order as brother knights must have been knighted already, and had to be the son of a knight or at least born legitimately from a knightly family. On the other hand, knights who attempted to enter the Order as sergeants would be severely punished. The rising status of knighthood was reflected in increasing status for knights within the Order. Under Master Bertrand de Comps (1236–39) knight-brothers were given a higher status than priest-brothers; in 1262 it was laid down that only a knight-brother could become master of the Order; and by the 1270s all high offices were reserved for the knights. At this period, knights were in a distinct minority within the Order; it was not until the early modern period that they became the majority of the brothers.

The fact that the leading brothers of the military orders were knights as well as religious meant that they were judged both as knights and as religious. Commentators who criticised all religious orders for being slack in their observance also criticised the military orders as religious orders. At the same time they were criticised by religious writers for the same faults as knights: for being too proud. Pride – or rather, self-confidence – was an essential part of knighthood; a warrior needs to have confidence in his own ability on the battlefield. Religious men, however, should be humble; pride was categorised as the first and most serious of the seven deadly sins. In this respect the dual nature of the members of the military orders brought problems.

In the fourteenth century the status of knighthood continued to rise into nobility. At the same time, because of the privileged position of the knight-brothers, the Order itself rose in status so that by the early modern period it appeared as an Order of nobility – a far cry from its lowly origins in Jerusalem. It was possible for a brother who joined as a sergeant to be raised to the rank of knight once in the Order, in recognition of his services in war: this was done in c. 1627 for Alonso de Contreras, a Spanish brother of poor but respectable birth and a professional soldier who had served the Order as a soldier for more than a decade and as a brother sergeant for around fifteen years.[13]

By the early modern period, the Order distinguished between 'knights of justice' who were of knightly status because of their noble birth, or – exceptionally – in recognition of their outstanding military achievements, and 'knights of grace' who were given the status of knights as a special honour and not because it was due to them. The 'knights of grace' were of lower status than the 'knights of justice' and were not eligible to hold high office within the Order.

[13] *The Life of Captain Alonso de Contreras, Knight of the Military Order of St John, Native of Madrid. Written by Himself (1582 to 1633)*, translated from the Spanish by Catherine Alison Phillips with an Introduction by David Hannay (London, 1926), pp. 225–8.

Knights joining the Order during the later middle ages and early modern period would have been imbued since childhood with the ideals of knighthood or *chevalerie* (anglicised as 'chivalry') developed and promoted by the noble knightly class: the concept of knighthood as a class chosen by God to protect the poor and defenceless, especially women and the Church, and to serve God through the profession of arms. The knight-brothers of the Hospital may have thought of their Order as a particularly suitable place in which they could live out their knightly vocation. Yet there is no evidence of this in medieval fictional literature, where ideals of knighthood were developed and expounded. Rather, the Hospital was portrayed in works such as Jean d'Arras's *Mélusine* (written in the late fourteenth century) as a support unit for individual secular knights engaged in serving God in the crusade, serving secular knights in their vocation rather than representing that vocation.[14]

Although the knight-brothers of the military orders were never generally recognised as the epitome of knighthood, they were respected as doughty and pious warriors. As they were also religious, bound by monastic vows, they were regarded as more honourable and trustworthy than secular knights. This must have been an important factor in their employment by popes and kings, discussed in chapter five below. As religious, they were not supposed to become involved in the normal pursuits of knighthood such as hunting, tourneying or courting ladies, but when not involved in fighting the enemies of Christendom they should be saying the hours in chapel, or involved in the work of their Order. By the early modern period it is clear that members of the Order did become involved in duelling, but this was always regarded as a vice to be avoided. Away from the frontiers of Christendom, the Hospitallers' houses in Europe were not normally built as fortresses and should not normally contain weapons. Numerous papal bulls and records of legal cases give witness that in the middle ages the Hospitallers and their houses frequently came under attack from violent neighbours and suffered considerable damage. This was normal in a violent age.

The brother sergeants (or servants) were of two types, sergeants-at-arms, who fought but with less expensive equipment than the knight-brothers, and sergeants who served, or 'serving brothers', who worked as (for instance) carpenters, blacksmiths or shepherds. In the twelfth, thirteenth and early fourteenth centuries they formed the majority of the brothers. Unlike in the Order of the Temple, where only the brother knights could wear the distinctive white mantle over their dark tunics, the brother knights and brother sergeants of the Hospital wore identical habits. In the house, they all wore black mantles with a white cross. From 1259, Pope Alexander IV (1254–61) attempted to differentiate between the ranks of the Order on the battlefield. Whereas Pope Innocent IV in 1248 had allowed all the fighting brothers to wear a red surcoat with a

[14] On this see Helen Nicholson, *Love, War and the Grail: Templars, Hospitallers and Teutonic Knights in Medieval Epic and Romance, 1150–1500* (Leiden, 2001).

white cross on the battlefield, Pope Alexander noted that this ruling was discouraging nobles from joining the Order because they could not be distinguished from those of non-noble status. He therefore decided that only the knight-brothers should wear the red surcoat with white cross, while the sergeant-brothers had to wear black. The general chapter of 1278 reversed this ruling: in battle, all brothers-at-arms should wear a red surcoat with a white cross, and all brothers should wear a black mantle with a white cross in the house.[15] In this respect at least the brother sergeants had secured equal status with the knights. In other respects, however, they were not equal, as their access to higher office was limited. In the 1630s Alonso de Contreras noted that there were few commanderies available to be held by brother sergeants, and they were small with low revenues.[16] In 1671 the grand master and his council decided that there were too many brother sergeants in the Order and decreed that no more were to be received for the time being: in 1726 Abbot Vertot noted that there were very few left.[17] Nevertheless, the rank of sergeant survived until after the loss of Malta in 1798.

The sisters of the Hospital lived either in houses of sisters or as one or two individuals attached to a house of brothers. The houses of Hospitaller sisters were sometimes associated with a house of brothers, as at Buckland in Somerset, where there was a house of fifty sisters in 1338, with an attached house of six men. Even in 1539 at the dissolution of the monasteries there were still fourteen sisters at Buckland. In 1207 Pope Innocent III laid down that there should be thirty sisters at Sigena (a double house presided over by a prioress), in 1250 a maximum of twenty had been imposed on the Hospitaller house at Alguaire, and in 1298 the grand master limited the number of sisters at Beaulieu in France to thirty-nine. These figures are far higher than the number of brothers usually resident at commanderies in the West: we know from Philip de Thame's report to the central convent in 1338 that there were ten brothers at Chippenham in England at that date, and that this was then the largest male house of the Order in England.

The largest and most wealthy houses of sisters were in Aragon, where the Hospital had royal patronage and where women's landowning rights were more extensive than elsewhere in Europe. Hospitaller sisters did not usually run hospitals, although they sometimes did acquire hospices; they contributed to the Order through the running of estates and contributing their responsions, and through spiritual service in prayer. By the early modern period the remaining houses of sisters in Spain, France and Italy were very prestigious institutions, and no lady could enter who was not of proven noble descent.

The Order of the Hospital also had many associate members, who had not taken full vows but who shared in some of the spiritual benefits of the Order.

[15] *Cartulaire*, nos 2479, 2928, 3670.

[16] Alonso de Contreras, p. 224.

[17] Vertot, *Histoire*, 5, pp. 263, 323–4.

Plate I. Grand Master Pierre d'Aubusson gives instructions regarding the defence of the city of Rhodes against the Turks, 1480. Bibliothèque Nationale ms. Lat. 6067, fol. 33v. Photo copyright: Bibliothèque Nationale de France, Paris.

Plate II. The Grand Master holds court: Guillaume Caoursin presents his account of the 1480 siege of Rhodes to the Grand Master, Pierre d'Aubusson. The eight conventual bailiffs of the Order sit behind him; petitioners and townspeople bringing cases before the Grand Master stand in the foreground. Bibliothèque Nationale ms. Lat. 6067, fol. 3v. Photo copyright: Bibliothèque Nationale de France, Paris.

Plate III. *The Decapitation of St John the Baptist*, by Michelangelo Merisi da Caravaggio (1571–1610), in the Conventual Church of St John in Valetta, Malta. Photo copyright: Bridgeman Art Library.

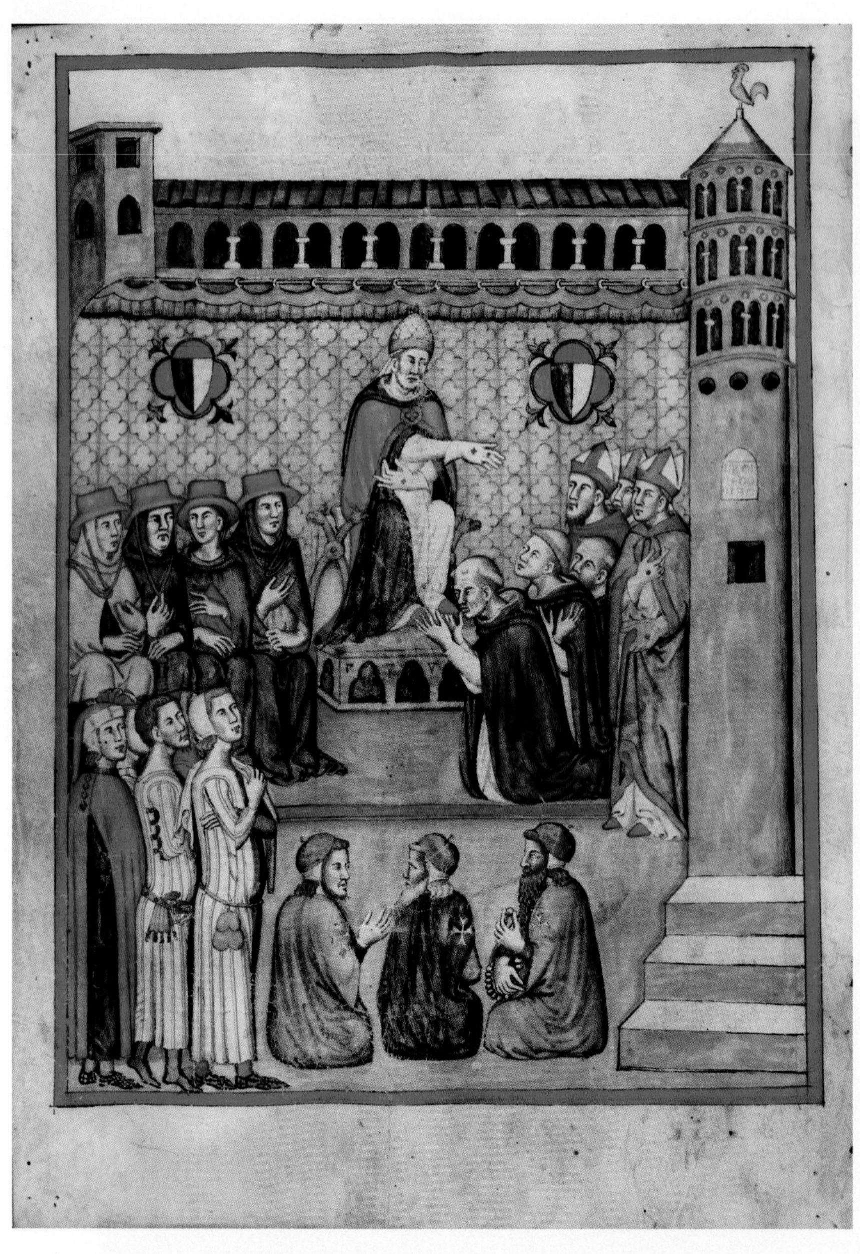

Plate IV. Three Hospitallers (seated) attending Pope Benedict XI (1303–4): Perugia, Biblioteca Augusta, Ms. 975. Photo copyright: Biblioteca Augusta, Perugia.

Plate V. Matteo Perez d'Aleccio, modello for his fresco of the Turkish batteries around Fort St Elmo, 27 May 1565, in the National Maritime Museum, London. Photo copyright: The National Maritime Museum.

Plate VI. Portrait of Grand Master Alof de Wignacort, with his page, by Michelangelo Merisi da Caravaggio (1571–1610). Photo copyright: Bridgeman Art Library.

Plate VII. H. Letter, 'The Battle of Lepanto', in the National Maritime Museum, London. Photo copyright: National Maritime Museum.

Plate VIII. The capture of the Algerian ship *Bequicogia* by galleys of the Hospital in the Maltese Channel commanded by the Marshal and General of the Hospitallers' galleys, 16 January 1647: watercolour from an eighteenth-century album. Photo copyright: Hill Monastic Manuscript Library.

Plate IX. Battle between the Hospital's ship *St George* with three vessels of Tunis, 23 May 1721: watercolour from an eighteenth-century album. Photo copyright: Hill Monastic Manuscript Library.

Men, women and married couples took vows of obedience to the grand master and promised to join the Order in the future: they were known as *donati* and *donatae*, literally 'persons given to the Order'. The status and actions of donats varied. They might remain in their own homes and only enter the Order on their deathbed, or they might take the Order's habit – possibly in an altered form to differentiate them from full members of the Order – and live in one of the Order's houses. It is not clear whether they lived alongside full members of the Order; it seems likely that as they had not taken full vows they lived separately, joining the full members of the Order for divine service. As associates, they should not be able to attend chapter meetings, for instance.

Confratres and *consorors* (*confrères* and *consoeurs* in French) were more loosely associated with the Order. They were attached to their local house of the Order, but remained in their own home. They made an annual donation as token of their association, and in return the Order guaranteed to take care of them in their old age and to give them Christian burial on their death, provided that they were not excommunicate by name. They did not take the habit. There were often complaints that such associates were claiming the legal privileges of the Order without actually being members, and the papacy tried to limit the Order's privileges to those who had actually taken the habit and physically entered a house of the Order. However, it is difficult for scholars now to be certain of the level of commitment of an associate to the Order, as by the fourteenth century and sometimes earlier the terms 'donat' and 'confrater' or 'consoror' were also used of people who had become full members of the Order.

There were also persons, men and women or married couples, who had made a one-off, large donation of their property to the Order in return for maintenance in their old age: a room in the Order's house and an allowance of food, clothing and fuel. This maintenance was called a 'corrody'. If the donor lived a long time after making the donation, the corrody could prove a serious strain on the Order's finances. It is clear that not all recipients of corrodies actually lived within the Order's house, and they could receive a payment in lieu instead.

Also within the houses of the Order were paid servants, men and women, who were not members of the Order and had taken no religious vows. A house might also contain pensioners, retired servants of the Order being supported by the Order in their old age. In the East (after 1530, on Malta) there were slaves, Muslims who had been taken prisoner in battle or on raids. The Order was expected to free its slaves if they converted to Christianity, but it was unenthusiastic about doing so. Long-serving slaves of the Order could rise to positions of respect and responsibility; the Turkish slaves on Malta had their own imam, or spiritual leader. But in times of siege, the Order was aware that its Muslim slaves were a security risk.

It appears that by the thirteenth century those joining the Hospital were professed as full members immediately, without a novitiate or period of instruction. This originated in the need to replace quickly members of the

Order lost in action in the East. Instead, members of the Order were taught the statutes of the Order through hearing them read out in chapter each week. By the early seventeenth century there was less urgent need for professed brothers, so that Alonso de Contreras had to complete a year's novitiate before taking the vows as a brother sergeant. New knight- and sergeant-brothers of the Order were expected to complete a period of active service in the East in order to qualify for any sort of office within the Order, such as control of a commandery, but sisters and those not eligible for office seem to have remained in their own area throughout their lives in the Order.

The need to complete a period of service in the East before being eligible for an income or control of a commandery continued after the loss of the Holy Land, but now it was service at sea in the Hospital's fleet for a whole sailing season (spring to autumn) – although the service was still called a 'caravan', a term derived from military service on land. In the late seventeenth century a chaplain of the Order was expected to complete two periods of service at sea in order to receive a pension, and four in order to receive a commandery; at various periods a knight-brother had to complete three or four 'caravans'. Alonso de Contreras, who returned to Spain and the service of the king of Spain almost immediately after making his profession, discovered to his annoyance fifteen years later that he was barred from receiving a commandery because he had not completed the required period of residence on Malta.[18]

□

The origins of those who joined the Hospital and their motivations for doing so cannot be completely reconstructed. Research by Dieter Wojtecki into the social origins of Teutonic Knights in the thirteenth century revealed that the majority of those whose origins could be discovered originated in the lower knightly class. For this group, entry into a religious order opened up opportunities for social improvement not available to them in their own class. However, the traditional monastic orders were largely closed to them; entry was restricted to those of noble birth, who could afford to give a large donation to the house on their entry. The military orders did not demand that an entrant make such a large financial commitment. Moreover, the military orders valued warrior skills, which were the main asset of the lower knightly class, and did not demand that members be literate, that is able to read and write Latin. Members of the military orders could achieve high office through hard work within the Order, and could be given important secular responsibilities, such as acting as almoners, ambassadors or treasurers for secular lords, kings and popes. In short, entrance to a military order was a means of career advancement for members of the lower knightly class.

This pattern continues into the fourteenth century, where we find prominent members of the English Hospital coming from families which were not of

[18] Alonso de Contreras, pp. 173, 224.

knightly origin but who became 'esquires' in the fourteenth century; sub-knightly, yet with a sense of social status and definitely rising in the social scale. The Archer (Larcher) family, which supplied several prominent Hospitallers to the English tongue during the fourteenth century, is the best-researched example of this trend. Another example in the same pattern is the Inge family. Hildebrand Inge was a leading English Hospitaller in the last quarter of the fourteenth century: the Inges were landholders and were involved in the royal administration, but were not of knightly origin.[19] As knights became *de facto* noble, entrance to the Hospital was a means of career advancement for members of the class just below the knightly class. Even in the seventeenth century, entry to the Hospital as a brother-sergeant offered a means of gaining a substantial rise in social status for a professional military man of humble birth such as Alonso de Contreras.

Other motivations mingled with the urge for self-improvement. The military orders allowed members to serve God, doing penance for their sins and winning an assurance of Heaven, while not having to give up their warrior vocation. For men and women of all landed classes the military order offered a secure life if they had no inheritance to support them and no means of acquiring one through marriage. Men and women might choose to enter the Hospital rather than another religious order because it was the geographically nearest religious house, or because their relatives had already joined the Order, or because their family had a tradition of donation to the Order (especially if their family had founded the local house of the Order) or because the Hospital had done them services in the past – such as lending them money. There were also many individual circumstances which could lead a person to join the Hospital. A man or woman might join on the death of their spouse, seeking solace for their soul and security for their old age. A letter of Pope Innocent III tells of a priest, B., who left the Augustinian canons and joined the Hospital in order to travel and see the Holy Land, but then grew anxious about his soul because the Hospital was not as strict an Order as the Augustinian canons, and asked the pope for permission to return to his original order.[20]

Brother B.'s spiritual concerns were based on the fact that the Hospital was an active rather than a purely contemplative order. In traditional Christian ideology, the contemplative lifestyle was of higher spiritual value than the active lifestyle. This belief was based on Christ's reply to Martha when she complained

[19] Peter Coss, 'Knights, Esquires and the Origins of Social Gradation in England', *Transactions of the Royal Historical Society*, 6th series, 5 (1995), 155–178: here p. 175 and note 95; see also Anthony Luttrell, 'English Contributions to the Hospitaller Castle at Bodrum in Turkey: 1407–1437', in *The Military Orders*, vol. 2, *Welfare and Warfare*, ed. Helen Nicholson (Aldershot, 1998), pp. 163–72: here p. 164; Paul Brand, *The Earliest English Law Reports*, 2, Selden Society (1996), pp. lxi–lxv on William Inge (died 1322). By the mid-fourteenth century some Inges had achieved knightly status: *Calendar of the Patent Rolls Preserved in the Public Record Office. Edward III*, vol. 13: *AD 1364–1367* (London, 1912), pp. 211, 402.

[20] *Die Register Innocenz' III*, ed. O. Hageneder and A. Haidacher, 2 vols in 4 (Graz–Cologne, 1964–8, Rome–Vienna, 1979–83), 2, p. 101, year 1199/1200, no. 54.

that her sister Mary was not helping her with the housework, preferring to sit and listen to Christ teaching: that Mary had chosen the better way (Luke 10 vv. 39–42). The Templars in particular seem to have suffered from fears that their Order was spiritually inferior, as an early letter of encouragement to the Order points out that the active life was absolutely essential for the survival of Christianity.[21]

Nevertheless, the changes in religious practice and ideology in the late eleventh and early twelfth centuries favoured a more practical Christianity which worked itself out in action, and the military orders were part of this new movement in faith. The Hospitallers, with their dual hospitaller–military function, were in the fortunate position of being able to draw upon two strands of Christian activity: holy war and care for the sick. At times of military failure, the Hospitallers could always revert to their original vocation, and hence could escape some of the opprobrium which fell on the more purely military Order of the Temple.[22] This was not, however, purely cynical manipulation of their Rule: the Hospitallers were genuinely dedicated to the care of the sick. The brothers were told at their reception into the Order that they were to regard the sick poor as their lords. The 'Rule' of Raymond du Puy states that the only things which the members of the Order may demand of the Order are bread, water and humble clothing. The clothing should be humble because Christ's poor 'whose serfs we claim to be' go naked: 'and it is a filthy and ugly thing that a serf should be proud and his master humble'. Those received into the infirmary to be cared for are the brothers' 'lords the sick'. The Rule lays down the procedure by which the sick poor should be received, an indication of the centrality of the care of the sick within the Order.

Documents survive from the twelfth century which describe the care of the sick within the Hospital at Jerusalem. These emphasize the importance of prayer, comfort and diet, but place less importance on the role of the doctor. In 1184/5 Pope Lucius III (1181–5) laid down that there should always be five doctors and three surgeons in the Hospital at Jerusalem, a pitifully small number in comparison to Byzantine and Muslim hospitals of the same period, but impressive in comparison to hospitals in western Europe. As contemporary sources indicate that there were usually around 1,000 sick poor in the Hospital's infirmary at any one time, this would make the doctor: patient ratio so low as to make any effective individual care by the doctor impossible. It is clear that the Hospital did not set out to give patients an intensive course of medical care, but rather to provide somewhere for them to rest and recuperate. There were one master and eleven assistants in each of the Hospital's eleven wards, whose task

[21] Jean Leclercq, 'Un document sur les débuts des Templiers', *Revue de L'Histoire Ecclesiastique*, 52 (1957), 81–91: here 87, para. 2; G. Schlafert, 'Lettre inedite de Hugues de Saint-Victor aux chevaliers du Temple', *Revue d'Ascetique et de Mystique*, 34 (1958), 275–99.

[22] Helen Nicholson, *Templars, Hospitallers and Teutonic Knights: Images of the Military Orders, 1128–1291* (Leicester and London, 1993), pp. 120–2.

was to care for the patients rather than to diagnose or prescribe. John of Würzburg, who visited the Hospital's infirmary in Jerusalem in the early 1160s, refers to fifty dead being carried out each day, and immediately being replaced by new patients; but he does not criticise the Hospital for this high death rate (5% a day). This does not indicate a hospital which set out to cure patients, but rather to make their last days more bearable.

The Hospital would take in anyone who needed care, of whatever religion. Its patients were mostly Christian pilgrims, but it also cared for casualites of war, and had a field-hospital service to bring the wounded to the hospital. When the infirmary was full, the brothers had to give up their own beds to the sick poor and sleep on the floor.

Male and female patients were segregated. Pregnant women received special care, and if they were not able to take care of their babies the Hospital took them into their care and found wet nurses for them, who received a wage from the Order. Orphaned children and abandoned children were also cared for by the Hospital. The Hospital required the wet nurses to bring the children frequently to the Hospital so that they could be checked over by the sisters to ensure that they were being properly cared for – and assigned to other carers if they were not. When they were adults the children could enter the Order or remain in the secular world, as they preferred.

After the loss of Jerusalem the Hospital lost the use of its infirmary in the city, although the building remained and was still used by Christian pilgrims to the city. When the Order's headquarters was moved to Acre in 1191, the infirmary at Acre (constructed by 1155) became the centre of its hospital operations. This was probably extended after 1191. Excavations carried out in the 1990s have revealed much of the Hospitaller buildings in Acre, but, at the time of writing, the precise location of the infirmary within the Hospitaller complex is not known. It may lie to the south of the main courtyard, next to the large latrine tower. The Hospital also had a women's house at Acre, dedicated to St Mary Magdalene, but there is no evidence that the sisters there also cared for the sick.

The fact that the Hospital would take in any needy pilgrim and would give them anything that they required was greatly admired in the West; in the mid-thirteenth century the so-called 'minstrel of Reims' recounted a story of how Saladin had visited the Hospital's infirmary at Acre to discover whether the Hospital was really as generous to pilgrims as he had been told, and established that the master was even prepared to sacrifice his priceless war horse for the sake of a sick pilgrim.[23]

In 1291 the Hospital moved its central convent to Limassol on Cyprus. The Order planned to build a hospital there, but so far as is known nothing was done. By 1306 the Order was involved in the conquest of Rhodes, and the construction of a hospital there was decided on in 1314. This hospital or infirmary was built in

[23] *Récits d'un Ménestrel de Reims au Treizième Siècle*, ed. N. de Wailly, Société de L'Histoire de France (Paris, 1876), pp. 104–9, 112, sections 198–208, 219.

Plate 8. The fourteenth-century infirmary of the Hospital, Rhodes town. Photo copyright: Nigel Nicholson.

the Collachium, the area of the town of Rhodes reserved for the Hospitallers. It is generally agreed that it was the building which later became the knights' arsenal, opposite the Inn of Auvergne. It seems to have been mainly concerned with the care of pilgrims, although it also cared for the Order's own battle casualties. It is not clear whether it received Greeks, Jews and Muslims as well as Latin Christians, unlike the Jerusalem Hospital which had received anyone who asked.

In 1437 Grand Master Fluviá bequeathed money for a new infirmary to be built, on a larger scale. This was built near the old infirmary, on the south side of the Street of the Knights, near the harbour. The main ward is on the first floor, along the east side of the building, above the main entrance. Each bed had a cubicle built into the thickness of the wall behind it. There is a small chapel half way down the infirmary on the main street side. A small refectory adjoins at the south-west end. There were also, for noble patients, smaller private rooms on the first floor, accessed from the gallery which ran around the courtyard at first-floor level. These each had a window looking outwards and a stone fireplace set into the wall.

The infirmary in Rhodes was obviously a showcase building, intended to impress visitors from the West with the Order's dedication to its vocation. The Order also had responsibility for some hospices in the West, although these were never significant. In England, the brothers had the privilege of collecting the bodies of executed criminals and seeing to their burial, which occasionally caused problems when an apparently dead criminal revived in Hospitaller care. The Order had some responsibilities for pilgrims: it had a hospital at Genoa, a major staging post for pilgrims to the East, and in the fifteenth century some hospices were founded by the Hospital on the Santiago pilgrim route, specifically for the care of pilgrims to Santiago.

After the loss of Rhodes the Hospitallers re-established their conventual hospital wherever the central convent was: for a time it was on a galleon at sea. On their arrival on Malta the brothers found that there was already a hospital on the island, but they constructed their own at Birgu. The infirmary was not needed to care for sick pilgrims, as Malta was not on the western European pilgrimage routes, but it did care for the local Maltese. A new infirmary was built at Valletta after 1565. This was built on the same plan as that on Rhodes, with a large central courtyard and the main ward on the first floor – although this is now at street level, with the ground floor at basement level. The main ward again had small cubicles built into the walls behind each bed. A large chapel leads off the main ward of the infirmary about half-way along its length; far larger than the chapel in the infirmary ward on Rhodes. A contemporary illustration shows doctors attending the patients, each of whom has his own bed which can be curtained off from the rest of the ward. The Valletta infirmary complex was badly damaged during the Second World War but has since been rebuilt; the central courtyard has been covered over and converted to a theatre.

The Order on Malta was also involved in relief of the poor, in particular elderly men and poor women; it also took in unwanted infants, orphans and children whose parents could not support them and arranged for their care. In 1675 an English chaplain, Teonge, was very impressed by what he saw in the holy infirmary, although by 1789 when John Howard, prison and hospital reformer, visited Malta, the standard of care had apparently declined, with privies unemptied, ruffianly nursing staff, and a lower standard of cleanliness than the grand master's stables. Yet in the seventeenth and eighteenth centuries brothers of the Hospital were involved in medical advances, and hospital care had become more proactive, in line with developments in Europe. Patients came to Malta for operations to treat cataracts and to remove stones. In 1676 Grand Master Nicolas Cotoner (1663–80) founded a Chair of Anatomy and Surgery in the Hospital. In 1783 the Order organised relief for the earthquake victims of Sicily and Calabria: a field hospital was set up outside Messina, providing medicine, beds, tents and food for the homeless. Presumably standards of hospital care in 1789 had been affected by the Order's growing financial difficulties, which would come to a head with the sequestration of its estates in France following the 1789 Revolution.

After the loss of Malta in 1798, the Order's hospitaller activities were all that remained of its original vocation. When it moved to Rome a conventual

Plate 9. The interior of the infirmary of the Hospital at Valletta, Malta. Photo copyright: Nigel Nicholson.

hospital was founded there, and the modern Order continues its service for the poor sick.

□

Despite its continued devotion to Hospital care, the Order of St John has never been particularly renowned for piety. Like all religious orders, all members followed a daily routine of religious services, which could be adapted if they were on active service in the field, and all members were expected to conform to certain standards of religious behaviour as laid down in the Rule. But as the houses in the West were increasingly let out to tenants and one brother could hold several commanderies and never live in any of them, so the communal religious life of the local commandery declined during the later middle ages. The Order has produced a number of saints, although none of these were canonised for their military activity. It seems that the Order did not attempt to win canonisation for its military martyrs, as this would encourage brothers to act individually on the battlefield rather than together as a military unit. All brothers-at-arms were potential martyrs and none should be raised above the rest.

The Hospital was never an order which would attract the most spiritually minded persons, who would be more likely to join a contemplative order. The spiritual life of individual lay members is difficult to reconstruct. The autobiography of Alonso de Contreras, sergeant-brother and then knight-brother, offers some insight into the spirituality of one member of the Order in the first three decades of the seventeenth century: he depicts himself as a conventionally pious man, proud of the fact that he came from an 'old Catholic' family which had never been investigated by the Inquisition, respectful of the Blessed Virgin Mary and Her Son, regarding the war against the Muslims as a religious conflict as well as a means of self-enrichment, and retiring into a hermitage at a time of personal crisis, but determined that he would never become a monk.[24]

In the middle ages the Order produced no great theologians, and few widely educated men – Brother William of Santo Stefano in the late thirteenth century and Grand Master Heredia being the most obvious exceptions.[25] The brothers produced or commissioned some historical works, notably Giacomo Bosio's history of the Order, first published in 1602 and not yet superceded for the period after 1421. The Order also produced some lawyers (notably, again, Brother William of Santo Stefano), while Grand Master Heredia had Greek histories translated and built up a considerable library of classical literature. Yet in general the Hospitallers were not renowned for their learning, and this was the cause of some criticism. To be fair, however, the Hospitallers were as educated as most people of the class from which they were drawn, and as the status of knighthood increased and the membership of the Order became more noble, the members' level of education improved.

Nevertheless, despite occasional accusations in the thirteenth century that the Order was too friendly towards heretics (notably during the Albigensian crusade and by Pope Gregory IX in 1238),[26] the Order was consistent in its devotion to the Catholic Christian faith of its day. It was its religious practice which attracted donations from the Christian faithful in Europe. Donations were given in free alms, without feudal obligations attached; but in return the donors required the Order's prayers, and a share in the good works of the Order. The more spiritually worthy a person, it was believed, the more God would listen to her prayers; if the Order had not been regarded as spiritually worthy, then donors would have given their lands and money to another, more spiritual order whose prayers would be more valuable on their behalf. Hence the very fact that donors did give in alms to the Order is an indication of its perceived spiritual worth.

For reasons described in chapter three, from the early thirteenth century all

[24] Alonso de Contreras, pp. 11, 32–45, 45–7, 48–90, 118–26, 133–8, 264.

[25] Anthony Luttrell, 'Fourteenth-Century Hospitaller Lawyers', *Traditio*, 21 (1965), 449–56: here 450; reprinted in his *The Hospitallers in Cyprus, Rhodes, Greece and the West (1291–1440)* (London, 1978), ch. 16; Anthony Luttrell, 'Greek Histories Translated and Complied for Juan Fernández de Heredia, Master of Rhodes: 1377–1396', *Speculum*, 35 (1960), 401–7: reprinted in his *Hospitallers in Cyprus*, ch. 20.

[26] On the Hospital and the Albigensian Crusade see Dominic Selwood, *Knights of the Cloister: Templars and Hospitallers in Central-Southern Occitania 1100–1300* (Woodbridge, 1999), 43–7; for Gregory IX see *Cartulaire*, no. 2186.

donations to religious orders by the high nobility were reduced, and donations from other social groups also declined. Nevertheless, the Order continued to receive gifts from the Christian faithful in western Europe throughout its career on Rhodes, and westerners did respond to its appeals for aid against the Muslims; they also bought the indulgences sold through the Order. This indicates that the Order's religious devotion, while not of the highest, was certainly regarded as satisfactory by Catholic Christians during the middle ages. The devotion of members of the Order was representative of the social class from which they were largely drawn: not deeply spiritual nor well-educated in theology, but for the most part genuine in their faith and anxious to demonstrate their piety in practical action. For many, religious belief, personal ambition and a desire to win honour in the world were equal motivations in life.

Certainly there were cases of scandal during the Order's history, as in all religious orders; and as the Order was not enclosed and the brothers in particular had to move around Europe and the East on the Order's business, acquiring money and property and dealing with the secular and ecclesiastical authorities, there was more opportunity for breaking the three vows than if they had been enclosed in a traditional monastic house – despite the fact that the Order had a well-deserved reputation for strict discipline. In line with trends in other religious orders, attitudes towards private property became more lax in the later middle ages: in the fifteenth century the Hospitaller sisters in the kingdom of Aragon had extensive personal property; and in 1638 Pope Urban VIII (1623–44) allowed even commanders of the Order to make wills leaving their personal property to whomever they wished – previously all property had to be returned to the common treasury of the Order on a brother's death.

Predictably, lapses in chastity aroused the most attention outside the Order. In 1238 Pope Gregory IX complained that he had heard that the brothers kept harlots in their houses; in 1236 the same pope had informed his judges in England that the sisters of the Hospital's house at Aconbury, Herefordshire, had complained that the priest whom the Hospitallers had appointed to their house had been behaving *nimis inhoneste*, excessively dishonourably. Sisters were particularly vulnerable, as it was impossible to protect them entirely from rapacious men: even if all men were excluded from the house, a brother priest had to enter the house regularly to provide the sacraments. In 1427 the Hospitaller women's houses at Alguaire and Sigena in Aragon were involved in a scandal involving Sister Margarida d'Erill, who had become pregnant, and implicating at least three Hospitaller brothers: her cousin, who was currently commander at Alguaire, the priest at Sigena and the priest at Alguaire. In around 1314 Brother Ramon d'Ampurias, prior of Catalonia, was accused of having impeded two of his squires from giving their confessions when they were dying at Rhodes, so that his homosexual relations with them would not become public. He was also accused of raping many ladies and having many illegitimate children. Ramon d'Ampurias was eventually deprived of office after a long armed resistance and a papal excommunication. Grand Master Juan Fernández de Heredia, formerly castellan of Amposta, fathered at least four illegitimate children by two or more women. Less high profile cases included the Greek woman who died a martyr fighting at Rhodes against the Turks in the siege of 1522, who was apparently the partner of a Hospitaller officer, and Alonso de Contreras, who continued to enjoy the company of women after becoming a brother of the Hospital.[27]

Appearances of the Order in fictional literature from the thirteenth century onwards implicated the Order in romantic love affairs in one way or another. In Joanot Martorell's famous romance *Tirant lo Blanc*, written in Valencia between 1460 and 1468, the love of a Navarrese Hospitaller brother, Simó de Far, for a lady plays a crucial role in saving the Order of the Hospital from the Muslims. Joanot Martorell's work is notable for its historical accuracy rather than its flights of fancy, and his inclusion of a Hospitaller love affair indicates that the Hospitallers of Rhodes were not viewed as immune from the attractions of women. The Order has long been depicted as a suitable refuge for those disappointed in love: most famously for Raoul de Bragelonne in Alexandre Dumas's *Le Vicomte de Bragelonne* (1847).[28]

Lapses aside, the Hospitallers were nevertheless members of a religious order. The brothers' chief devotion, after Christ and the Blessed Virgin Mary, was to St John the Baptist, whose head appears on some of the seals of the Order in England. Other images of the saint also appear on plaques attached to houses of the Order in England. The conventual church of St John on Rhodes was destroyed in the nineteenth century and its iconography is lost, but the conventual church of St John in Valletta, Malta, has over the high altar a painting of the beheading of St John the Baptist (see plate III), an outstanding work of art by Michelangelo da Caravaggio (1571(?)–1610), who was briefly a knight of the Order. The ceiling of the church shows scenes from the life of St John the Baptist, painted by Mattia Preti (1613–99).

[27] *Cartulaire*, nos 2186, 2140; Anthony Luttrell, 'Margarida d'Erill, Hospitaller of Alguaire: 1415–1456', *Anuario de Estudios Medievales*, 28 (1998), 219–49; idem, 'Gli Ospitalieri di San Giovanni di Gerusalemme dal Continente alle Isole', in *Acri 1291: La Fine della Presenza degli Ordini Militari in Terra Sancta e I Nuovi Orientamenti nel XIV Secolo*, ed. Francesco Tommasi (Perugia, 1996), pp. 75–91: here p. 83; reprinted in his *Hospitaller State on Rhodes and its Western Provinces, 1306–1462* (Aldershot, 1999), ch. 2; idem, 'Gli Ospitalieri e l'Eredità dei Templari, 1305–1378', in *I Templari: Mito e Storia – Atti de Convegno Internazionale di Studi alla Magione Templare di Poggibonsi-Siena (29–31 Maggio 1987)*, ed. G. Minnucci and F. Sardi (Singaluna-Siena, 1989), pp. 67–86, here p. 75; reprinted in Luttrell, *The Hospitallers of Rhodes and their Mediterranean World* (Aldershot, 1992), ch. 3; idem, 'Hospitaller Life in Aragon', in *God and Man in Medieval Spain. Essays in Honour of J. R. L. Highfield*, ed. D. W. Lomax and D. Mackenzie (Warminster, 1989), pp. 97–115: here p. 111; reprinted in Luttrell, *Hospitallers of Rhodes*, ch. 15. On the martyred Greek mother see Vertot, *Histoire*, 3, pp. 342–3 and note. See also Alonso de Contreras, pp. 174–5.

[28] Joanot Martorell and Martí Juan de Galba, *Tirant lo Blanc*, ed. Marti de Riquer, 2 vols, 2nd edn (Barcelona, 1970), 1, pp. 295–8, ch. 98. See also Helen Nicholson, *Love, War and the Grail: Templars, Hospitallers and Teutonic Knights in Medieval Epic and Romance Literature 1150–1500* (Leiden, 2001).

In the twelfth century the Order sometimes built its commandery churches with circular naves, in imitation of the Church of the Holy Sepulchre which it helped to protect in Jerusalem, and whose pilgrims it cared for. One such church still exists at Little Maplestead in Essex; the priory church at Clerkenwell, Middlesex, was another. However, by the late thirteenth century this architectural style was abandoned by the Order – perhaps because it had lost its iconographic purpose following the loss of Jerusalem – and the church at Clerkenwell was rebuilt with a rectangular nave. As was usual in the middle ages, the interior of the Order's churches and chapels were decorated with wall-paintings illustrating religious subjects: such paintings survive at Crac des Chevaliers and Marqab; paintings at Sigena also survived into modern times. These sometimes showed military martyr-saints such as St George, for example at Crac des Chevaliers; they would also show images of female martyr-saints such as Catherine of Alexandria, whose patient and faithful suffering under pagan torment was a potent example to the warriors who fought non-Christians and must be prepared to face martyrdom on the battlefield. Catherine had a particular appeal for the Order in that it claimed to possess her arm, which in 1458 was kept in the chapel of the palace of the grand master in Rhodes town. The Order also had a relic of the martyr St Sebastian, which was stolen during the move from Rhodes and taken by a Greek deacon to Majorca.

This preference for martyr-saints continued in the art of the post-medieval Order, although St John the Baptist remained an important subject. Christ – particularly His crucifixion – and the Blessed Virgin Mary also appear, unsurprisingly; again, the emphasis on Christ's suffering and death had a particularly edifying function in a religious order dedicated to martyrdom on the battlefield. The works of art commissioned by the Hospitallers on Malta for the conventual church included the martyrdom of St Sebastian (seventeenth-century, anonymous Italian Master) and St Sebasian being tended by the holy women after the martyrdom attempt (seventeenth-century, by Cassarino). *The Martyrdom of St Catherine* was painted for the Order by Mattia Preti in the late 1650s; he also sent the Order an altarpiece of *St George on Horseback*, for the conventual church. Preti received the commission to decorate the ceiling of the conventual church in 1661, a work he completed in less than five years. After completing the ceiling, Preti remained on Malta and produced many other works of art; he also ran a workshop that produced work for the local and foreign markets, and trained many artists, Maltese, knights of the Order and Italians. He was patronised by grand masters Rafael and Nicolas Cotoner (1660–63; 1663–80). His works for the Order included another *Saint Catherine*, and a *Saint George and the Dragon* commissioned by the knight governor of Gozo for the basilica of St George in Victoria. His work was a significant stimulus to artistic development on Malta, and through him the Order of St John had some notable impact on baroque art.

The Order's piety also revealed itself in the collection of holy relics. It was believed in the middle ages that the possession of holy relics was in itself an indicator of spiritual worth, for relics would not remain with an unspiritual person. Through the relic, a physical token of a saint's existence on earth, God could operate, as if the relic were a conduit for God's power. Alternatively, the saints could operate through their relics. The Hospital owned many relics, which it collected from its earliest days in Jerusalem. These were proudly displayed to pilgrims, who would have venerated them and given gifts to the Order in response. A pilgrim's guide to Jerusalem of around 1170 mentions the 'very holy relics' kept at the Hospital's church of St John the Baptist. Another guide states that the Hospital had the stone water-pot in which the Lord turned water into wine (John 2 vv 1–11).[29] After the dissolution of the Templars the Hospital received many of their relics, including the supposed relics of St Euphemia of Chalcedon. In 1458 it was also recorded as having the arm of St Catherine and relics of St Anthony, as well as a holy thorn from Christ's crown of thorns. Its acquisition of the arm of St John the Baptist from the Ottoman sultan has been described in chapter three; Sultan Suleiman wanted this relic returned after the fall of Rhodes, but the grand master succeeded in dissuading him, although he did have to give the sultan a painting of the Annunciation. In 1501 Brother Emery d'Amboise, then prior of France, gave the Order a gold plate with a portion of St John the Baptist's skull set into it; this was taken by the brothers to Malta in 1530.

Despite changes to Catholic devotion during the middle ages and early modern period which resulted in a reduction in the veneration of relics, the Hospital retained its relics and took care to keep them properly housed. For the Order they represented its long, active and illustrious history, and gave validity to its vocation. Brother Paul de Forbin, the Order's ambassador to King Louis XIII (1610–43) and Queen Anne of France (died 1666), on the birth of the dauphin Louis in 1638, declared: 'This Order has always held God and His saints in the highest esteem. Throughout its defeats, its sieges, its retreats and losses, it has always venerated relics with the profoundest respect.'[30] Even if it might seem to outsiders that the Hospitallers' main interest was in gaining wealth and influence for themselves, the brothers could always point to the visual symbols of their devotion, their infirmary and their military activity against the Muslims, as proof that they were still primarily a religious order, serving Christ and His Mother.

[29] *Jerusalem Pilgrimage, 1099–1185*, ed. J. Wilkinson, J. Hill and W. F. Ryan, Hakluyt Society, 2nd series, 167 (London, 1988), pp. 11, 178 and pp. 21, 239. For the relics after 1291 see Anthony Luttrell, 'The Rhodian Background of the Order of Saint John on Malta', in *The Order's Early Legacy in Malta*, ed. John Azzopardi (Valletta, 1989), pp. 3–14: here pp. 12–14; reprinted in his *Hospitallers of Rhodes and their Mediterranean World* (Aldershot, 1992), ch. 18.

[30] Quoted by David F. Allen, 'The Order of St John as a "School for Ambassadors" in Counter-Reformation Europe', in *The Military Orders*, vol. 2, *Welfare and Warfare*, ed. H. Nicholson (Aldershot, 1998), pp. 363–79: here p. 373.

5

Relations with the Rest of Christendom: the Hospitallers' economic and political activities in Europe

ALTHOUGH medieval religious orders claimed to stand apart from 'the world', that is, everyday society, in fact they were inevitably an integral part of it. They depended upon the secular authorities for gifts of property, exemptions from taxes and other dues, and for protection. They depended on ordinary people for labour and for small-scale support, such as gifts of rent and money and confraternity payments. The lands which they were given were useless unless they were exploited through agriculture or industry; and the act of exploiting their assets had an impact on the society around them, which often aroused ill-will. In return for the gifts and protection which they received from secular lords they were expected to perform various services, which in turn gave them enormous political impact on society but which deflected them from their religious vocation and aroused criticism.

For the military orders, as international landowners and with a high-profile vocation which was of interest to the whole of Christendom, these factors were particularly significant. Their military operations required enormous financial investment, as did even the hospitals, although on a lesser scale. Some money came from booty from military campaigns and the ransom of prisoners; while the Order was based on Malta, these were a major source of income.

Economic and commercial development were safer and more reliable in raising funds than were the fortunes of war. Yet the exploitation of landed estates and winning the favour of secular authorities involved the Hospitallers in various activities which seem a long way from their proper vocation and which won them much criticism. By the early modern period the Hospital became an important and influential political power in the West; Hospitallers served popes and kings in important, trustworthy offices. Yet this led to a divergence of interests among its members, for kings expected them to put royal interests

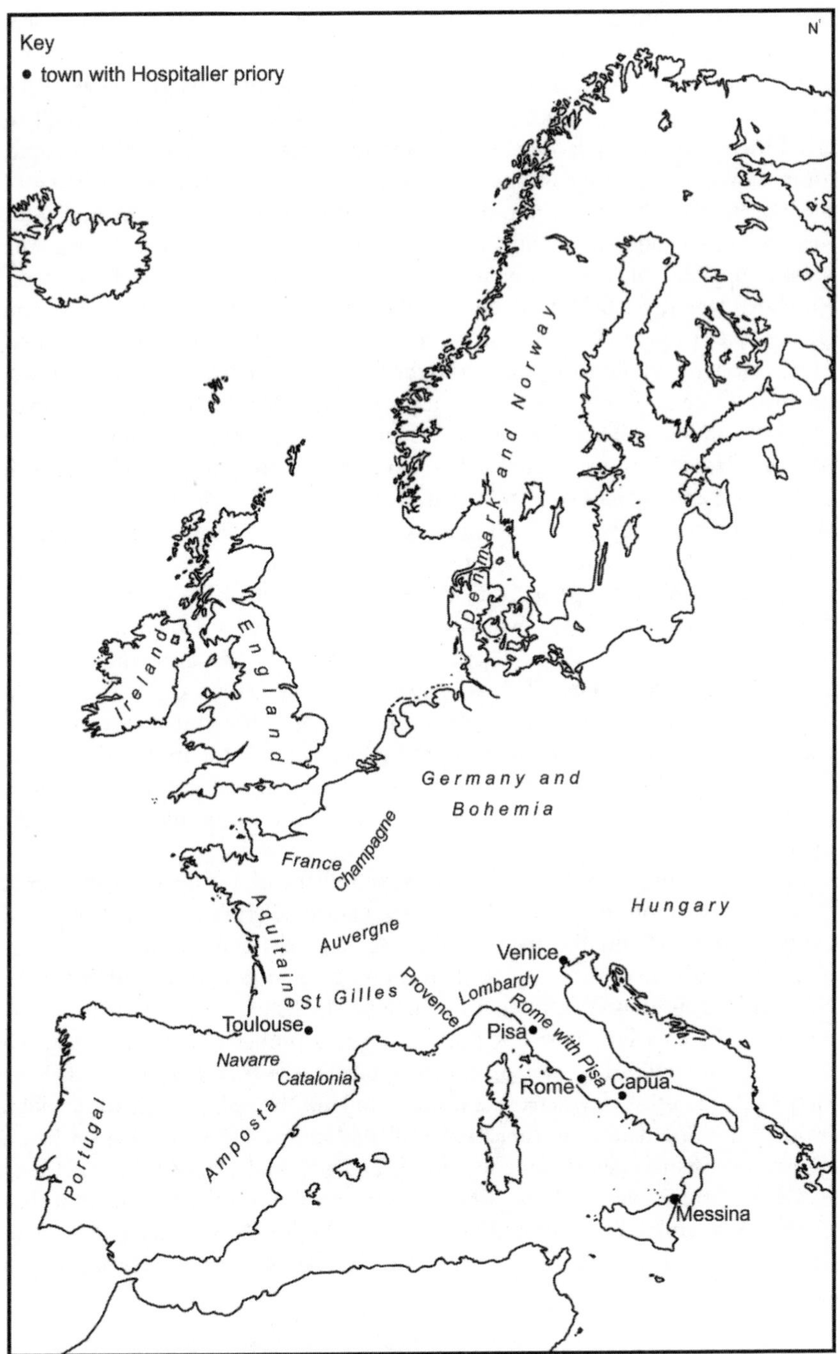

Fig. 4. The provincial officials of the Hospital recorded in the proceedings of the General Chapter of 1330.

before those of the Order, and brothers were tempted to put their national interests before those of the Order.

The Order's economic activities were important in the East as well as in the West. Everywhere that the Order produced grain in its fields it needed mills to grind the grain; but mills were also an important means of generating income, for as they were expensive to build and maintain there were still relatively few of them in the twelfth century and those who owned them could charge highly for their use. The majority of mills in the twelth century were water-driven. The most notorious of the Hospital's water-driven wheat mills was on Nahr Kurdaneh (the River Belus), which flowed over the low-lying land from Kurdani (Recordane) to Acre. At Da'uk (Doc), downstream from the Hospital's mill was a mill belonging to the Templars. From the first decades of the thirteenth century the two Orders were in constant disputes over the water supply to their respective mills, which twice had to be settled by arbitration arranged by the papacy.[1] These disputes illustrate the economic importance of mills to both Orders, but also the lack of respect that the personnel of each Order could show towards the other. It was this sort of petty incident which earned the two leading military orders a reputation for constant rivalry.

The supply of water pressure to drive a mill did not have to come from a river or stream. The Order owned a tide mill in Horsley Down meadow on the south bank of the River Thames in London, just downstream of where Tower Bridge now stands.[2] This was operated by the action of the tide; when the tide came in it filled a 'tidepond' behind the mill, which remained full when the tide went out. The water in the pond then ran the mill until the tide came in again. As this sort of mill is cheap and practical around the British coast where tidal ranges are high, tide mills were common during the medieval period.

In 1220 the Hospital in Ireland came into conflict with the burghers of Dublin over their mill on the River Liffey. The Hospitallers at Kilmainham had constructed a mill on the river with a weir and millpond which completely blocked the course of the river, so that shipping could not go up and down the river and fish were unable to cross, damaging the fisheries of the king and the people of the city. From the description, it seems probable that this was also a tide mill. The political power of the Hospitallers was such that although King Henry III (1216–72) instructed the justiciar to have the mill pond made smaller, by 1223 nothing had been done. The mill was still *in situ* in 1269–70, when a dispute over fishery rights came to a head. The king had a fixed fishing net next to the city bridge over the Liffey which was let out to the citizens of Dublin. The prior of Kilmainham complained to the mayor, Roger of Ashbourne, that it was damaging his fishery rights in the river. The prior and his men then broke the net

[1] *Cartulaire*, nos 2117, 3045; J. Riley-Smith, *The Knights of St John in Jerusalem and Cyprus: c.1050–1310* (London, 1967), p. 446

[2] Geoffrey Day, *Tide Mills in England and Wales* (Ipswich, 1994), p. 13.

'by force and arms' whereupon the mayor and citizens went to the prior's mill and demolished it.[3]

Not all mills were for the production of wheat flour. Sugar was an important product in the Latin East. It was produced from sugar cane, which was ground in mills. The remains of pottery sugar cones for the manufacture of sugar have been found at the sugar factory (mill and aqueduct) at Khirbat Manawat (also known as Manot or Manueth), which was given to the Hospitallers in or after 1217. From 1210 the Order held Kolossi in Cyprus, a centre of sugar production, and in the fourteenth and fifteenth centuries the output of sugar here produced a significant income for the Order.

There were other forms of produce from the Hospital's estates in the East: there was apparently a salting at their tower of Burj al-Malih; there was an olive press at Khirbat Manawat. In Rhodes sugar, soap and linen cloth were produced. In Malta the Order produced luxury goods for export, such as oranges and orange-flower water, and bred falcons; high quality cotton was also produced. By the late eighteenth century cotton was the major product of Malta and Gozo.

The Hospitallers owned wide agricultural estates throughout Europe, varying from small Italian farms to vast areas in Catalonia. Their methods of exploitation varied depending on the location. In Italy the brothers of the commanderies preferred to farm the land themselves; in Essex, England, the Order appointed non-brothers as managers, leased out its lands to farmers and used hired rent-collectors. The Order traded the production from its estates, which varied from one area to another: in Aragon it sold pine trees from its woods; on Sicily it had orchards and vineyards which were destroyed during 1267–8 in the wars between Charles I of Anjou (died 1285) and Conradin. From Sicily it exported grain and vegetables to the Holy Land in its own ships: in 1289–91 King Charles II of Naples (1285–1309) demanded guarantees from the masters of the Temple and the Hospital that wheat they exported from his kingdom would not be sold in the lands of his enemies. In 1240 the prior of England bought part of Leicester Forest from Earl Simon de Montfort of Leicester (died 1265), the rest being purchased by the canons of Leicester Abbey. The two groups of religious then set about felling and selling the timber.[4]

Like other religious orders, the Hospital also engaged in mining activities, where conditions allowed. Charles I of Anjou licensed the brothers to mine for lead, silver and gold on the kingdom of Sicily. In 1373 the Order was recorded

[3] J. T. Gilbert, *Historical and Municipal Documents of Ireland, 1172–1320*, Rolls Series, 53 (London, 1878), pp. 75–6, 79–80; *Calendar of Documents Relating to Ireland*, vol. 5, *1302–1307*, ed. H. S. Sweetman (London, 1886), pp. 81–2, no. 239.

[4] Sicily: *Cartulaire*, 4, no. 3308; 3, nos 3351, 3360, 3362; *I Registri della Cancellaria Angioina Ricostruiti da Riccardo Filangieri*, 35 (Naples, 1985), p. 247, no. 390: for a reference to a ship of the Hospital at Marseilles in 1289–91, see ibid., pp. 125–6, no. 322. For Leicester Forest: Matthew Paris, *Chronica Majora*, ed. H. R. Luard, 7 vols, Rolls Series, 57 (London, 1872–83), 4, p. 7.

Plate 10. The Hospitallers' castle of Kolossi, Cyprus. Photo copyright: Juan Fuguet Sans.

as owning a coal mine at Fenham St Andrews in Newcastle upon Tyne, England.[5]

The Order's reliance on its European estates to support its operations in the East is made clear in Master Hugh Revel's letter of 1268 to Ferrand de Barres, prior of St Gilles, in which he declares that wars in Sicily, Italy and England, and problems in France, prevent him from obtaining anything from these countries; 'we have never received anything from Spain except sometimes a number of animals', while drought in Armenia and the invasions of Sultan Baibars have left the Order in desperate straits in the Holy Land. Therefore he is calling on the priories of St Gilles, Auvergne and Germany for help.[6] Yet the Order did produce some of its needs in the East and its sugar production in particular was a valuable source of income.

Much of the land given to the Hospital in the West, in common with many such donations to religious orders, was of little agricultural productivity and required investment to make it profitable. In frontier areas, both within and on the outskirts of Christendom, landowners gave unproductive lands to religious orders with the intention that they would colonise them and make them productive. In south Wales, disputed territory on the frontier between the Cymro-Norman marcher lords and the Welsh princes was given to the Hospital as a means of winning God's favour, demonstrating concern for the defence of Christendom and stabilising the frontier. In Ireland, Cymro-Norman donations to the Hospital were far from the frontier but nevertheless served the purpose of stabilising the acquired territories. On a much larger scale, the Hospital was engaged in encouraging the colonisation of its lands in the Iberian peninsula. Extensive lands were given to it in north-eastern Europe for colonisation. After 1309 the Order also attempted to attract colonists to Rhodes, although here it was less successful.

The Order was also engaged in wider commercial undertakings. Many donations of rents were given to it; not only rents on land but also on houses in towns. The twelfth and thirteenth centuries were times of rapid economic and commercial growth in which agricultural production and the population rose, towns grew, new towns were founded and trade expanded. Many markets and fairs were licensed, at which this expanding trade could take place. In 1246 King Henry III of England granted the Hospital the right to hold a weekly market on Tuesdays at their manor of Kirkby, as well as an annual fair.[7] Rhodes was a centre of eastern Mediterranean commerce, although not of major importance. In contrast, Malta under the Order became a transit port for international trade,

[5] In Sicily: Jean Dunbabin, *Charles I of Anjou: Power, Kingship and State-Making in Thirteenth-Century Europe* (London, 1998), p. 157. In Northumberland: *Calendar of the Patent Rolls Preserved in the Public Record Office. Edward III*, vol. 15, *AD 1370–1374* (London, 1914), p. 389.

[6] *Cartulaire*, 4, no. 3308.

[7] *Cartulaire*, no. 1088; *Calendar of the Charter Rolls preserved in the Public Record Office*, vol. 1, *Henry III, 1227–1257* (London, 1903), p. 305.

Plate 11. A frontier far from Jerusalem: the Hospitallers' church of Llanrhidian, Gower Peninsula, south Wales. Built by the Order in the thirteenth century following local architectural styles, the church was designed to be used as a refuge for local people against bandits and pirates. Photo copyright: Nigel Nicholson.

and the Maltese dealt in the exchange of money and goods; this development is reflected in the vast warehouse buildings built on Grand Harbour by Grand Master Emanuel Pinto de Fonseca (1741–73).

The Order also engaged in moneylending, although to a lesser degree than the Order of the Temple. The first occasion that the Order is known to have loaned money to a king was to King Louis VII of France (1137–80) during the Second Crusade (1147–49). The Order also lent money to the English royal administration during the minority of Henry III (1216–27), and to King Charles II of Naples in 1289–91.[8] Such money-lending formed the foundation of a close relationship between the Order and European monarchs throughout its history.

The Order's widespread economic and commercial operations, coupled to its exemptions from royal and ecclesiastical dues and legal exemptions, aroused a good deal of local resentment. During the inquests in England during 1274 the burghers of Plympton St Maurice and of Dartmouth, Devon, complained about the Hospitallers' liberty of buying and selling without paying tolls, which gave them an unfair advantage in trade. The burghers of Totnes protested at the privileges of the Hospitallers which exempted their 'men' from paying merchantile dues in the port or the market and enabled them to have anyone who tried to exact from their 'men' tolls or other dues on merchandise, buying and selling, summoned to answer cases in courts at the other end of the country. At Wirksworth in Derbyshire the jurors declared that the Hospitallers abused the privileges that they had obtained from the pope to bring many people to court in London and elsewhere, which was causing much inconvenience.[9] In the Parliament of 1385 a 'petition from the commons' asked that the money in the hands of the prior of St John of Jerusalem in England 'called responsions' be used to the profit and honour of the lord king, to relieve and support his poor people, rather than being sent to the East. In England in the 1380s, after the expenses of wars with France and with Scotland, repeated epidemics of plague and the Peasant's Revolt, the sending of so much money to support a war at the other end of Europe must have seemed to some an unjustifiable luxury. The king's reply was that he wished the money to be taken to the convent on Rhodes to maintain the war against the infidel; but if the prior preferred, he would take advice from his nobles and his council as to how

[8] For Louis VII, see *Cartulaire*, no. 185. For Henry III, see: *Roll of Divers Accounts for the Early Years of the Reign of Henry* III, ed. F. A. Cazel, Publications of the Pipe Roll Society, 82 (n.s. 44) (London, 1982), pp. 51, 57; *Rotuli Litterarum Clausarum in Turri Londinensi Asservati*, ed. Thomas Duffus Hardy, vol. 1 (London, 1833), p. 456; *Patent Rolls of the Reign of Henry III Preserved in the Public Record Office, 1216–1232*, 2 vols (London, 1901–3), 1, pp. 455, 529. For Charles II of Anjou, see: *I Registri della Cancellaria Angioina*, vol. 32, *1289–90* (1982), p. 100, no. 38, p. 187, no. 316, p. 188, no. 320, p. 190, no. 327, p. 236, no. 509, p. 239, no. 523; ibid., vol. 35, *1289–91* (1985), p. 165.

[9] *Rotuli Hundredorum Temporis Henricis III et Edwardi I in Turri Londoniensis et Curia Receptae Scaccarii Westm. Asservati*, 2 vols (London, 1812–18), 1, pp. 58, 77, 83, 95, 96.

the money could be best used.[10] Clearly the prior was under moral pressure to allow his responsions to be used for poor relief nearer to home; but he continued to send the money to the East.

The Order's location in the Holy Land in the first two centuries of its existence, and its continued commitment to holy war and the recovery of the holy places, meant that any monarch who supported it was demonstrating a commitment to holy war and the holy places, an essential aspect of European kingship. Support for the Order could also demonstrate support for the papacy, although this was less certain. It is certainly the case that the Order of the Hospital has always been close to the papacy: it was taken directly under papal protection, *tutela apostolica*, by the papal bull *Pie postulatio voluntatis* of 1113, a privilege which brought with it freedom from any other ecclesiastical power. Papal support for the Hospital underlined the papal responsibility for the holy places of Christendom. In turn, the Hospital could give the papacy valuable political support. Pope Innocent II gave two important bulls of exemption to the Hospital and one to the Temple; his pontificate was marked by a schism and the election of antipopes Analectus II (1130–38) and Victor IV (1138). In times of uncertain authority, supporting the religious Orders which defended the Holy Land strengthened the pope's position. Likewise, Pope Alexander III was faced by a succession of antipopes supported by the emperor Frederick Barbarossa (1152–90). The Welsh cleric Gerald of Wales (died 1223) recorded that Alexander declared a particular affection for the Templars, the Hospitallers and the Cistercians. These happened to be Orders which Gerald hated, so that he may simply be underlining his own dislike of this pope. However, they were also all new religious orders with a high standard of spiritual life which were directly under papal protection. At the Third Lateran Council of 1179 the secular clergy attempted to have the Templars' and Hospitallers' privileges restricted to prevent their misusing them, but this was unsuccessful because the pope's interpretation of their rulings was more generous than the council had intended.

From the twelfth to the early fourteenth centuries, popes appointed Templars and Hospitallers to honourable offices and positions of trust. The prior of the Hospital in Acre was a papal chaplain under Pope Urban IV (1261–4); a Hospitaller held the post of papal porter under Pope Martin IV (1281–5). A Templar and Hospitaller often appear as papal chamberlains. During the Fifth Crusade (1217–21), Pope Honorius III entrusted the transportation of a large volume of cash destined for his legate Pelagius in Damietta to Templars and Hospitallers because, he said, he had no other messengers that he could trust better. In 1274, Pope Gregory X (1271–6) appointed Brother William de Villaret of the Hospital as vicar of the county of Venaissin; this appointment was

[10] *Rotuli Parliamentorum ut et Petitiones, et Placita in Parliamento*, collected by R. Blyke, P. Morant, T. Astle, J. Topham, ed. J. Strachey, 6 vols (London, 1767–77), 3, pp. 179, 213; *Calendar of the Patent Rolls Preserved in the Public Record Office, Richard II: 1385–1389* (London, 1900), p. 95.

renewed by Popes Nicholas III (1277–80) and Martin IV (1281–5). Papal confidence in the Hospital continued into the following centuries. In around 1340 every province of the papal states was governed by an Italian Hospitaller, and in 1347 Pope Clement VI asked the queen of Naples to appoint the Hospitaller prior of Capua as her seneschal of Provence.

In particular, Pope Innocent VI favoured Juan Fernández de Heredia, who was already castellan of Amposta through royal favour. Innocent supported his appointment as prior of Castile, then as prior of St Gilles, appointed him as his ambassador, and employed him as papal captain in the defence of Avignon and the county of Venaissin. In 1358 he became captain-general of the papal forces. As a member of the suite of Cardinal Talleyrand, papal legate to France, he fought on the French side at the battle of Poitiers (1356) and was captured by the English. As castellan of Amposta he fought on the Aragonese side in the war against Castile. His military experience and wide contacts made him an invaluable papal servant; he was also simultaneously a trusted servant of King Peter IV of Aragon, who relied on him to represent his interests at the papal court in Avignon and also used him as an ambassador and as a military commander. After the death of Pope Innocent VI, his important role in papal service continued under Urban V and Gregory XI. The fact that Heredia also ran up enormous debts to the Hospital did not worry him; when his Order proceeded against him in 1359 he turned to the pope for aid, and the debts were cancelled. His career in the Order did not suffer a setback until the election of Raymond Bérenger as grand master in 1365. Raymond Bérenger was from Provence, part of Heredia's 'empire', and he was determined to curb Heredia's abuses of his position. The grand master appealed to Pope Urban V (1362–70) against Heredia's pluralism and non-residence, and as a result he lost St Gilles and Castile and was forced to reside in his priory of Aragon. He was not able to return to Avignon until after Urban V's death in 1370. The new pope, Gregory XI, recalled Heredia as papal general and in 1377 had him elevated to the post of grand master of the Hospital. Despite his abortive campaign in north-west Greece, Heredia was a largely successful grand master who governed the Hospital efficiently, gave it good military leadership and ensured that its interests were protected at Avignon. Hence in this case a good papal and royal servant also made a good grand master; but during his career Heredia's pluralism, non-residence, nepotism and retention of the Order's funds did his Order a great deal of damage.

The royal minister who served his king or pope before his Order was an increasing problem for the Order by the fourteenth century. Religious houses had long been important as centres of administration and a source of royal administrators. Brothers of the Military Orders had won prominent positions in royal government since the twelfth century. As warriors who were also religious, they were regarded as being particularly trustworthy. Under Philip II Augustus of France (1180–1223), Brother Guérin of Glapion of the Hospital rose to be one of the most powerful men in royal service. A contemporary, the 'Anonymous of

Béthune' tells us that he was of lowly birth. He had risen to be vice-chancellor of France by 1201. In 1213 he became bishop of Senlis. He supported Philip II during the king's attempt to divorce his wife Ingebourg of Denmark (died 1236), which won him a rebuke from Pope Innocent III. He was present during Philip's campaigns against Flanders and at the battle of Bouvines in 1214, where he played an important role. He accompanied Philip's son, Louis VIII (1223–6), to invade English-held Poitou in 1224, and on his Albigensian Crusade of 1226, by this time as chancellor of France. On Louis's early death, he was advisor to the young heir Louis IX (1226–70) and his mother Queen Blanche (died 1252). He died in 1227. Charles Petit-Dutaillis summed up his career in royal service: 'Guérin was not a Richelieu, but he was a great man of his day'.[11]

For Philip II, Guérin was a man whom he knew he could trust. Guérin's position in the administration was based not on his birth or his wealth but on his own skill and hard work and the king's trust and friendship. He had nothing to gain by treachery to the king, and everything to win from faithful service. To the modern historian of the Hospital, Guérin the Hospitaller appears to be a typical example of the lowly born career man who entered the Order with a view to gaining opportunities normally unavailable to those of his status.

In England, Brother Joseph of Chauncy, formerly treasurer of the Hospital, served King Edward I (1272–1307) as royal treasurer between October 1273 and June 1280. He was also prior of England during this period. Presumably Edward met him in the Holy Land during his crusade of 1271–2, and he returned with the king. In 1281 he returned to the East, from where he continued to keep Edward informed of events in the East. He was given wide responsibilities as royal treasurer, and was clearly competent, hard working and trusted by the king. Like Guérin the Hospitaller, we can only speculate about Joseph of Chauncy's origins; he was of non-noble birth, and rose through the ranks of the Hospital through his efficiency and dedication, qualities also valued by the king.[12]

Members of the military orders were particularly valued by monarchs when the monarch could not use members of the local nobility to undertake administrative duties without their acquiring so much authority and power that they would become a threat to royal authority. This could be a problem in the kingdoms of the Iberian peninsula; it was also a particular problem for the English monarchs in Ireland, where the ambitious Cymro-Norman nobility were as much a threat to the English monarch's authority as were the native Irish kings. Brothers of the Hospital acted as deputy chief justiciar and as treasurer of Ireland for periods during the thirteenth century; in the fourteenth century, Hospitallers acted as chancellor, justiciar and treasurer. Most notable of

[11] Charles Petit-Dutaillis, *L'Étude sur La Vie et Le Règne de Louis VIII (1187–1226)* (Paris, 1894), pp. 43, 197, 221, 225, 239, 244, 295, 335–6; Jim Bradbury, *Philip Augustus, King of France 1180–1223* (London, 1988), pp. 201, 243, 249–50, 252–3, 281–2, 299–300, 302–3, 305, 307, 310.

[12] Riley-Smith, *Knights*, p. 312; *Cartulaire*, no. 3518; *Calendar of the Patent Rolls Preserved in the Public Record Office: Edward I, 1272–1281* (London, 1901), p. 382.

Hospitallers in royal service in Ireland was Brother Stephen of Fulbourn, who held high office from 1280 to 1288. He was a priest-brother of the Hospital in England, who had held high office in the English priory before being sent to Ireland in 1270 by Queen Eleanor of England (wife of Henry III) on her service. He had returned to England by 1273 collecting the tax of a twentieth granted to the king in aid for the Holy Land, and collecting a tallage on the Jews. Then in 1274 he was elected bishop of Waterford and appointed treasurer of Ireland. In 1281 he was also made chief justiciar of Ireland; in 1285 he became archbishop of Tuam. He involved his brother and nephews in his administration and was accused of absolutism, nepotism and embezzlement. On his death there was a long investigation into his affairs.[13] However, it is clear that those who complained about his activities were at least as great criminals as he, and that the king had raised him to high office because he knew him to be an efficient administrator whom he could trust better than anyone else in Ireland.

Royal service was not always so beneficial to a member of the Hospital. Robert Hales was another example of the non-noble gentry who rose in the priory of England during the second half of the fourteenth century. His precise origins are unknown. He took part in King Peter I of Cyprus's expedition to Alexandria in 1365, and was commended by his Order. He then returned to England, where he appears in English government records as the prior's representative. He became prior of England in 1372. As prior, he was expected to contribute troops to the defence of England against possible French and Spanish invasion. He had been appointed admiral of the fleet to the westward by 1 May 1377, before the death of Edward III. He was made a member of the council governing for the young Richard II (1377–99). On 1 February 1381 he was made royal treasurer. The contemporary chronicler Thomas Walsingham remarked that Hales was a great-hearted and active knight, but that he would not please the community of the realm. Subsequent events give some indication of why Hales was not popular.

Hales was beheaded by the rebels during the Peasant's Revolt of early summer 1381. His death can be attributed to a combination of causes: his association with the hated third poll tax, collected while he was treasurer; his position as one of Richard II's counsellors, blamed for the government's bad policies and particularly for advising him not to negotiate with the rebels; and personal vendettas against him, notably that of Thomas Farndon or Farringdon who claimed that the prior had expelled him unjustly from his inheritance. As one of the rebel leaders, Farndon went to meet King Richard II at the assembly at Mile End, grabbed the bridle of his horse and exclaimed: 'Avenge me on that false traitor the prior for my property which he falsely and fraudulently stole from me. Do me justice because otherwise I will get justice done myself.' Farndon was later

[13] *Calendar of Documents Relating to Ireland, preserved in Her Majesty's Public Record Office, London*, ed. W. S. Sweetman, 5 vols (London, 1875–86), 2, p. 177, no. 1034, no. 1883, p. 489, no. 2114 and see the index, pp. 726–8; 3, pp. 1–15; no. 2; pp. 254–7, 290–4; James Lydon, 'The Years of Crisis, 1254–1315', in *New History of Ireland*, vol. 2, *Medieval Ireland, 1169–1534*, ed. Art Cosgrave (Oxford, 1993), pp. 179–204, here p. 191.

accused before the king's bench of being chiefly responsible for Hales's death. He was imprisoned, but released.[14]

Like Brother Guérin and Joseph of Chauncy, Robert Hales worked his way up through the ranks of the Hospital to a position of great power, close to the king, but unlike them he was the servant of an unpopular regime. It appears that he had also been using his position to acquire property by legally doubtful means, and at a time of political instability this proved his final undoing. Hales's death was noted, but not mourned by the chroniclers.

Political ambition was less fatal for Brother Henri d'Estampes de Valençay, whose career has been traced by David Allen.[15] In the early modern period the knight-brothers were usually of noble birth, but brothers still used the Order as a gateway to opportunities otherwise unavailable to them. Valençay's good reputation as a brother of intelligence and piety led to his being appointed as his Order's ambassador to the papal court, but as he became embroiled in political scheming he lost the confidence of the grand master, Jean Paul de Lascaris (1636–57). After the rise to power of Cardinal Mazarin (died 1661) at the French court, Valençay became a client of the cardinal, to such an extent that he put his loyalty to Mazarin before his loyalty to his Order. He described Mazarin as 'the miracle of our times, the hero of the age, the glory of Italy and the reputation of France' and dedicated his life to the advancement of France over Spain. Mazarin made good use of his service on behalf of France during the Neopolitan revolt of 1647–8. Valençay was made French ambassador to the papal court, where he singularly failed to keep the grand master informed of events as he was now primarily serving Mazarin and France. As French ambassador in Rome, he supported the French alliance with the Ottomans even as his Order was struggling to prevent the Ottomans from conquering Crete. In return for his faithful service, Valençay seems to have hoped that Mazarin would nominate him as a cardinal. Mazarin in fact supported him as next grand master of his Order, but he was unsuccessful, and in 1657 Valençay's rival Martin de Redin, prior of Navarre, was elected by the Order instead.

[14] Charles Tipton, 'The English Hospitallers During the Great Schism', *Studies in Medieval and Renaissance History*, 4 (1967), 91–124: here 96, 99–100; *Calendar of the Close Rolls. Edward III*, vol. 13: *AD 1369–1374* (London, 1911), p. 568; vol. 14, *AD 1374–1377*, p. 495; *Calendar of the Patent Rolls Preserved in the Public Record Office. Richard II: AD 1377–1381* (London, 1895), p. 589; Thomas Walsingham, *Chronica Monasterii S. Albani Thomae Walsingham quondam Monachi S. Albani, Historia Anglicana*, ed. Henry Thomas Riley, Rolls Series, 28, 2 vols (London, 1863–64), 1, pp. 449–50; P.R.O., KB 145/3/6/1, printed in André Reville, *Le Soulèvement des travailleurs d'Angleterre en 1381, Études et Documents Publiés avec une Introduction Historique par Ch. Petit-Dutaillis*, Mémoires et Documents Publiées par la Société de l'École des Chartes, 2 (Paris, 1898), pp. 194–5, no. 10; Charles Oman, *The Great Revolt of 1381*, new edn with introduction by E. B. Fryde (Oxford, 1969), pp. 211–12; and translated in R. B. Dobson, *The Peasants' Revolt of 1381* (Basingstoke, 1970, 1983), pp. 218–19; P.R.O., KB27/484 rex 3r.

[15] Allen, 'Order of St John as a School for Ambassadors', in *The Military Orders*, vol. 2, *Welfare and Warfare*, pp. 368–70, 376–9.

Arguably Valençay's political activities had alienated his brothers, thereby reducing his chances of winning the grand mastership.

From the first, the brothers of the military orders had been expected to serve the kings of the country in which they were based. This could involve acting as ambassadors, lending money, or holding offices close to the king, for example porters, chamberlains or almoners. They also came under pressure to commit their military resources to European Christian monarchs in their wars against each other; sometimes monarchs took their resources without the permission of the Order. In the twelfth and thirteenth centuries the military orders strove to avoid such entanglements, generally with success. By the fourteenth century they were no longer being so successful. In theory the Order maintained its neutrality in disputes between Christian rulers, but in practice it had to recognise that monarchs insisted that brothers within a realm had a natural duty to assist their sovereign in its defence.

During the thirteenth and fourteenth centuries it was becoming accepted that as kings were appointed by God, and the realm was under God's protection, war in defence of the realm was a type of holy war. Brothers helping their 'natural' sovereign in his wars were therefore fighting a holy war – even though they could be fighting against other brothers of their Order who were fighting for the other side. Already during the crusade of King Philip III of France (1270–85) against Aragon, King Peter III of Aragon (1276–85) had expected the military orders to give him military aid in the defence of the realm, and his successor Alfonso III (1285–91) had complained bitterly to the Hospitallers that some of the French brothers had joined the crusade against him.[16] Throughout the fourteenth century, the prior of England, in common with other leading ecclesiastics in England, was expected to provide military aid for the defence of England, and he was restricted in sending his responsions to Rhodes on the basis that they were being sent to the king's enemies – France being the dominant 'tongue' within the Hospital. The prior of France and the castellan of Amposta fought on the French side at the battle of Crécy in 1346 and were killed. It has already been noted above that Juan Fernández de Heredia fought on the French side at the battle of Poitiers in 1356 and on the Aragonese side in the wars between Aragon and Castile during the fourteenth century. In 1511, during the Franco-Spanish wars in Italy, the Hospitaller prior of Messina, Sir Pedro de Coignes, knight of Rhodes, was present among the troops of the Spanish captain Saint-Croix at Ferrara, and acted as second in a duel between Saint-Croix and the Spanish lord Azevedo.[17]

Alonso de Contreras, who had served the king of Spain as a soldier and as a commander before joining the Hospital, returned to Spain almost immediately after making his vows and applied for the post of captain in the service of King

[16] *Cartulaire*, no. 4007.

[17] *La Très Joyeuse, Plaisante et Récreative Histoire du Gentil Seigneur de Bayart Composée poar le Loyal Serviteur*, ed. M. J. Roman, Société de l'Histoire de France (Paris, 1878), pp. 253–5.

Philip III (1598–1621). His autobiography indicates that he continued to serve the Spanish crown and its officials for the rest of his life, while wearing the habit of the Order. Coming from a poor family, service in the Order alone was insufficient to provide for his livelihood, and even as a brother of the Order he looked to the Spanish crown to provide him with promotion and the opportunity to win honour in service. When he finally won promotion to knight-brother, it was with the support of the count and countess of Monterey, who were ambassadors extraordinary to Rome for King Philip IV (1621–65) and currently his employers.[18] He was not the only brother of the Order who continued to serve his national monarch before his Order, irrespective of his vows. The French and Spanish brothers fought on opposite sides in the Franco-Spanish war of 1638–9 and again during the Neopolitan revolt of 1647–8. During these wars, the French brothers used their ships against the Spanish and Sicilians. In retaliation the Spanish viceroy in Sicily forbade the export of grain to Malta, resulting in famine on Malta.[19] Throughout the Order's history, brothers of the Order fought against each other and against other Christians in national wars.

Even when the Order was able to enforce its neutrality, it still suffered as it was suspected by both sides: as in the war of the Spanish Succession (1701–13) when grain supplies from Sicily to Malta were cut off because of a suspicion that the Order was aiding the British, and all parties attacked Maltese shipping. French influence on Malta was regarded with suspicion by the Spanish, the British and the Dutch.

Nevertheless, the Order was occasionally able to avoid such entanglements. In 1617 the Spanish duke of Osuna asked Grand Master Alof de Wignacort (1601–22) for the assistance of the Hospital's galleys in his projected expedition against the Turks; but the grand master had been tipped off by the Venetians that the expedition was actually intended to attack Venetian property in Dalmatia. He informed the duke that he would only allow the Hospitallers' galleys to join his expedition if he could be assured 'that the Hospitaller squadron would serve no other purpose than to fight the Turk and the infidel'. The duke was unable to give this assurance, and the grand master refused assistance. In 1619 the Hospital decided to send naval forces to assist the duke of Savoy against the Turks, but the grand master wrote to assure the Venetian Republic that the fleet was intended to attack 'the common enemy' (the Turks) and his captains had been strictly instructed not to harm Venetian interests. In 1740 the Hospital successfully refused to allow its fleet to assist the Spanish fleet to harass British shipping in the Mediterranean, or to allow privateers to be armed on Malta in order to attack the British. Grand Master Ramon Despuig (1736–41), himself a Spaniard, appealed to the sacred college (then in the process of electing a new pope) to defend the Hospital against Spanish pressure to misuse his fleet against a

[18] Alonso de Contreras, pp. 173–4, 182, 211, 226–7.

[19] Allen, 'Order of St John as a School for Ambassadors', pp. 374–5; Vertot, *Histoire*, 5, pp. 195, 209, 213–16.

Christian nation. The sacred college supported his claim, and the Spanish crown was forced to withdraw its demands.

Although brothers could justify fighting in defence of the realm on behalf of their 'natural' lord and king, they also became involved in civil wars within their realm, against the crowned monarch. During the reign of King John II (died 1479) and Queen Blanca of Navarre, Prior John of Beaumont of the Hospital of Navarre was chancellor of the kingdom and also guardian of the heir to the throne, Charles, prince of Viana. In 1451 he joined the prince's revolt against the king, and became one of the leaders of the revolt. In 1468, during the wars of the Roses in England, the English Hospitallers gave their support to Richard Neville, earl of Warwick, against King Edward IV after that king had tried to make his brother-in-law Richard Woodville prior of England, against the brothers' decision to appoint Brother John Langstrother. When the earl of Warwick deposed Edward IV and reinstated King Henry VI, Langstrother became royal treasurer and enjoyed the earl of Warwick's trust. Edward IV's fortunes rallied in 1471 when he defeated first the forces of Warwick at Barnet and then Queen Margaret and Prince Edward at Tewkesbury. John Langstrother was executed with the other Lancastrian leaders after the latter battle. He could claim that he had sided with the earl of Warwick in the interests of his Order, because King Edward IV threatened the Order's liberties. His actions had also won him enormous prestige and political influence – and led directly to his own death, which was hardly of benefit to his Order.

It is easy to criticise brothers of the Hospital for their involvement in the politics of their times, on the basis that those dedicated to a religious life should stay out of worldly affairs. However, the brothers were acting in the same way as religious in other religious Orders, who were called to secular courts to give advice and act as ambassadors and trustworthy officials. It was very difficult for members of religious orders to stay apart from political life, as they were dependent upon the secular authorities for their properties and for protection. In 1338 Philip de Thame informed the grand master in his report of the state of the English priory that the Order had to pay two magnates of Wales forty shillings a year each to maintain and protect the *bailie* of Slebech in Pembrokeshire, because of the fierce bandits and malefactors in Welsh parts. The brothers also had to give gifts to the king and other religious houses to have their friendship – and, hence, protection and support. In North Wales they had to give many gifts, amounting to a hundred shillings a year, to various lords and their seneschals and private officials in order to have guarantees that the Order's liberties would be respected and to have their aid, favour and friendship. At Lopen in Somerset they had to give twenty shillings a year to the sheriff and his clerks and bailiffs and to the bailiffs of other lords.[20] In short, the Hospital could

[20] *The Knights Hospitallers in England: Being the Report of Prior Philip de Thame to the Grand Master Elyan de Villanova for AD 1338*, ed. L. B. Larking and J. M. Kemble, Camden Society, lst series, 65 (1857), pp. 36, 39–40, 186.

not remain untouched by worldly affairs because worldly affairs would not leave it alone. If the Order attempted to stand aside and refused to serve secular lords or to put its resources at the disposal of secular lords, those same lords could quickly destroy it. Alternatively, if the Order co-operated with secular lords, the rewards were many, both for individuals and for the Order as a whole.

The Hospital of St John possessed many estates and buildings throughout Europe, was entitled to collect many rents and tithes, and owned the right of advowson (to present the priest) over many churches. It had many privileges such as exemption from episcopal authority and from many royal dues, customs dues and mercantile tolls and had many legal rights. It had enormous influence due to its possessions and their wide extent, and due to its religious vocation. It was an ally worth winning; its properties were too valuable for a secular lord to ignore them. Kings expected to have a voice in the appointment of the prior who was responsible for the Order's houses within their realm: James I of Aragon wrote that he had asked the master of the Hospital to make Hugh of Forcalquier prior of the Hospital in Aragon, because he was a man he trusted and liked.[21] The king might seek to have even more influence over a priory by having one of his relatives made prior, as in 1412 King Janus of Cyprus paid the pope the sum of 6,000 florins so that his illegitimate son could be made grand commander of Cyprus.[22] The Hospitallers protested and the donation was revoked, but the Order had to reimburse the king. During two years of negotiations the king gave the Hospitallers so much trouble that they had to recall all their knights from Cyprus. In 1414 the grand commandery of Cyprus was brought under direct administration from Rhodes, a move promoted by the need to ensure that the profits of sugar manufacture went straight to the Order's treasury.

In Aragon, relations between king and Order were always close. This originated in the Order's role in the *reconquista*, although by the late thirteenth century, with its resources stretched, the Order was trying to avoid involvement in military activities outside the East. Nevertheless King James II insisted that the Order commit resources to his campaigns against Granada. The kings of Aragon were also interested in the Order's castles, especially those which had originally been given to the Order of the Temple but had been transferred to the Hospital after the dissolution of the Templars. These were important and strategic castles, originally given away because the king did not have the means to hold and defend them, but now essential for royal authority. However, an attempt by the crown to acquire them in the 1320s was vetoed by the pope. The inevitable result of the close relations between king and military orders in the Iberian peninsula was that the latter came under increasing royal control and were increasingly seen as royal servants rather than as independent agents. In 1523 Pope Hadrian VI (1522–3) ratified the incorporation of the Spanish military orders in the crown of Spain, at that point represented by the emperor Charles V. The crown

[21] *Chronicle of James I, King of Aragon*, p. 183, ch. 95.
[22] Delaville le Roulx, *Hospitaliers à Rhodes*, pp. 319–21, 324–5.

then gained complete control over their revenues and the conferment of their prestigious offices. The Hospital remained theoretically independent, but in reality the Spanish brothers were as much servants of the Spanish king as of the Order.

In the eighteenth century the bailiwick of Brandenburg actually became a royal Order, under the control of the ruling house of Hohenzollern. The master was a member of the house of Hohenzollern; military units in the Prussian army used the Hospitallers' cross on their flags and the commanders and members of the Order placed a royal crown above the Hospitallers' cross on their banner. Despite its close connections with the kings of Prussia, however, the Order in Prussia maintained its connections with Malta and continued to pay its responsions.

Whereas in the thirteenth century the English chronicler Matthew Paris depicted the prior of the Hospital defying King Henry III, by the fourteenth century when king and Order came into conflict the members of the Order within the realm were likely to side with the king. When in 1540 King Henry VIII of England (1509–47) dissolved the monasteries in England, including the priory of St John, the turcopolier of the Order on Malta – one Brother Clement West – supported the king's actions. According to West, the grand master had offered to make him the next prior of England if he renounced the king, but he retorted that the king was entitled to take the Order's possessions as they already belonged to him. 'What does the bishop of Rome have to do in England?' West lost his position as turcopolier and his habit for his words, but to judge by the actions of other members of the Order throughout its history, he only said what many believed.[23]

The Hospitallers' involvement in worldly affairs inevitably brought them into conflict with other interests, and won them opposition and criticism. This could range from armed conflict with the burghers of Dublin over a fishery to the execution of a prior on a battlefield because he had supported the losing side in a civil war. However, the Order's worldly wealth and influence also made it very valuable to those with political authority, both kings and popes, and they made great use of the Order in their service. This benefited the Order in that such rulers gave it protection and could assist it in sending military supplies to the East; but it also diverted the Order's resources, particularly its best administrators, away from service to the Order into papal and royal service. Hence the Order became a potential route into royal service for many of its members, diverting them from the Order's real vocation of caring for the sick and the defence of Christendom. In these conflicts of interest the brothers' attitude was typical of Catholic religious orders; as the monarch was appointed by God, service for the monarch was merely another way of serving God.

[23] Matthew Paris, *Chronica Majora*, 5, p. 339; *Letters and Papers, Foreign and Domestic, of the Reign of Henry VIII* (London, 1864–1932), 14, 2, no. 579, pp. 204–5.

6

The Order of Malta, 1530–1798

THE Hospitallers arrived on Malta in 1530 at a low point in their history. They had lost their base in the East; they were no longer based on the pilgrim routes to Jerusalem or caring for pilgrims on their way to and from the holy places. They were in serious financial straits after the loss of Rhodes and its islands. Malta in 1530 reflected culturally its past domination by the Muslims (who conquered the island in 830) and by the kingdom of Sicily (Roger II, Norman king of Sicily, had conquered it in 1127). As a dependancy of Sicily it had passed into the Aragonese orbit in 1282 following the revolt of the Sicilian Vespers (1282), and so in 1516 to the hands of Charles, soon to be Holy Roman Emperor. Herewith lay one of the major problems of accepting responsibility for the island from the Hospitallers' point of view: the Order would become a dependant of Spain, which was frequently at war with France; yet most of the brothers of the Order were French.

The brothers had had an investigation made into the state of the island, which did not impress them. Malta was described as lacking in trees, very hot and short of drinking water in summer, with stony fields and suffering attacks from pirates. Yet Malta produced olives, honey, cotton and flax; the trees bore fruit twice a year and farmers could get two yields from their lands in a year by sowing first barley and then, when this had been harvested, cotton.

The only town of any size was Mdina (literally, in Arabic, 'the fortress'), a walled city on high ground in the centre of the island which dated back to Roman times. Around this was Rabat, 'the suburb'. The Maltese government of the island was based at Mdina (also known as the *Città Notabile*): the government was known as the *Università*. The civic nobility had their palaces at Mdina and there was a small Jewish population. There was a hospital at Rabat, with wards for men and women. Rabat also had a flourishing community of artisans, formed into guilds. On the island of Gozo to the north there was a sizeable community at the fortress in the centre of the island. On the eastern coast of Malta, on one of the narrow peninsulas of land jutting out into the deep waters of the Grand Harbour, there was a castle and a settlement called Birgu. This was a busy port by 1530. The Sicilian captain who represented the Sicilian monarchy on the islands was based at the castle, with a force of mercenary soldiers and various officials who levied taxes and were in charge of justice. There was no official navy, but many nobles had their own ships, and a flourishing piracy industry was carried on from Malta, a *corso* which was allowed to prey upon Muslim shipping – although by the early fifteenth century the Sicilian Admiralty was taking a portion of the profits. There were various look-out towers about the coast of Malta, Comino and Gozo, which were not in a good state of repair by the early sixteenth century. The brothers' own researchers reported in 1524 that even the castle at Birgu was not equipped to face a modern siege with gunpowder.

The people of the Maltese archipelago were Catholic Christians. Various monastic orders were present on the islands by the sixteenth century. The islands had a tradition of fine architecture and church paintings; there was a school at Mdina teaching Latin and music.

The Order initially set up its base at the castle at Birgu, where an infirmary was established. Its first task was to fortify its new acquisition to make it defensible against attack from pirates and the Turks, but without money little could be done. The fortifications of Birgu were strengthened with a new fortress, San Angelo, and a wall along the southern end of the peninsula; each of the tongues was given responsibility for defending a section of these defences, as on Rhodes. A fort dedicated to St Michael was built on the peninsula to the west of Birgu, the Isola San Michele, and a new town founded, Sanglea (so named after Grand Master Claude de la Sengle, 1553–7); another fort was built at the end of Mount Sciberras, which lies along the opposite side of the Grand Harbour from Birgu and the Isola. This last, dedicated to St Elmo, controlled the entrance to the Grand Harbour; but it was very small and could hardly hold off a major siege. A new town was also planned on Mount Sciberras, but this was delayed by lack of funds. The bulk of these defensive works were built after 1551, when the Order lost Tripoli and it was clear that its future lay on Malta.

□

While the Hospitallers had been losing Rhodes and taking over Malta, momentous events had been taking place in the religious life of Europe, as the Protestant Reformation broke out in Germany and spread to Sweden and Denmark – and, later, to England. The Protestants did not believe that religious orders were spiritually valid, and dissolved them. Members of religious houses abandoned their Orders, married and settled down in the secular world. However, not all religious Orders did this. In Brandenburg, the Hospital survived the conversion of the margrave to Lutheranism in 1538. Although some commanders married, the Order continued to be distinctive, the brothers electing their own master who paid homage to the Protestant duke. The Order became effectively a royal order under the protection of the house of Hohenzollern, and survived until 1811. The Teutonic Order had likewise reached a compromise in Livonia in 1526, where the Order became Lutheran, but continued its monastic way of life.

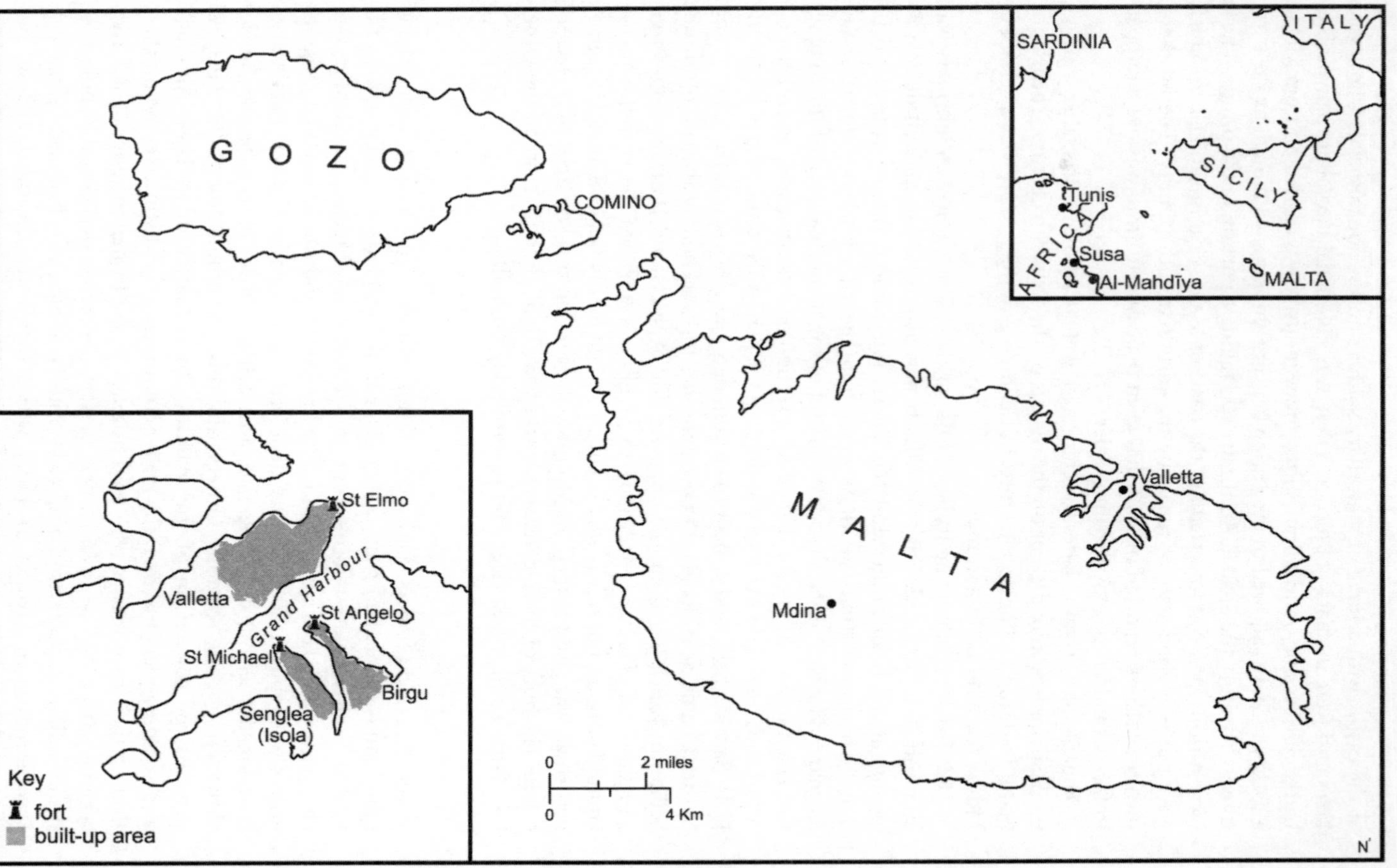

Fig. 5. Map of Malta and its environs during Hospitaller rule.

Plate 12. The Isola San Michele and Sanglea from Valletta, Malta. Photo: Nigel Nicholson.

In Switzerland, the Hospitallers managed to retain some of their houses within the Protestant cantons, by dint of agreeing to pay rent and give charitable contributions to the poor. Although most of these properties ceased to function as religious houses, the Hospital was able to continue drawing revenues from their estates. Other houses of the Order – especially those in strategic positions – were sequestrated by the Protestant cantons, although after negotiations the Order generally succeeded in obtaining financial compensation in the form of a formal sale of the house to the canton. The Order was able to retain its house at Basel partly because the grand prior of Germany, who was conducting the negotiations, had just returned from the successful defence of Vienna against the Turks (1529) and was able to point out that his Order still played an essential role in the defence of Christendom. The Order also agreed to pay rent to the canton.

These religious changes meant considerable financial loss to the Hospitallers. They were followed by the dissolution of the monasteries in England, prompted more by King Henry VIII's political manoeuvring than by religious devotion, which meant the loss of the English and Irish priories of the Order (1540). In Scotland, where there had been very few brothers of the Order since the Anglo-Scottish wars early in the fourteenth century, the Order survived until 1563/4.

Even before surrendering the Order's estates to Queen Mary (1542–67), the grand prior of Scotland had married.

The Hospital itself came under fire at the Council of Trent in 1545–63, where the Order endeavoured to avoid the institutional reforms which swept through the Catholic Church and retained its ecclesiastical privileges intact – stressing that these were necessary so that it could continue its war against the Muslims. Nevertheless the general chapters of the Order did reform aspects of the brothers' lifestyle, and stressed the religious and hospitaller aspects of the Order. From the late sixteenth century the popes sent an inquisitor to Malta to ensure the Catholic orthodoxy of the brothers; this official regularly clashed with the grand master over the limits of their respective jurisdictions. On the other hand, the papacy continued to support holy war, ensuring that the Order's reason for existence continued unchallenged by the Church. As late as 1743 Pope Benedict XIV (1740–58) issued a bull for Malta, offering a plenary indulgence (i.e. cancellation of all penance for confessed sins) to anyone who served a year in the Order's ships against the infidel, or who appointed a deputy to do so.

Even in countries which remained Catholic, the Hospital suffered loss of revenue and damage to its property through the religious wars which raged during the sixteenth century and later. The wars of religion in France, where the bulk of the Order's territories lay, disrupted half the revenues due to the Order's treasury. The wars of independence in the Netherlands also damaged the Order. This problem was to continue. The Order also faced other problems: the dependence of Malta on Sicily for grain supplies sometimes resulted in famine on Malta, for instance because the viceroy of Sicily stopped shipments of grain because of suspicions of French influence on Malta or clashes with the grand master over jurisdiction; plague also struck the islands periodically – there was a particularly severe epidemic in the 1590s. In short, the islands' small size, lack of self sufficiency and subordination to the kingdom of Sicily meant that the Order on Malta was always more vulnerable than it had been in the East.

Despite these problems, the Hospital continued to be involved in military operations against the Turks. As on Rhodes, it did not have large forces at its disposal: typically it had six to seven oared galleys plus irregular corsair ships which were licensed to raid Turkish and other hostile shipping. Hence it could only harass the enemy, and play a supporting role. By the late seventeenth century it had eight galleys; in the early eighteenth century the Order introduced heavy sailing vessels known as 'ships of the line' to supplement the galleys. In 1798, just before the loss of Malta, the fleet consisted of four galleys, two ships of the line and two frigates. The Order's centres of operations varied throughout the period, including the Balkans, the central Mediterranean, the North African or Barbary coast, and the eastern Mediterranean or Levant.

The aim of the Hospitallers' aggressive naval activity was not to destroy the Islamic enemy (impossible with so few ships) but to harass and raid, taking booty and prisoners who could be ransomed or enslaved. The prudent withdrawal was as much a part of their strategy as the bold attack; likewise, the

Ottomans and the Barbary corsairs preferred to raid and take booty and prisoners rather than conquer. Yet holy war remained an issue. Even in the seventeenth century the Order hoped that a Christian prince – such as Louis XIV – would lead a crusade against the infidel to recover the holy places, and then the Order would be ready to support him;[1] until then it was keeping alive the concept of holy war and supporting itself through its raids on the enemy. In theory it was also encouraging Christian shipping at the expense of non-Christians; but as the Hospitallers and their licensed corsairs also attacked the shipping of any country with trading agreements or alliances with the Turks, which included France, Genoa and Venice, their activities became a danger to Christian shipping which incurred papal censure.

□

In the 1530s holy war was being fought on two fronts: in the central Mediterranean, where Charles V was attacking Algeria, and in the Balkans, where the front stretched from Vienna through Hungary to Greece. The Hospitallers' involvement in the defence of Vienna in 1529 has just been mentioned. In Greece, in 1531 the Hospitallers sacked Modon, a coastal town in the south-west Peloponnese. They also supplied galleys to assist other Christian fleets: in 1532 four Hospitaller galleys took part in the conquest of Coron, to the east of Modon, and in 1533 assisted in its defence against the Turks. In 1538 their ships joined other Christian ships raiding off Corfu. In the central Mediterranean, the Hospitallers assisted the Spanish fleet in its raids along the North African coast. They assisted King Charles V when he captured Tunis in 1535, in his attack on Algiers in 1541, and in his capture of Al-Mahdīya (east of Tunis). The Hospitallers' ships also attacked corsairs based on the North African coast which were preying on Mediterranean shipping, and in 1550 successfully carried out attacks on corsair strongholds along this coast.

In retaliation for what the sultan regarded as the Hospitallers' corsair activities, the Turks raided Malta and Gozo, capturing the fort on Gozo and carrying many of the people away as slaves. In 1551 the corsair and Ottoman naval commander Dragut Reis attacked and captured Spanish-occupied Tripoli on the North African coast, which had a Hospitaller commander and garrison. In 1553 the emperor Charles offered the Order Al-Mahdīya to replace Tripoli and suggested that the Order should move its headquarters to the North African mainland and expand into the interior, but the council of the Order declined, stating that the Order did not exist to expand its own domains but to help other Christians.[2]

In 1559 an expedition of fifty ships was launched by King Philip II of Spain

[1] See David F. Allen, 'The Order of St John as a "School for Ambassadors"', in *The Military Orders*, vol. 2, *Welfare and Warfare*, p. 373.

[2] Vertot, *Histoire*, 4, pp. 351–7.

(1556–98) under his admiral Juan Andreas Doria to recapture Tripoli, with three galleys supplied by Pope Pius IV (1559–65) and five galleys and other craft from the Hospitallers. When Dragut Reis reinforced Tripoli, the fleet went instead to attack Jerba (Djerba), which was captured but immediately relieved by Piali Pasha. The Christian fleet was routed and Jerba was lost (1560). For the Hospitallers, this defeat was particularly unfortunate because King Philip II would henceforth be very reluctant to risk his fleet against the Turks.

In 1565 Suleiman the Magnificent sent a fleet to attack Malta. His motives were varied. The major stimulus was the Order's persistent harassment of Turkish shipping: in particular, the Order had recently captured a Turkish ship carrying pilgrims to Mecca and (allegedly) a well-laden merchant ship belonging to the sultan's chief eunuch and the leading ladies of the harem. A contemporary writer and eyewitness of the siege of 1565, Francesco Balbi di Correggio, states that the Order had also captured an island which had been taken a short while before by the sultan; this may refer to Hospitaller aid given to a Spanish expedition to recapture Ceuta, on the North African coast to the south east of the straits of Gibraltar. Another possible explanation was that Suleiman, having failed to destroy the Order of the Hospital in 1522, may have wanted to complete the Order's destruction before he died.

According to Balbi, the force which attacked Malta was 48,000 strong. The sultan commissioned the casting of heavy artillery to fire cast iron shot; there was a basilisk of 180 hundredweight firing a shot weighing one hundredweight; two 80–pounders of 130 hundredweight and four 60-pounders of 110 hundredweight. There was also a gun which fired stone shot which had been used at the siege of Rhodes in 1522.

Suleiman's fleet was commanded by Mustafa Pasha, described by Balbi as 'an old general of great experience', and Piali Pasha, the general who had relieved Jerba in 1560. According to Balbi, Mustafa Pasha was made commander in chief from the start; another account states that the two set out as joint commanders, but *en route* Mustafa Pasha produced secret orders from the sultan giving him special authority over the army, which infurited Piali Pasha. In any case, the two leaders appear to have been rivals. Dragut Reis and his fleet were to join them on Malta, but after landing on Malta in May the Turks attacked St Elmo at once, without waiting for him. Balbi considered that this was an error: firstly attacking St Elmo, a minor fort, rather than the Hospital's main fortress of San Angelo; and secondly not waiting for the great admiral.

The Hospital, lacking the resources to launch a major counterattack, concentrated on defending its lines and waited for relief. Pope Pius IV sent money for the payment of troops and encouraged Philip II of Spain to send aid, for Malta lay within Philip's domain. He stressed that Malta was of strategic importance and that the Order deserved aid, because it had always been a loyal guardian of Christendom. Yet Philip and his Sicilian viceroy Don García de Toledo were unwilling to risk the Spanish fleet, preferring to lose Malta. As they delayed, the pope decided to send 600 foot, but they would not set out until

September. Men and women took the cross to aid the Hospital, presumably not all intending to go themselves but with the intention of sending money in redemption of their crusading vow. A relief force of 700 men arrived at Birgu in early July.

Dragut Reis arrived in Malta and was angered that St Elmo had been attacked rather than Birgu. The Turks kept up a continual bombardment of the small fort, but the Hospitallers held on doggedly. On 18 June Dragut Reis was mortally wounded by a gun shot, a terrible blow for the Turks. The Turks finally captured the battered fort on 23 June and the defenders were massacred; but it had taken over a month to capture St Elmo, and in the meanwhile the Hospitallers had been able to reinforce their other fortresses.

The Hospitallers, under the strong generalship of Grand Master Jean de la Valette (1557–68), kept up a determined defence, with help from the Maltese. An attack on the Isola San Michele was foiled by the chain across the inlet which sank nine large Turkish ships. While the Turks attacked the Isola and San Angelo a cavalry force from Mdina fell on them from the rear; the Turks, thinking that a relief force had arrived from Europe, retreated to their main camp. By the time they discovered that this was actually a small local force, the cavalry had returned to Mdina.

By the beginning of September the Turks were growing short of food and water, and had suffered heavy losses. In addition the weather was changing and becoming wet, which hampered the Turkish cannon. Finally on 7 September a part of the Spanish fleet arrived from Sicily under the viceroy Don García de Toledo, and the Turks retreated to St Elmo. They attacked the relief force on 11 September but were defeated and withdrew from Malta on 12 September 1565.

In his letter to Pope Pius IV giving an account of the siege, Grand Master La Valette gave chief credit for the victory to God, and stated that the relief force which had arrived in early July had saved Birgu and the Isola San Michele. The troops of Don García de Toledo had forced the Turks to withdraw, but they had come at the very end. The Hospitallers were very grateful to the king of Spain for sending them – but it was clear that La Valette would have been far more grateful if they had come in July.

The pope was furious with Philip II. In his view, God and the Hospitallers' own courage had won the victory. Don García de Toledo was annoyed that La Valette did not give him much credit for his help at the end of the siege. While some modern historians believe that his aid was decisive, others consider that the Turks were already defeated by 7 September and all Don García achieved was to force them to retreat more quickly than they would otherwise have done.

In 1565 the Turks had very long supply lines. They suffered from divided leadership; the death of the great admiral Dragut Reis was a serious blow to morale; the concentration on St Elmo may have been decisive in their failure, as it lost them over a month in which the Hospitallers could build up their defences elsewhere. Most of Suleiman's military effort was focused on the Balkans, and it was here that he died in 1566. Although the Turks were led by experienced generals, the Maltese expedition was of secondary importance.

The Hospitallers, on the other hand, were well led, and were fighting for the very existence of their Order. It had faced such crises before: in Acre in 1291, on Rhodes in 1444, 1480 and 1522. As an Order whose members' vocation was to lay down their lives on the battlefield for Christendom, the brothers gave their best in such emergencies. In 1291 and 1522 they made an heroic defence and only retreated when all was completely lost. In 1444, 1480 and 1565 they forced the enemy to retreat and lived to fight again.

Their successful defence of Malta raised the profile and reputation of the Hospital throughout Europe, among both Catholics and Protestants. It did much to re-establish the Order's prestige after the loss of Rhodes. Jean de la Valette set about fortifying the island, and building a new capital city which was named after him: Valletta. He was able to use the Order's success against the Turks to encourage donations from Europe. The city was built on Mount Sciberras, with the sea on three sides and only a thin strip of land on the fourth, land side. It was fortified using the latest defensive technology, with massive walls all round and a dry ditch across the land side, reinforced by two huge bastions, one each side of the entrance gate. Small look-out towers, vedettes, were spaced along the top of the city walls, giving good visibility without presenting a target for cannon fire. Fort St Elmo was rebuilt, larger, with sharply angled exterior walls forming a star-shaped plan as defence against cannon fire. Later grand masters extended and improved the defences, but the basis of the city is Valette's.

Yet the Ottoman tide was far from turning. In 1570 the Turks, under Mustafa Pasha and with assistance from Piali Pasha, attacked Cyprus. Famagusta held out for ten and a half months, after all else had been lost, and only surrendered at last because of the lack of relief from the West. Philip II had again refused to risk his fleet: almost 200 galleys financed by Venice, Spain and the papacy were stationed off Crete, but withdrew in September 1570 on Philip's instructions rather than engage the Turks. The Christians' success at Malta but failure at Cyprus underlines the importance of supply lines for the Turks and the importance of relief forces for the Christians. Both at Malta and at Famagusta the Christians had excellent generals, but in these circumstances the best of generals could do no more than hold out and wait until either the besiegers' supplies ran out or relief came. The geographical position of each island was clearly decisive: Malta was much further from the Ottoman capital of Constantinople and nearer to Europe than Cyprus.

While Cyprus was under siege, the Hospitallers were involved in the formation of a Holy League. This was agreed in spring 1571 in response to Ottoman advances in the Balkans and the siege of Cyprus, and was financed by Venice, Spain and the papacy. The Hospitallers contributed only three galleys: three had been lost to the naval forces of Calabrian renegade Uluj 'Ali in 1570 and the Order had no more to send. There were also five galleys and a hundred knights contributed by the new military order of St Stephen founded by Cosimo I de' Medici, duke of Tuscany, in 1562. This order and the Hospital would later co-operate in naval operations against the Turks.

The league's fleet set out in September 1571, after the fall of Cyprus. Don John of Austria (died 1578), an illegitimate son of Charles V and already proven in action, was commander in chief. In early October the fleet found the Turkish fleet in its winter quarters in the Gulf of Corinth. At the battle of Lepanto on 7 October, 208 Christian galleys fought 275 Turkish ships, with around 100,000 combatants. Muezzinzade Ali Pasha, commander of the Turkish fleet, was killed; Don John of Austria captured the Turkish flagship and the Turks were routed. The Christians lost fifteen to twenty ships and around 8,000 men, serious losses but minor in comparison to the Turkish loss of eighty vessels destroyed or crippled and 130 captured, with losses of over 30,000 men.

The Christian victory sparked Europe-wide rejoicing, in both Protestant and Catholic countries. The Ottoman reputation for invincibility at sea had been destroyed. Yet the Christian victory did not halt Ottoman advances in the Balkans nor enable the Venetians to recapture Cyprus. The Holy League was renewed in spring 1572, but achieved nothing notable. In 1573 Venice withdrew from the League and made peace with the Turks. Meanwhile, Sultan Selim II (1566–74) rebuilt his fleet. Don John of Austria captured Tunis in October 1573 (although the grand master of the Hospital, Jean l'Evêque de la Cassière, declined to send aid), but in the summer of 1574 the Turks recaptured it and expelled the Spanish from North Africa.

There were fears in the 1590s that the Ottoman sultan was planning an attack on Spain, or at least on Malta. In the event, the attack fell on Hungary, and the worst that hit the Hospitallers was reprisal raids from the Ottomans in revenge for their attacks on Ottoman shipping. In 1614 the Turks did land on Malta, but withdrew. The Hospitallers continued to be involved in attacking Muslim shipping off the North African coast and in the Levant: mostly in a piecemeal fashion through the *corso*, but also through their own fleet, manned by brothers of the Order and professional soldiers who hoped to get rich from booty. This fleet could co-operate with other Christian fleets, as at Lepanto, or in independent raids on Muslim shipping and the shipping of nations with trading agreements with the Turks, such as Venice. The Order was also involved in raids on Muslim ports, not all of which were particularly successful. Two attempts to recapture Tripoli failed. In 1606 the Order attacked Maometta (Hammamet, on the Tunisian coast) and in 1619 the neighbouring city of Susa (Sousse), both of which were repelled with heavy losses to the Order. Other attacks were more successful. In 1611 the Hospitaller fleet attacked Corinth in Greece and took part with thirty other Christian galleys in an attack on Kerkennah off the coast of Tunisia. In 1639 and 1640 it made raids against Tripoli in North Africa and La Goletta, to the north-west of Tunis.

Yet the Hospital also made agreements with Muslims: while they were responsible for the defence of Tripoli the Hospitallers had an alliance with the neighbouring Muslim ruler of Tunis, while in the following century Alonso de Contreras refers to the emir of Tyre as friendly towards Malta and defiant of the authority of the Ottoman sultan. Ships flying the Hospital's flag were welcomed in his port, and his brother was welcomed on Malta. In the late 1730s the Order helped the deposed Bey of Tunis recover his throne and in 1740 his son was received honourably at Malta. In the early 1780s the emperor of Morocco was received honourably by the Order.[3]

Where the Hospitallers were involved in large-scale action, it was in conjunction with the remaining Christian secular power in the East, namely Venice. This was a problem for the Order in that political relations with Venice were consistently poor because the Hospitallers' corsairs disrupted Venetian trade and antagonised the Turks.

Some of the corsairs were members of the Order, such as the Chevalier de Fressinet who was killed in a naval engagement with the Ottoman admiral Khalil Pasha in 1609, and his three galleons captured. Others were independent operators, licensed by the Hospital and allowed to bear the Hospitaller cross. In the 1580s the Venetians dubbed them 'corsairs parading crosses'; after his visit to Malta in 1716, Giacomo Capello complained that it was very rare for these violent pirates ever to be punished by the Order as justice required. However, many of the corsairs operating out of Malta were not licensed by the Hospital but by the representatives of foreign states who were resident on Malta. The Hospital allowed this practice without being directly responsible for the activities of these corsairs (enabling it to distance itself from their more outrageous activities), and possibly also benefited from it in some more material way. The Order did make various attempts to curb the corsairs operating out of Malta. In 1732 Pope Clement XII (1730–40) instructed that no ships should operate out of Malta under any flag except that of the Hospital, in an attempt to ensure that all Maltese corsairs were officially under control of the Order.

There was a series of incidents in the 1570s when the Hospitallers plundered the merchandise of Venetian Jews from Venetian ships, on the basis that not only were the Venetians in alliance with the Ottoman Turks but that non-Christians could fairly be plundered. From 1577 the Order also worked in co-operation with the Order of St Stephen of Tuscany, theoretically against the Turks, but in practice still hitting the Venetians at least as hard as the Turks. While the Hospitallers maintained that they were carrying on a holy war against the enemies of Christendom and their allies, the Venetian Republic saw this as a mere pretext for piracy. It is tempting to regard Hospitaller naval action of this period more as economic warfare than as religiously inspired; yet the brothers' own writings indicate that they truly believed that their activities formed part of

[3] Vertot, *Histoire*, 4, pp. 62–85, 98, 114–19, 157; Alonso de Contreras, p. 79; Roderick Cavaliero, *The Last of the Crusaders: the Knights of St John and Malta in the Eighteenth Century* (London, 1960), pp. 119, 167.

a holy war against the Turks.[4] In contrast, the brothers believed that the Venetians were too ready to sacrifice the interests of Christendom in their own commercial interests.

In 1578 Grand Master La Cassière, under pressure from the Venetian Republic and Pope Gregory XIII (1572–85), issued instructions to the Hospitaller fleet and the privateers licensed under the *corso* that Venetian ships were not to be molested, although Turkish vessels and vessels bound for Ancona which were not Venetian could be searched, and all property of non-Christians (Turks, Moors and Jews) seized. This did not prevent other, non-Hospitaller corsairs or Hospitallers sponsored by other nations from attacking the Venetians, who blamed the Order. In 1583 Don Diego Brochero de la Paz y Añaya, a knight Hospitaller, was arrested by the Venetian authorities at the island of Cerigo for piracy, although his Order protested that he had not attacked Venetian vessels and had been operating outside Venetian waters. Despite the interventions of Philip II of Spain and the duke of Savoy, Diego was taken to Venice and imprisoned. He was finally released two years later and allowed to return to Malta, where he died shortly afterwards as a result of his experiences in prison.

Another serious incident followed in 1573, when two Hospitaller galleys returning from a successful raid against a Turkish galleon were attacked and captured by seven Venetian galleys based on Crete. The Venetians killed and wounded the Hospitallers, even cutting off the Hospitallers' fingers to take their rings; and they dragged the Hospitallers' banner, the white cross on a red field, behind them as a sign of defeat. The repercussions of this event led to the Hospital declaring war against Venice in 1584, despite all the attempts of the Spanish and the papal see to mediate.

The Hospitallers' activities in the Mediterranean received a severe blow when in 1585 Pope Sixtus V (1585–90), anxious to facilitate commercial activity and reduce piracy, issued bulls favouring Jewish trade and forbidding the Hospitallers and ships flying their cross from attacking any vessel going from Christian ports to Turkish lands or vice versa, whether it was Christian, Turkish or Jewish. The Order nominated ambassadors to carry the Order's defence of its activities to the papacy. This argued that the papal injunctions would prevent the Order from carrying on its war against the infidel at sea, and endangered the Order's very existence; and it set out all the benefits which the Order's activities brought Christendom: training naval commanders (until 1748 the Order would officer and train the French galley fleet founded by Cardinal Richelieu (died 1642), and in the late eighteenth century provided naval training for the officers of Tsarina Catherine the Great of Russia, 1762–96), joining other Christian nations in fighting the Turks and distracting the Turkish fleet from attacking Christian coasts. The booty and prisoners from its naval operations were also essential to the Maltese economy. The pope, however, refused to withdraw his injunctions

[4] See, for instance, Allen, 'A Parish at Sea', *Military Orders: Fighting for the Faith*, ed. M. Barber (Aldershot, 1994); Allen, 'Order of St John as a "School for Ambassadors"', pp. 365–8, 371–3.

and actually extended them. The Hospitallers were forced to redraft their instructions to their corsairs not to attack any Christians and their goods, or those who were vassals or subjects of the king of Spain or of the Republic of Venice, or Jews.

The efforts of Grand Master Alof de Wignacort (1601–22) went some way towards restoring relations with Venice. He took steps to regulate the granting of licences for the *corso*, by which owners and captains of ships had to declare under oath that they would not attack Christians or even infidels who had a safe-conduct from the grand master or any Christian prince, which included the Venetian Republic. Relations were also improved after an incident in March 1614 when one of the Order's galleons rescued a Venetian ship, the *Monda*, which had been captured by the Turks, and restored the ship to her owners. Venetian fears of Spanish naval action in the Adriatic (ostensibly against the Turks but actually against Venice) encouraged Venetian friendship towards Malta; the Hospitallers refused to join the duke of Osuna's expedition to the Adriatic in 1617 because the duke was unable to guarantee that it would not be used to attack Christians. Yet Venetian officials were still arresting Hospitaller and Maltese ships on the grounds that they were pirates, despite all Wignacort's efforts to demonstrate to the Republic that the Order's ships and corsairs were being rigorously controlled.

In 1644 some Maltese corsairs seized a Turkish galleon on its way to Alexandria with cargo and important dignitaries on board. They went to Crete, a Venetian possession, to share out their spoils, although in fact the Venetian authorities had had nothing to do with the raid. In the following year the Ottoman sultan attacked Crete in retaliation. The Venetians appealed to the Hospital for help, but the Hospitallers were slow to react, because of recent events in Italy. Pope Urban VIII (1623–44) had called the Hospitaller fleet to his assistance after the forces of Venice, Modena, Parma and Tuscany had devastated papal shipping in the so-called war of Barberini; the Venetian government had retaliated by confiscating the property of the Hospital's grand priory of Venice.

At last, two months after the Turkish attack on Crete, the Hospitallers sent six galleys, with papal, Tuscan and Neapolitan forces, to Corfu to assist the Venetians on Crete; and the Venetian senate then agreed to return the Hospitallers' possessions. The war continued until 1669, with assistance from the Hospital throughout this period, and also from the Teutonic Order and the Order of St Stephen of Tuscany. The Christian defence was unsuccessful: in 1669 the Venetians and the Hospitallers withdrew from Crete.

The Hospitallers also assisted the Venetians against the Turks in the Morea, from 1684–99 and from 1714–18, with varying degrees of enthusiasm. In 1684, after the repulsion of the Turks from Vienna (1683), the pope formed a Holy League against the Turks with Venetian and Hospitaller aid. The Venetians attacked the Morea in 1685 with twenty-eight of their own galleys plus other ships, eight Hospitaller galleys, five from the papal states and four from Tuscany. The Turks had forty galleys plus other ships, but were unable to defeat the

Christian attacking force, although the Venetians were also unable to extend their conquests to recover Chios or Crete. Battles were indecisive. Peace was finally made in 1699, with some gains for Venice.

In 1714 Sultan Ahmed III (1703–30) launched an attack on Venetian territories in the Greek Archipelago. In late 1715 Giacomo Capello was sent by the Venetian Republic to Valletta to ask for the aid of two Hospitaller squadrons for the coming Venetian campaign in the Morea. Although the grand master, Ramon Perellos y Roccaful (1697–1720) assured him that the Order would give aid, the Order was very slow to respond; eventually it sent some assistance in conjunction with papal forces. Capello wrote a description of Malta soon after his departure, which accused the convent of sheltering pirates and profiting from piracy: the grand master received a tenth of all plunder; the whole island was a hotbed of pirates; the Order had lost all pretension to chivalry or honour.

After 1723 the war against the Ottomans was effectively over: French and Venetian pressure was brought to bear on the Order to cease troubling Ottoman shipping, and in addition many Turkish merchants were sailing under French passports so that they could not be attacked by the Order. The Hospital's new 'ships of the line' sailed to the East in summer 1732 and won an impressive victory against Ottoman fleet in the vicinity of Damietta on the Egyptian coast, but after this there was little activity.

Off the North African coast, raiding against the Barbary corsairs continued. Here the Hospitallers had been employing a squadron of ships of the line since 1705: these ships had been developed in response to recent developments in shipping and the realisation that the Order's old galleys were no longer capable of matching the Barbary corsairs. The Order assisted in the unsuccessful defence of Spanish Oran against Algiers in 1707. It also won a number of notable victories over Tunisian corsairs. During the first half of the eighteenth century the Order's fleet was increased to six sailing ships and four oared galleys. These ships were heavily armed: in 1723 commander Jacques de Chambray's ship *Saint Vincent* had 52 guns and a crew of 300; three of the ships of the fleet in the 1740s had 60 guns. The Order's ships were so successful against Tripoli that the city temporarily ceased to be a naval power and relations with Malta became peaceful.

The Hospital's corsairs continued their activity until the mid-eighteenth century, as ever, not only against Muslim corsairs but also against Christians suspected of trading with Muslims. In 1741 the Hospital and the Venetian Republic were virtually at war because of the behaviour of Hospitaller corsairs. The immediate cause of the crisis was the misdeeds of one Captain Grillo, originally a Venetian subject from the Dalmatian coast, who had been settled in Malta for some years. In retribution against the Hospital for the activities of its corsairs and particularly Grillo, the Venetian Senate ordered that all the Hospital's possessions within Venetian territory should be sequestrated, and that all ships flying the Hospitaller cross should be sunk. In return, Grand Master

Emanuel Pinto (1741–73) and his state council passed a decree against the Venetians, which forbad the reception of Venetian patricians into the Order as long as the sequestrations lasted, and ordered all Hospitaller galleys and Maltese corsairs to give all ships flying the Venetian flag of St Mark the same treatment as they themselves received. The situation was not resolved until 1747, when an agreement was made between the two powers by which the Hospitallers' properties were returned and Maltese privateers were not to harass Venetian shipping.

By 1751 the Republic of Venice was again complaining of harassment to Venetian shipping by Maltese corsairs. It was clear that the policy of sequestration was not working, so instead the Republic resorted to the expedient of suspending from office the Maltese consuls on the Venetian islands of Corfu and Zante (Zakynthos), forcing the consuls' offices to close down. Grand Master Pinto retaliated by dismissing his consul in Venice. The situation was resolved in 1754 through the Venetian magistracy of trade suggesting that the Republic appoint one of the Knights of St John, an Italian, to represent its interests on Malta. This was done, thereby giving the Republic access to the grand master's court and ministers and more information about events on Malta.

The Republic's appointee, Brother Massimiliano Buzzaccarini Gonzaga, sent on average one letter a fortnight to the magistracy of trade, and a regular news report. Enlightened by these reports as to Malta's reliance upon imports for most commodities, the Venetian magistracy of trade decided to promote a Veneto-Maltese trading link, both as a market for its goods and as a central Mediterranean entrepôt. In the 1762 a bilateral commercial agreement was concluded between Venice and the Hospitallers of Malta. This lapsed in 1767, but was renewed on more favourable terms to the Order in 1782. The Hospital may also have provided intelligence which assisted in the Venetian peace treaties with Algiers and Tunis in 1763, Tripoli in 1764 and Morocco in 1765. Between 1784 to 1792 the Republic used Malta as a naval base in its war against Tunis. At the same time, from the 1750s the Hospitallers' privateering activities in the eastern Mediterranean were reduced. So at last, after centuries of conflict, Venice and the Hospitallers became allies rather than rivals.

During the second half of the eighteenth century the Order also assisted various other European powers in attacks on North Africa: France in an attack on Tunis in 1752 and 1770, and Spain in attacks on Algiers in 1772, 1775, 1783 and 1784, leading to a peace treaty between Algiers and Spain in 1784. After the confiscations of Hospitaller property by the revolutionary government in France in 1792 the Order briefly revived the *corso* in an attempt to bring in much-needed funds.

□

The Order of the Hospital benefited the Maltese people through political stability and defence against the raiding of corsairs. It brought money to the island and employment opportunities, most notoriously in the form of the *corso*. Alonso de

Contreras recorded that the booty which he brought back to Malta as a soldier on board the Hospital's ships at the beginning of the seventeenth century enabled his 'young lady' to build herself a fine new house.[5] The Hospital also improved the lives of the people more generally: it imported food to the islands, and it also developed medical care for the Maltese people, as described above in chapter four. However, there was resentment that the Maltese nobility were not allowed to enter the Order except as conventual chaplains, and that few brothers could speak the Maltese language. There was resentment at new taxes, laws and courts and the reduction of local rights. Some Maltese protested against the Order's administration, but others were glad to see the power of the Maltese nobility reduced. The Maltese assisted the Order in its defence against the Turks in 1565.

The Order of the Hospital of St John had a considerable impact on Maltese culture during its sejourn of nearly three centuries on the island. The presence of the Hospitallers on Malta with their building activities and international contacts brought in Renaissance and Baroque culture, including leading artists such as Caravaggio and Mattia Preti, as described in chapter four. A university was founded by Grand Master Pinto. The brothers also brought the ostentation and pageantry appropriate to the court of an influential European ruler, as the grand master of the Order had become.

It was noted above in chapter four that the grand master and the convent had often been in conflict over the power and authority which the grand master should be allowed to wield over the Order. By the early modern period the grand master had enormous influence through the commanderies which were reserved for him, which he could grant out to whichever brothers he chose, and the various household posts and various other offices he could grant, all of which brought an income plus the opportunity for further gains, authority and influence. The grand master was not all-powerful; he still had to consult the convent and general chapter and the pope could overrule him. But he was effectively the sole ruler of a small independent state, and he acted like other Christian rulers of the period, with similar ceremonial and public performance.

Through public performance the grand master reaffirmed his authority over the island and the islanders, presenting himself as a rich, powerful and cultured ruler in contrast to his poorer, less glorious subjects.[6] The arrival of the Order on Malta in 1530 and its taking possession of the ancient capital of Mdina were marked with solemn processions of the brothers, Maltese nobles and clergy in magnificent dress, and sumptuous banqueting. Each grand master of the Order would make a ceremonial entry into Mdina when he took office, and the ceremony became more elaborate with time. By the end of the sixteenth century

[5] Alonso de Contreras, pp. 54, 86.

[6] For this, see Vicki Ann Cremona, 'Spectacle and "Civil liturgies" in Malta During the Time of the Knights of St John', in *The Renaissance Theatre: Texts, Performance, Design*, vol. 2, *Design, Image and Acting*, ed. Christopher Cairns (Aldershot, 1999), pp. 41–60.

when Ramon Perellos (1697–1720) became grand master, he rode in a carriage into Mdina, with his horse led behind; there were races in the evening, with a temporary stage erected from which the grand master and his retinue could watch; and the fine costumes of those taking part in the spectacles throughout the day was changed several times, with a new robe for each ceremony. The people of Malta and Gozo flocked to watch the events, and silver coins were thrown for them.

The induction of a grand master became more like a coronation. Grand Master Hugh Loubenx de Verdalle (1582–95) added his own ducal coronet to the traditional symbol of office, the cap, with a cardinal's ring and an admiral's baton. Grand Master Pinto took a closed crown as his symbol of office, effectively claiming that he was a king, and ruled like a benevolent despot, in line with many European monarchies of his day. The grand master was addressed as 'Prince'.

Other regular public ceremonies included the ceremonial feeding of the poor by the grand master before sitting down to dinner. Twelve poor men were fed, analogous to the twelve Apostles; the grand master himself waited upon them, fulfilling the role of Christ at the Last Supper. The grand master himself ate in public, and many travellers recorded the spectacle. Sixty knights waited on him at table; his plate was of silver, his cup of gold; the food was beautifully prepared and arranged. Onlookers, however, had to leave after the third course, emphasising the importance of the occasion; only the chosen few who were invited to eat with him could remain. Such ceremonies reinforced the grand master's image as a noble sovereign.

The brothers did not always agree with the powers the grand master assumed, particularly when these threatened their liberty to live as they chose. In July 1581 the council of the Order voted to depose Grand Master Jean l'Evêque de la Cassière and appoint a successor. Their declared reason for their action was that the grand master was autocratic and senile, but in fact it appears more likely that the brothers objected to his reforms within the Order. He had passed a decree ordering all loose women to be expelled from Valletta and the neighbouring villages – except those living with dignitaries of the Order. He also lacked tact in his dealings with the Maltese ecclesiastical hierarchy: he was so anxious to stamp out any danger of heresy becoming established on Malta that he set up an Inquisition, independent both of himself and of the bishop; and he asked the archbishop of Monreale, in Sicily, to consecrate the Order's new conventual church of St John in Valletta, rather than waiting for the new bishop of Malta to be installed. In short, although he was a devout man and determined to improve the religious state of Malta and the Order, he seems to have gone about his reforms in a manner well-calculated to raise hackles. The pope intervened in the quarrel and summoned both claimants to the grand magistracy to Rome, where both died, and a new grand master, Hugh Loubenx de Verdalle, was appointed in their place.

In the 1620s the general chapter demanded that the process for the election of the grand master should be reformed to make it quicker and to give the general chapter more influence in the appointment. The 1631 general chapter passed a number of reforms, simplifying the procedure for electing the grand master as well as legislating on the lifestyle of the brothers and administrative matters. However, the power of the grand master was not reduced; while it was in the interests of the great officials of the Order to ensure that their opinions were heard, they did not want to downgrade the office of grand master as they all aspired to achieve it one day.

The next general chapter was not summoned until 1776. While the grand master consulted his council, rewarded powerful and influential brothers with valuable offices and upheld his authority and dignity and those of his retinue through the grandeur of court ceremonial, and provided that he ruled reasonably benevolently so that the ordinary people did not revolt, he could argue that there was no need to call a general chapter – even though the customs and statutes of the Order demanded that he should. Special committees were set up to deal with specific areas of administration. Knight-brothers of the Hospital were appointed to lead these councils, so that the demand for a voice in the Order's administration were met without the grand master having to sacrifice his supreme authority to a general chapter.

The 1776 general chapter was summoned by Emanuel de Rohan Polduc (1775–97), who ruled the Order and Malta as a secular monarch at a time when the Order was facing increasing financial problems, threats to its autonomy, and its dedication to holy war was under attack. Even with the help of the general chapter, he could do little to improve the Order's position. Rohan's relations with the Church indicate that he regarded himself as absolute sovereign of Malta with even the Church subject to him, and believed that the Order and he himself were independent of the jurisdiction of the papacy. His stance led to a serious clash with the papacy, so that in 1793 Pope Pius VI (1775–99) threatened to dissolve the Order, and the grand master was forced to allow papal orders to be promulgated on Malta without first being approved by his council.

The pope's delegate in Malta, Mgr Gian Filippo Gallarati Scotti, was critical of the grand master: without papal protection for its property, which was scattered across Europe, the Order would be destroyed. Brother Deodat de Dolomieu, a knight-brother of Auvergne and a famous geologist (dolomite is named after him), wrote to a friend in 1788 that the grand master was mistaken if he believed that he was a prince of the same rank as the princes of France, Spain and the Empire. These sovereigns would not unite to protect the Order if its independence came under threat. He compared the Order to an ant which considers itself to have a very important role in the scheme of things, yet it and its nest are crushed in a moment by a passer-by's foot.[7]

Dolomieu and the papal delegate saw that the European situation had changed dramatically since the Order of the Hospital had come to Malta. The Ottoman

[7] On Deodat Dolomieu, see Cavaliero, *Last of the Crusaders*, p. 25, *passim*.

Turks were no longer an active threat to Christendom; in contrast, they were allied with western nations who were coming to see Russia as a greater threat to the West than the Turks. The philosophical and religious ideas of the Enlightenment were not sympathetic to the old ideals of crusading and holy war, which were regarded by educated writers of the eighteenth century as barbaric activities based on superstition. The military orders' status as supranational eccelesiastical institutions independent from the jurisdiction of the sovereign secular states in which they held their property was regarded as anomalous. They were seen as out of place in the modern world. The logical conclusion was that they should be abolished and their property taken over by the state.

The Hospital had played some part in the medical developments of the early modern period and a few brothers such as Dolomieu were involved in scientific advance, while Grand Master Pinto was interested in alchemy. Yet overall the Order was orientated towards holy war. There had been some attempts to expand operations outside this field: some estates had been purchased in the New World, in Canada and the Caribbean, but were sold again. In 1735 the Order was approached by a Franciscan missionary, Francesco Rivarolo, with a plan to found an Ethiopian Company to help the Ethiopians to clear the Arab slavers from the Red Sea ports, and to carry out missionary work and trade. Grand Master Ramon Despuig (1736–41) rejected the plan because he saw that it would interfere with British and French interests in the area, and that the Order could not compete with these powers. In 1793 Grand Master Rohan was negotiating an alliance with the new United States of America, seeking a grant of lands which the Maltese would be encouraged to clear, cultivate and settle – just as during the middle ages the Order of the Hospital had been given grants of frontier and marginal land to clear, cultivate and settle. In return he offered port and trading facilities and services at Malta. The US appears to have been favourable to these overtures, but nothing came of them. Meanwhile, in the 1780s negotiations with the Tsarina Catherine of Russia over the Order's property in Poland were hampered because the Tsarina's envoy, a Greek and a schismatic, could not be received by the Order in an official capacity; and a potentially lucrative trading treaty proposed by the Ottoman sultan Selim III in 1796 was turned down by the grand master because it would be against the Order's statutes.[8]

Rohan died in July 1797 and Ferdinand von Hompesch was elected in his place, the first brother of the German tongue to be elected grand master. He was to be the last holder of the office on Malta.

The Order had long had close relations with France; the three richest 'tongues' of the Order were French, although by the late eighteenth century the official language of the Order was Italian. France had an interest in Malta as a strategic

[8] Vertot, *Histoire*, 5, pp. 216–18, 252; Cavaliero, *Last of the Crusaders*, pp. 124–6, 167; Victor Mallia-Milanes, *Venice and Hospitaller Malta, 1530–1798: Aspects of a Relationship* (Marsa, 1992), pp. 290–4.

stronghold in the Mediterranean; as did the kingdom of Naples and Sicily (as legal overlord of Malta), and Great Britain, and as did Russia and Austria, which aimed to break up the Ottoman Empire to their own advantage and become Mediterranean maritime powers. The French revolution of 1789 did not change French ambitions in the Mediterranean, and also weakened the Order by removing a significant portion of its European revenues. In 1789 Church tithes were abolished in France, and it was decided to confiscate Church property. The Order petitioned vigorously, and others petitioned on its behalf. The Order argued that the Hospitallers were not clergy and that the destruction of the Order was not in French interests as France would lose influence in the Mediterranean through the loss of this ally; it was also pointed out that the Order protected French shipping against pirates. The National Constituent Assembly of France nevertheless continued with its reforms. In July 1791 the Assembly withdrew the right of French citizenship of all the Frenchmen who were members of orders of chivalry outside France – which ended the three French 'tongues' – and in 1792 the Order's property in France was confiscated.

In 1793 the new French envoy to Malta was instructed that although the Order in Malta was scorned by the Republican Government as 'a shameful monument, erected by religion and by the pride of the nobles',[9] Malta was the key to the East and therefore of crucial importance for trade. Russia and Great Britain had a keen interest in Malta and it was feared that the Order would surrender it to Britain. Therefore the French Republic must support the Order, and if there was any sign that the island might be invaded by the British the French fleet must defend Malta against them.

The execution of King Louis XVI in January 1793 caused great upset in Malta, for the French monarchy had long been a protector of the Order. Grand Master Rohan forbad the French fleet to hoist the national flag, and refused to acknowledge the French Republic. The French envoy on Malta saw this as a declaration of war, but the new Republic had other problems and could not attack Malta at this time. After negotiation the Order returned to a policy of neutrality and war was averted.

This situation continued until September 1797, when the Directory which then ruled France became alarmed at reports, prompted by the election of Ferdinand von Hompesch as grand master, that Austria intended to take over Malta. Moreover, following the partition of Poland, the Polish priory of the Order had been converted into a Russian Grand Priory, confirmed by the new Tsar Paul I (1796–1801): marking an increasingly close relationship between Russia and the Order. The Directory decided that the best course of action was to force Spain to confiscate the Order's possessions in the Iberian peninsula, which would leave the Order unable to survive; and then to force it to surrender Malta

[9] Quoted in Alain Blondy, 'Malta and France, 1789–1798: the Art of Communicating a Crisis', in *Hospitaller Malta, 1530–1798: Studies on Early Modern Malta and the Order of St John of Jerusalem*, ed. Victor Mallia-Milanes (Msida, 1993), pp. 659–85: here p. 670.

to France. The Maltese people were known to favour the French Republic because they hoped for freedom from the Order's government. To encourage the Order to surrender Malta to France a French fleet was sent to Malta in spring 1798, *en route* to Egypt, commanded by Admiral Brueys with an army of 29,000 men under General Napoleon Bonaparte.

The grand master had been informed of French intentions, and apparently decided that the island was not defensible. Its fortifications were in good order, but he lacked trained defenders. He did not trust the Maltese to fight alongside the brothers, and appealed to the British fleet for assistance. The British fleet, under Horatio Nelson, was attempting to follow the French, but had been delayed by gales and did not receive Hompesch's appeal until Napoleon had captured Malta.

General Napoleon Bonaparte and the French fleet arrived at Malta on 9 June 1798. A message was sent to the grand master asking for permission for the fleet to enter and take on water. The request was refused by the grand master's council, which replied that only four ships at a time might enter – a regulation dating back to an incident with the British in 1758. Bonaparte responded that he would take the water by force, and ordered an attack. On Malta the old arrangements for defence of the island were put into play, and the French were courageously opposed, but the defence soon broke down. In the aftermath of the defeat accusations of treachery were made against various brothers. Yet the situation was deeply problematic simply because the brothers were vowed to defend Christians, not to fight them. The fact that the grand master himself did not enter the field may have been decisive – by this period kings did not usually enter the field, but as a general as well as a king the grand master was expected by his subjects to fight. Not only did the brothers not trust the Maltese to fight, but the Maltese did not trust the brothers to defend them. The Maltese *Università* called on the grand master to treat with the French, saying that they would not fight Christians. A rumour went around that the Order had already surrendered.

The grand master and council agreed to ask for a truce. Bonaparte demanded the surrender of the island. The grand master and the knights left the island on 17 June 1798, leaving behind their archives and their treasure, although they were allowed to take some of their relics including the hand of St John the Baptist, the icon of the Virgin of Philerimos (brought by Rhodian refugees to Malta in 1530) and the relic of the True Cross. Some relics, such as the reputed skull of the blessed Gerard, remained on Malta. The Order's churches were looted by Napoleon's soldiers and some of the relics were carried off with their reliquaries in the French flag ship *L'Orient.* On the evening of 1 August the British fleet under Nelson caught up with the French fleet in Aboukir Bay off the north Egyptian coast and defeated it in the battle of the Nile. *L'Orient* was blown up and sunk, with the Order's relics on board.

Scholars still debate why the Order surrendered so rapidly to Napoleon, rather than waiting to be relieved by the British, or defying Napoleon in the hope that he would sail on if he were unable to take the island within a few days. It appears that Hompesch had no confidence that the British would come to his assistance, could not rely on the Maltese to assist the brothers, and lacked the military and diplomatic skills to defy Napoleon. As grand master he must take principal responsibility for the surrender; perhaps he felt that he had to give consideration to preserving life and that resistance would only defer the inevitable. The French were to show in 1798–1800 how impregnable were the fortifications of Malta, but that ultimately a defending garrison could not withstand a prolonged blockade by a determined enemy with control of the sea. Hompesch's speedy surrender spared the Maltese in June 1798 the agonies which they would endure over the following two years under the French.

7

The Order of St John from 1798 to the present day

GRAND MASTER HOMPESCH with twelve knight-brothers, two sergeants-at-arms and a few of the Order's most precious relics left Malta for Trieste on the Adriatic on 17 June 1798. Here the Emperor Francis II (Holy Roman Emperor 1792–1806, Emperor of Austria 1804–35) gave him asylum. The fate of the Order now appeared to be in the hands of the Holy Roman Emperor; but this situation soon changed. The news of the loss of Malta reached the brothers of the newly formed Russian priory in August; the priory chapter, believing that Hompesch had betrayed Malta, declared him deposed as grand master, and the brothers 'threw themselves into the arms' of their protector Tsar Paul I. They repudiated the terms of surrender which had been negotiated with Bonaparte, 'the Convention'. Tsar Paul I agreed to maintain the Order and its institutions and to do all he could to re-establish it. His capital city of St Petersburg would become the Order's centre of administration. He invited the other tongues to accept this arrangement. The priories of Russia and Germany agreed, although the German grand prior did not. The priories of Spain, Bohemia and Bavaria did not. The other priories of the Order had been destroyed or reduced to impotence in the recent upheavals in France and Italy.

In Trieste, Hompesch defended his actions and denied accusations of treachery. The priory of Castile supported him. It was left to Pope Pius VI to decide what to do. Meanwhile, the tsar had taken the Order's habit – although he had taken no religious vows, and could not enter the Order as he was of the Russian Orthodox faith and therefore a schismatic in Catholic eyes. The priory of Russia elected him as the new grand master, and the ambassadors of two countries whose priories still recognised Hompesch as grand master – Spain and Bavaria – were told to leave Russia. The tsar created new Russian Orthodox commanderies, and gave the Order money and a small fleet. It appears that the tsar did not do this for political motives or hopes of recovering Malta and dominating the Mediterranean so much as from romantic dreams of chivalry and a hatred of the French revolutionary republicans. He declared that the

Orders' rules and statutes 'inspire love of virtue, form good manners and cement the ties of obedience . . . The Order is for every state a means of increasing its strength, security and glory.'[1] He was expressing the motives which had encouraged monarchs for the last six hundred years to support the Order and use its members as administrative officials in positions of trust.

Acting as grand master, the tsar worked to promote the Order's interests. The elector of Bavaria, in need of funds, had sequestrated the Order's property; the tsar ordered it returned, on pain of Russian attack. The elector, who needed Russian support against Austria, complied. The tsar refused to assist the Holy Roman Emperor in Italy against the French unless he supported him as grand master of the Order of St John. Emperor Francis II put pressure on Hompesch to resign as grand master. Hompesch finally agreed on 6 July 1799, and in token of his surrender he sent the Order's precious relics, carried from Malta, to the tsar: the hand of St John the Baptist, the icon of Our Lady of Philerimos, and the relic of the True Cross.[2] In this way he symbolically transferred custody of the Order to the tsar. Pope Pius VI eventually recognised the tsar as grand master of the Order, despite his own serious objections. The bulk of the Order was now based at St Petersburg with 249 members including many Russian Orthodox. Hompesch and a handful of brothers remained in Trieste; a number of brothers were resident in commanderies across Europe. Of the rest of the brothers left on Malta, around fifty knights accompanied Bonaparte to Egypt.

This appeared to be the effective end of the Order. Its hospital was lost; its role of fighting holy war against the enemies of Christendom was ended; its most holy relics were in the hands of a schismatic. Its European possessions had either already been secularised or would be sequestrated in the years to come as Bonaparte's armies conquered mainland Europe. Even the Lutheran bailiwick of Brandenburg was abolished in 1811.

However, while the Order could still be of use to secular powers it was not completely finished. In 1799 the island of Malta was still in the centre of the war. The Maltese were in revolt against the French, and the island was being blockaded from the sea by the British under Captain Alexander Ball. The British could not land an army as they lacked troops, but they could blockade effectively, and since the battle of the Nile they controlled the Mediterranean by sea. They were determined to capture Malta, and that the Russians should not have it; so far as the British were concerned, the tsar's protection of the Order of St John was a cover for his ambitions in the Mediterranean. Already he was in alliance with the Turks against the French, and their fleets captured Corfu in February 1799. The Order of St John had refused an alliance with the Turks in 1796, but now, as a puppet of the tsar, it had no choice in the matter.

The British were encouraged by the fact that the Maltese disliked the Russians

[1] Quoted by R. Cavaliero, *The Last of the Crusaders: the Knights of St John and Malta in the Eighteenth Century* (London, 1960), p. 239.

[2] *The Order's Early Legacy on Malta*, ed. John Azzopardi (Valetta, 1989), p. 22.

and would prefer British rule, but had to take into account the opinions of the king of Naples, who was an ally for the British against the French but also had a claim to Malta. Meanwhile, the British blockade of Malta had reduced the French garrison and the Maltese to starvation. Seeing an opportunity, in June 1799 Hompesch sent three knight-brothers to Malta with an appeal to the Maltese to support him; if they agreed to help Hompesch recapture Malta he would recognise Ferdinand IV, king of Naples (1759–1806; king of the two Sicilies 1816–25), as his sovereign and expected Ferdinand to send them help. Hompesch's representatives were arrested by the British and sent back to Trieste. The following month Hompesch resigned as grand master.

The Russians were expected to capture Malta, but did not; troops sent for the attack on Malta were diverted by Ferdinand of Naples to defend his capital city. Austria was also opposed to Russia taking Malta. The British refused any terms which allowed the island to be divided between the powers. Matters were complicated as the tsar opened peace negotiations with the French. Finally Valletta fell to the British in September 1800, and Major-General Pigot, in charge of the British troops, claimed it for Britain. Captain Ball advised the incoming governer, Charles Cameron, not to allow the Hospitallers to have any authority on the island, and the British government, cautiously eyeing Russia and wondering whether the tsar could be trusted, decided to hold on to Malta.

The tsar demanded that a Russian garrison be admitted; and he continued to negotiate with Bonaparte. These negotiations were ended by his murder in March 1801. His successor, Tsar Alexander I (1801–25), took the Order of St John under his protection and promised to do what he could to restore what it had lost, but did not become grand master. He appointed a lieutenant grand master until a general chapter could elect a grand master following the proper procedures.

The intervention of Tsar Paul I had saved the Order – but for what? The Order's subordination to a secular prince, who was unchaste and did not recognise the pope, had brought it into disrepute as a religious Order and reduced it to the level of one of the new pseudo-religious Orders of nobility of the Enlightenment, such as the Rosecrucians or the Free Masons. The Order's most precious relics were now in the hands of the Russian monarchy, and remained there, surviving the Bolshevik revolution and then passing into the hands of the Russian Orthodox Church in exile. They were sent for safe keeping to a monastery in Montenegro in 1941, where they have been recently rediscovered. But without its relics the Order had lost its spiritual link with its past, and even its validity as a religious Order supported by God and the saints. What was more, due to Tsar Paul's enthusiasm in creating commanderies and members of the Order, various spurious branches of the Order grew up, which still cause problems to the Order.

In March 1802 the Treaty of Amiens laid down, among much weightier matters, that the Order of St John should call a general chapter on Malta and elect a grand master, and that the English and French tongues would be abolished as the Order no longer existed in those countries, but a Maltese tongue should be established. The British garrison should evacuate the island to the Neopolitans. The island would then be held by a force consisting half of Maltese and half of the tongues of the Order. Malta would be neutral and its independence guaranteed.

The Maltese tongue was set up, but the British were not willing to withdraw from Malta as they did not believe that the Order or the Maltese could hold it against French aggression. The priories of Spain had been taken over by the king of Spain; the priories of Italy had been damaged in the war or their property sequestrated; the priory of Germany refused to allow the Maltese to join the Order; the Order had no resources to carry through the terms of Amiens. Tsar Alexander I objected to the terms of Amiens regarding the Order, over which he had not been consulted. Eventually Pope Pius VII (1800–23) chose a new grand master from a short list submitted by the Russian priory: this was the Bailiff di Ruspoli, but he refused the office. The pope then appointed Bailiff Giovanni Battista Tommasi (1803–5), and the tsar recognised the appointment. Tommasi held a general assembly of all knight-brothers at Messina, but he could not return to Malta. He used an Augustinian convent in Catania as his centre of administration where the Order's convent could be said to be based, but he had no holy infirmary, no holy relics, little left as evidence that he was the successor to grand masters Pinto and de Rohan.

The tsar still refused to recognise the Treaty of Amiens, and Britain still refused to evacuate Malta. Various plans were put forward to allow the Order to return to Malta, but none satisfied the British that French domination of the Mediterranean would be prevented. In short, the British were convinced that they alone could protect their own interests in the Mediterranean. The British remained on Malta. The pope, anxious to avoid angering any of the great powers, refused to approve another grand master on the death of Tommasi, but he approved successive lieutenant grand masters selected by the convent, and at the Congress of Vienna in 1814 the brothers asked for another Mediterranean island where they could maintain a hospital and conduct the *corso*. But a *corso* against whom? The Ottomans were now regarded as part of Europe, and a valuable ally against France or Russia as appropriate. Britain's possession of Malta was confirmed, and the Order received nothing.

In the years that followed there were a number of schemes to find the Order a new role in fighting the forces of Islam. Emperor Francis II of Austria retained an interest in the Order. His minister of foreign affairs, Prince Klemens von Metternich (minister 1809–48), offered the Order the island of Elba or various islands in the Adriatic, if the Order permitted the grand master to be under the authority of the Habsburgs. The Order was not prepared to concede this. In 1821 the Greeks revolted against Ottoman rule and asked the pope for help; they offered to give the Order an island in the Aegean in return for their assistance against the infidel. The Hospitallers were in favour of this: it was agreed that they would receive Rhodes, and the French brothers set about raising loans to finance the expedition, as well as raising money on the London Stock Exchange. The governments of France, Britain, Austria and Russia, however, were opposed to supporting the revolutionaries; and the scheme fell through. The French brothers continued with it in a different form, attempting to raise support from all Christians and not only the Order, and in the process recruited several Hospitallers in England, Protestant and Catholic; their efforts were aided by the fact that by 1829 most of the discriminatory legislation against Roman Catholics in England had been repealed. In 1830 some French brothers proposed to King Charles X of France (1824–30) that he should instal the Hospitallers in Algiers, but when the revolution of July 1830 deprived Charles of his throne, the Hospitallers lost all influence with the French government.

Meanwhile the Order was in constitutional turmoil. Some commanderies remained in Europe. The priory of Bohemia still existed after a scheme of 1811 to amalgamate it with the Order of Maria Theresa was abandoned in the face of the Order's protests. The Spanish commanderies had been nationalised in 1802, returned in 1814 but confiscated again in 1820 in the revolution. When royal authority was resumed the Spanish commanderies were not returned to the Order but remained under royal control, as a royal Order. The French commanderies had formed a capitular commission, which was recognised by King Louis XVIII of France (1814–24) and by the lieutenant-master in Catania, and which claimed to have papal recognition, but which ceased to operate after the French government withdrew its support over the Greek island scheme. The lieutenant-master remained in Catania, having been refused permission by the Sicilian government in 1806 to move his convent to Rome. Yet the commanderies outside Catania did not necessarily recognise his authority. In 1825 the Sicilian commanderies were sequestrated, and in 1827 the lieutenant-master Antonio Busca (1821–34) moved his convent to Ferrara.

Finally, in 1834 the new lieutenant-master, Carlo Candida (1834–45), was instructed by Pope Gregory XVI (1831–46) to move the convent to Rome, to a palace on the Aventine Hill. The pope gave the Order a hospital, the hospice of Cento Preti, and the members of the central convent of the Order were again able to dedicate themselves to the Order's original and primary vocation of caring for the sick poor. The Order was reformed, abandoning its military function completely. In the wars to come, it would only play a hospital role. Nevertheless its modern title is 'the Sovereign Military and Hospitaller Order of St John of Jerusalem, called of Rhodes, called of Malta', usually shortened to 'the Sovereign Military Order of Malta'.

The Order now began to rebuild. Only the tongues of Italy and Germany still survived. Commanderies were founded in Italy. It proved impossible, however, to re-establish the grand magistracy, as the Habsburg Empire still insisted on having a say in approving the candidates. It was not until 1879 that Pope Leo XIII (1878–1903) was able to appoint a new grand master, Johann Baptist Ceschi a Santa Croce (1879–1905). He was followed by two more grand masters appointed by the papacy, Galeas von Thun und Hohenstein (1905–31), who retired as grand master, and Ludovico Chigi Albani della Rovere (1931–51). After the death of Grand Master Chigi, the pope, Pius XII (1939–58), refused to appoint another grand master until the Order had been reformed, and lieutenant-masters were appointed. In 1962 the first legislative general chapter of the order since 1776 was held, and a new grand master was elected by the chapter: Brother Angelo de Mojana dei Signori di Cologna, who held the office until his death in 1988. He was succeeded by the British Andrew Bertie, who is grand master of the Order at the time of writing.

The restoration of the grand mastership in 1879 was an important step in the re-creation of the Order. The restoration of the Catholic Order was complicated by the existence of other branches of the Order which were not Catholic. The Lutheran Bailiwick of Brandenburg was re-established by the Prussian crown in 1852. In Britain, those who had been enrolled as Hospitallers by the French brothers in the 1820s for the abortive Greek expedition and who had been disappointed by the failure of the Algerian enterprise hoped that their new English priory would be recognised by the Order in Rome. The Order in England had been restored briefly in 1557 by Letters Patent of Queen Mary I of England (1553–8) and her consort Philip II of Spain, and although Elizabeth I of England (1558–1603) had sequestrated its possessions on her accession, Queen Mary's order had never been repealed. The English brothers, led by one Robert Peat, therefore claimed to be the successors to the old English priory. But by this time they had broken away from the French brothers and had no connection with the modern Order. In 1843 they attempted to approach the Order's headquarters in Rome. But lieutenant-master Candida, 'not without real pain', refused to recognise them: the fundamental problem was that they were Protestant and did not acknowledge the authority of the pope. The English brothers were deeply wounded, but there was enough interest in the Order in England to keep it alive.

By the late 1850s the Catholic Order was trying to re-establish a Catholic priory in England, and the English Protestant 'priory' hoped to be affiliated to it; but this fell through, as the Catholic English brothers of the Order did not wish to have anything to do with the Protestants.[3] The priory's charitable work in the British Isles, however, won it respect. In 1888 Queen Victoria recognised the English priory as an order of the British Crown. Today it is an associate order of the Sovereign Military Order of Malta, but has a separate identity. It is responsible for the St John Ambulance Association, and also runs an eye hospital in Jerusalem. Its title is 'the Most Venerable Order of the Hospital of St John of Jerusalem', and its head is the English monarch.

From the 1860s onwards the Sovereign Military Order of Malta in Rome began to approve Catholic associations of the Order in various European countries: in the Rhineland and Westphalia, Silesia, Britain, Italy, France and Spain. In effect, these replaced the old 'tongues' which had been effectively

[3] Jonathan Riley-Smith, 'The Order of St John in England, 1827–1858', in *The Military Orders: Fighting for the Faith*, ed. M. Barber (Aldershot, 1994), pp. 121–38.

destroyed in the Napoleonic Wars and their aftermath. The associations, which still operate, are part of the Sovereign Military Order of Malta but the majority of their members are not full brothers and sisters but associates, like the 'confratres' and 'consorors' of the medieval Order. The British Association of the Sovereign Military Order of Malta was formed in 1876. In the twentieth century further associations of the Order were founded all around the world.

During the First World War the associations of the Order of St John of Jerusalem set up hospitals in France, Germany, Austria and Italy for the care of the wounded. Its property and influence suffered as a result of the defeat of Germany and Austria, but during the inter-war years the Order maintained good relations with the kingdom of Italy. In 1912 Rhodes had been taken by the Italians and in 1928, after the governor of Rhodes had begun 'restoring' (or, rather, reconstructing) the Order's medieval buildings, the Order was given the old Auberge or Inn of Italy on the Street of the Knights. The Second World War destroyed this *entente* and the Order lost some of its members to Nazi persecutions. After the war, in Germany and Italy the Order was involved in caring for refugees. Its work brought it praise and money, but in the 1950s the Order was involved in a serious scandal when it transpired that thousands of dollars of money raised for the Order through its US association were being embezzled. The result of this and connected problems within the Order was its constitutional reform, which in effect set down in writing its position within the Catholic Church: the Order is a sovereign order, in that it is not subject to any other authority (except the pope's) and operates across national boundaries; it is a religious Order, with all that this entails; and it has certain traditional privileges, such as not being answerable to episcopal authority.

Today the Sovereign Military and Hospitaller Order of St John of Jerusalem, called of Rhodes, called of Malta, still cares for the sick poor. It organises annual pilgrimages for the sick and disabled. Its national associations are responsible for hospitals. The Order is involved in diplomacy, and maintains embassies in many countries. It recognises only four Protestant Orders of St John: the Most Venerable Order of the Hospital of St John of Jerusalem in Britain, the Grand Bailiwick of Brandenburg, the Johanniter Orde in the Netherlands and the Johanniterorden in Sweden.

□

The modern Order would still be recognisable to its medieval patrons. It is still a Roman Catholic order, independent of secular authority, answerable only to the pope on earth. The officials of the Order are still drawn from a class wealthier and more privileged than the average western European, but whereas during the middle ages the Order was a means to rise in social status, now the Order's officials are drawn from families which are already of high social status. This change was already occurring by the late middle ages and by the early modern period the Order had become what it is now, an Order of nobility. There are only a relatively small number of knight-brothers and priest-brothers; most of those involved in the Order are not fully professed religious, but take vows of obedience to the spiritual authority of the Order and promise to perform certain religious duties. These associates may be married and many are drawn from what could be loosely referred to as 'ordinary people'. The Order is involved in hospital work, and in diplomacy. Its finances have occasionally given rise to scandal; it has been accused of not being sufficiently careful in admitting suitable candidates to membership. It is even closer to the papacy today than it ever was in the middle ages.

There are also certain differences between the modern order and the medieval order. The professed members of the Order no longer follow a conventual lifestyle – this was a change already occurring in the late medieval period, although the conventual lifestyle survived on Malta until 1798. Having lost its great estates and revenues, the Order no longer supports any of its members, who have to have an independent income. The Order is no longer involved in holy war. Its physical connection to its long historical past was broken in 1798–1801 with the loss of its archives and its holy relics. Its tradition of hospital care was also interrupted between 1798–1834, but the fact that there was some continuity of membership between the loss of Malta and the re-establishment of the central convent at Rome in 1834 means that the modern Order is truly the survivor of the medieval Order, albeit in much reduced circumstances. In recent years the Order has returned to Malta on a small scale, opening an embassy in St John's bastion in Valletta, and restoring the fortress of San Angelo as a base for its hospital work.

□

A brief consideration of the Order's achievements over its more than nine-hundred-year existence will serve to sum up the history of the Sovereign Military and Hospitaller Order of St John of Jerusalem. Without the military assistance of the Order, the crusader states of the Latin East would probably have fallen more quickly to the invading Muslim and Mongol armies. The Order's support for the Christian kingdom of Cilician Armenia may have helped to prolong its existence. It also supported western European crusades to the East, and ensured that physical holy war remained a living reality at a period when most western Europeans would otherwise have been distracted by the Anglo-French wars and others in western Europe, even though the Ottoman Turks were beginning to become a real threat to Europe. The Order's harassment of Mamluk and Ottoman shipping in the Mediterranean did limit Muslim naval control of the seas during its periods on Rhodes and on Malta. During the sixteenth to the eighteenth centuries the Order's anti-piratical activities made the Mediterranean safer for some Christian shipping, if not always for all. The Order was never able to turn the tide of Muslim advance, but could slow it.

During the period under consideration here, the Order made no impressive advances in medicine; it cannot be said to have transferred Arabic advances in medicine to Europe during the middle ages, although its own standards of care in the Jerusalem hospital were somewhat in advance of those practised in Europe and may have encouraged some advance in European hospital care. Rather than the Order taking the lead in scientific advance, individual members made their mark, such as Brother Deodat de Dolomieu in geology. Many members played a significant, even a leading role in the courts of Europe. The Order patronised artists and inspired some great works of art. It has also left a great number of buildings across Europe and the Middle East, from tiny churches in western Wales to massive fortifications in the Middle East, Rhodes, Malta and the Iberian Peninsula. These physical mementoes of the great wars of the past – a stark contrast with the Order's current, peaceful role – perhaps form its most significant impact on the modern world.

Further Reading

This list concentrates on works in English.

GENERAL

For the medieval period:

Alan Forey, *The Military Orders: From the Twelfth to the Early Fourteenth Centuries* (Basingstoke, 1992)

Alan Forey, *Military Orders and Crusades* (Aldershot, 1994)

Anthony Luttrell, *The Hospitallers in Cyprus, Rhodes, Greece and the West (1291–1440)* (London, 1978)

Anthony Luttrell, *Latin Greece, the Hospitallers and the Crusades, 1291–1440* (Aldershot, 1982).

Anthony Luttrell, *The Hospitallers of Rhodes and their Mediterranean World* (Aldershot, 1992)

Anthony Luttrell, *The Hospitaller State on Rhodes and its Western Provinces, 1306–1462* (Aldershot, 1999).

Jonathan Riley-Smith, *The Knights of St John in Jerusalem and Cyprus: c.1050–1310* (London, 1967)

Militia Sacra: Gli Ordini Militari tra Europa e Terrasanta, ed. Enzo Coli, Maria de Marco and Francesco Tommasi (Perugia, 1994)

The Rule, Statutes and Customs of the Hospitallers, 1099–1310, trans. Edwin James King (London, 1934)

For the early modern and modern period:

Anthony Luttrell, 'The Military Orders, 1312–1798', in *The Oxford Illustrated History of the Crusades*, ed. Jonathan Riley-Smith (Oxford, 1995), pp. 326–64

Henry J. A. Sire, *The Knights of Malta* (New Haven and London, 1994)

For the whole period:

Jonathan Riley-Smith, *Hospitallers: The History of the Order of St John* (London and Rio Grande, 1999)

See also the volumes of proceedings from the Clerkenwell conferences on the Military Orders:

The Military Orders: Fighting for the Faith and Caring for the Sick, ed. Malcolm Barber (Aldershot, 1994)
The Military Orders, vol. 2, *Welfare and Warfare*, ed. Helen Nicholson (Aldershot, 1998)
The Military Orders, vol. 3, *History and Heritage*, ed. William G. Zajac (Aldershot, forthcoming)

See also the *Ordines Militares* series: *Ordines Militares – Colloquia Torunensia Historica*, ed. Zenon Hubert Nowak, Universitas Nicolai Copernici, 10 vols to date (Torún, 1983–),
And the new periodical *Sacra Militia: Rivista di Storia degli Ordini Militari* (Genoa, 2001–).

Chapter 1. THE ORIGINS OF THE HOSPITAL OF ST JOHN IN JERUSALEM

General:

Jonathan Riley-Smith, *The Knights of St John in Jerusalem and Cyprus, 1050–1310* (London, 1967)

Background:

T. S. R. Boase, *Castles and Churches of the Crusading Kingdom* (Toronto, 1967), chapter 1
Denys Pringle, 'Crusader Jerusalem', *Bulletin of the Anglo-Israel Archaeological Society*, 10 (1990–91), 105–13
Denys Pringle, *Secular Buildings in the Crusader Kingdom of Jerusalem: An Archaeological Gazetteer* (Cambridge, 1997), under 'Jerusalem'

On the beginning of the Order:

Alan Beltjens, *Aux Origines de l'Ordre de Malte: de la Fondation de l'Hôpital de Jérusalem à sa Transformation en Ordre Militaire* (Brussels, 1995)
Alan Forey, 'The Militarisation of the Hospital of St John', *Studia Monastica*, 26 (1984), 75–89; reprinted in his *Military Orders and Crusades* (Aldershot, 1994), 9
Alan Forey, *The Military Orders: From the Twelfth to the Early Fourteenth Centuries*, chapter 3
Rudolf Hiestand, 'Die Anfänge der Johanniter', *Die Geistlichen Ritterordern Europas*, ed. Josef Fleckenstein and Manfred Hellmann, Vorträge und Forschungen 26 (Sigmaringen, 1980), pp. 31–80: a major modern study
Luis García Guijarro Ramos, 'La militarización de la Orden del Hospital: líneas para

un debate,' in *Ordens Militares: Guerra, Religião, Podar et Cultura – Actas do III Encontra sobre Ordens Militares*, 2 (Lisbon, 1999), pp. 293–302
Anthony Luttrell, 'The Earliest Hospitallers', in *Montjoie: Studies in Crusade History in Honour of Hans Eberhard Mayer*, ed. Benjamin Z. Kedar, Jonathan Riley-Smith and Rudolf Hiestand (Aldershot, 1997), pp. 37–54
Michael Matzke, '*De Origine Hospitaliorum Hierosolymitanorum*: vom klösterlichen Pilgerhospital zur internationalen Organisation', *Journal of Medieval History*, 22 (1996), 1–23

The Order's traditions:

Karl Borchardt, 'Two Forged Thirteenth-Century Alms-Raising Letters used by the Hospitallers in Franconia', in *The Military Orders: Fighting for the Faith and Caring for the Sick*, ed. Malcolm Barber (Aldershot, 1994), pp. 52–56
Anthony Luttrell, 'The Rhodian Background of the Order of Saint John on Malta', in *The Order's Early Legacy in Malta*, ed. John Azzopardi (Valletta, 1989), pp. 3–14; and p. 45
The Hospitallers' Riwle (Miracula et Regula Hospitalis Sancti Johannis Jersolimitani), ed. K. V. Sinclair, Anglo-Norman Texts 42 (Oxford, 1984)
Helen Nicholson, *Templars, Hospitallers and Teutonic Knights: Images of the Military Orders, 1128–1291* (Leicester and London, 1993), pp. 112–16

On the origins of the concept of holy war and the crusade:

Jean Flori, *Idéologie du Glaive: Préhistoire de la Chevalerie* (Geneva, 1983)
John Gilchrist, 'The Papacy and the War against "the Saracens"', *International History Review*, 10 (1988), 174–197
Jonathan Riley-Smith, *The First Crusade and the Idea of Crusading* (London, 1986)
Jonathan Riley-Smith, *The First Crusaders, 1095–1131* (Cambridge, 1997)
Ian Robinson, 'Pope Gregory VII and the Soldiers of Christ', *History*, 58 (1973), 169–92

Primary sources in translation:

Gesta Francorum et aliorum Hierosolimitanorum, trans. Rosalind Hill (London, 1962)
Guibert of Nogent, *The Deeds of God through the Franks: Gesta Dei per Francos*, trans. Robert Levine (Woodbridge, 1997)
A History of Deeds Done Beyond the Sea, by William of Tyre, trans. E. A. Babcock and A. Krey, 2 vols (Columbia, 1944)
Jerusalem Pilgrimage 1099–1185, ed. J. Wilkinson, J. Hill and W. F. Ryan, Hakluyt Society, 2nd series, 167 (1988): descriptions of the city of Jerusalem and its surrounds in the twelfth century

Chapter 2. HOLY WAR IN THE LATIN EAST AND ON THE EUROPEAN FRONTIERS, 1130–1291

General:

Jonathan Riley-Smith, *The Knights of St John in Jerusalem and Cyprus* (London, 1967)
Alan Forey, *The Military Orders from the Twelfth to the Early Fourteenth Centuries* (Basingstoke, 1992), chapter 3

See also:

Alain Demurger, 'Templiers et Hospitaliers dans les combats de Terre Sainte', in *Le Combatant au Moyen Age, Montpellier 1987*, Société des Historiens Médiévistes de l'Enseignement Supérieur Public (Paris, 1991), pp. 77–96
Hugh Kennedy, *Crusader Castles* (Cambridge, 1994)

On the Crusades and the Latin East:

Hans E. Mayer, *The Crusades*, trans. John Gillingham, 2nd edn (Oxford, 1988)
Peter Edbury, 'The Crusader States', in *The New Cambridge Medieval History*, vol. 5, *c. 1198–1300*, ed. David Abulafia (Cambridge, 1999)
Jean Richard, *The Latin Kingdom of Jerusalem*, trans. Janet Shirley, 2 vols. (Amsterdam, 1979)
Jean Richard, *Histoire des Croisades* (Paris, 1996) trans. Jean Birrell, *The Crusades, c. 1071–c. 1291* (Cambridge, 1999)

See also:

M. Benvenisti, *The Crusaders in the Holy Land* (Jerusalem, 1970)
Carole Hillenbrand, *The Crusades: Islamic perspectives* (Edinburgh, 1999)

The Hospitallers' early military activity:

Alan Forey, 'The Emergence of the Military Order in the Twelfth Century', *Journal of Ecclesiastical History*, 36 (1985), 175–95: reprinted in his *Military Orders and Crusades* (Aldershot, 1994), 1
Alan Forey, 'The Militarisation of the Hospital of St John', *Studia Monastica*, 26 (1984), 75–89; reprinted in his *Military Orders and Crusades* (Aldershot, 1994), 9
Jonathan Phillips, 'Archbishop Henry of Reims and the Militarization of the Hospitallers', in *The Military Orders*, vol. 2, *Welfare and Warfare*, ed. Helen Nicholson (Aldershot, 1998), pp. 83–8

The East: twelfth century:

Peter W. Edbury, 'Propaganda and Faction in the Kingdom of Jerusalem: the Background to Hattin', in *Crusaders and Muslims in Twelfth Century Syria*, ed. M. Shatzmiller (Leiden, 1993), pp. 173–89
Jonathan Phillips, *Defenders of the Holy Land: Relations Between the Latin East and the West, 1119–1187* (Oxford, 1996)

R. C. Smail, 'Latin Syria and the West', *Transactions of the Royal Historical Society*, 5th series, 19 (1969), 1–21

On William of Tyre:

R. H. C. Davis, 'William of Tyre', in *Relations between East and West in the Middle Ages*, ed. D. Baker (Edinburgh, 1987), pp. 64–76

Peter W. Edbury and John G. Rowe, *William of Tyre: Historian of the Latin East* (Cambridge, 1988)

Rudolf Hiestand, 'Zum Leben und zur Laufbahn Wilhelms von Tyrus', *Deutsches Archiv für Erforschung des Mittelalters*, 34 (1978), 345–80

Helen Nicholson, 'Before William of Tyre: European Reports on the Military Orders' Deeds in the East, 1150–1185', in *The Military Orders*, vol. 2, *Welfare and Warfare*, ed. Helen Nicholson (Aldershot, 1998), pp. 111–18

D. W. T. C. Vessey, 'William of Tyre and the Art of Historiography', *Medieval Studies*, 35 (1973), 433–55

On the Latin Empire of Constantinople:

Peter Lock, 'The Military Orders in Mainland Greece', in *The Military Orders: Fighting for the Faith and Caring for the Sick*, ed. Malcolm Barber (Aldershot, 1994), pp. 333–9

Crusaders as Conquerors: the Chronicle of the Morea Translated from the Greek, trans. Harold E. Lurier (New York and London, 1964)

Cilician Armenia:

T. S. R. Boase, 'The History of the Kingdom', in his *The Cilician Kingdom of Armenia* (Edinburgh and London, 1978), pp. 1–33

Jonathan Riley-Smith, 'The Templars and Teutonic Knights in Cilician Armenia', in *The Cilician Kingdom of Armenia*, ed. T. S. R. Boase (Edinburgh and London, 1978), pp. 92–117

Frederick II's crusade:

David Abulafia, *Frederick II: a Medieval Emperor* (London, 1988), pp. 164–201

Keith Giles, 'The Emperor Frederick II's Crusade, 1215–1231', unpublished Ph.D. thesis, University of Keele, 1987

For a full bibliography of the crusade to 1962 see:

Thomas C. Van Cleve, 'The Crusade of Frederick II', in *The Later Crusades 1189–1311*, ed. Robert Lee Wolff and Harry W. Hazard, vol. 2 of *A History of the Crusades*, ed. Kenneth M. Setton, 2nd edn, 6 vols to date (Madison, 1969–1989), pp. 429–82: here pp. 429–30, note

1230–1250:

Marie Luise Bulst-Thiele, 'Zur Geschichte der Ritterorden und des Königsreichs

Jerusalem im 13 Jahrhundert bis zur Schlacht bei la Forbie am 17 Okt 1244', *Deutsches Archiv für Erforschung des Mittelalters*, 22 (1966), 197–226

Peter W. Edbury, *The Kingdom of Cyprus and the Crusades, 1191–1374* (Cambridge, 1991), pp. 81–2

Jonathan Riley-Smith, *The Feudal Nobility and the Kingdom of Jerusalem, 1174–1277* (Basingstoke, 1973)

Peter Jackson, 'The Crusades of 1239–41 and their Aftermath', *Bulletin of the School of Oriental and African Studies*, 50 (1987), 32–60

Joshua Prawer, 'Military Orders and Crusader Politics in the Second Half of the XIIIth Century', in *Die Geistlichen Ritterorden Europas*, ed. Josef Fleckenstein and Manfred Hellmann, Vorträge und Forschungen, 26 (Sigmaringen, 1980), pp. 217–29

After 1250:

Peter Edbury, *John of Ibelin and the Kingdom of Jerusalem* (Woodbridge, 1997)

D. J. Cathcart King, 'The Taking of Le Krak des Chevaliers in 1271', *Antiquity*, 23 (1949), 83–92

Peter Jackson, 'The Crisis in the Holy Land in 1260', *English Historical Review*, 95 (1980), 481–513

Peter Jackson, 'The End of Hohenstaufen Rule in Syria', *Bulletin of the Institute of Historical Research*, 59 (1986), 20–36

Peter Thorau, *The Lion of Egypt: Sultan Baybars I*, trans. Peter M. Holt (London and New York, 1992)

Peter M. Holt, 'Mamluk-Frankish Diplomatic Relations in the Reign of Baybars (685–76/1260–77)', *Nottingham Medieval Studies*, 32 (1988), 180–98

Peter W. Edbury, 'The Disputed Regency of the Kingdom of Jerusalem, 1264–6 and 1268', *Camden Miscellany*, 27 (Camden 4th series, 22, 1979), 1–47

1291 and after:

Alan Forey, 'The Military Orders in the Crusading Proposals of the Late Thirteenth and Early Fourteenth Centuries', *Traditio*, 36 (1980), 317–45; reprinted in his *Military Orders and Crusades*, 8

Silvia Schein, *Fideles Crucis: the Papacy, the West, and the Recovery of the Holy Land, 1274–1314* (Oxford, 1991)

Papers in:

Acri 1291: La Fine della Presenza degli Ordini Militari in Terra Santa e i Nuovi Orientamenti nel XIV secolo, ed. Francesco Tommasi (Perugia, 1996)

Spain:

Alan Forey, 'The Military Orders and the Spanish Reconquest in the Twelfth and Thirteenth Centuries', *Traditio*, 40 (1984), 197–234; reprinted in his *Military Orders and Crusades*, 5

Anthony Luttrell, 'The Aragonese Crown and the Knights Hospitallers of Rhodes: 1291–1350', *English Historical Review*, 76 (1961), 1–19, reprinted in his *The*

Hospitallers in Cyprus, Rhodes, Greece and the West (1291–1440) (London, 1978), 11

Eastern Europe:

Zsolt Hunyadi, 'The Knights of St John and the Hungarian Private Legal Literacy up to the Mid-Fourteenth Century', in *The Man of Many Devices, Who Wandered Full Many Ways . . . : Festschrift in Honour of János M. Bak*, ed. Balázs Nagy and Marcell Sebõk (Budapest, 1999), pp. 507–19

Walter Kuhn, 'Ritterorden als Grenzhüter des Abendlandes gegen das östliche Heidentum', *Ostdeutsche Wissenschaft*, 6 (1959), 7–70

Walter Kuhn, 'Kirchliche Siedlung als Grenzschutz 1200 bis 1250 (zum beispiel des mittleren Oderraumes', *Ostdeutsche Wissenschaft*, 9 (1962), 6–55

Maria Starnawska, 'Crusade Orders on Polish Lands during the Middle Ages: Adaptation in a Peripheral Environment', *Quaestiones Medii Aevi Novae*, 2 (1997), 121–42

B. Szczesniak, *The Knights Hospitallers in Poland and Lithuania* (The Hague and Paris, 1969)

See also:

Articles in *Expanding the Frontiers of Medieval Latin Christianity: The Crusades and the Military Orders*, ed. József Laszolovsky and Zsolt Hunyadi, Central European University (Budapest, 2001)

Other issues:

Alan Forey, 'The Military Orders and Holy War against Christians in the Thirteenth Century', *English Historical Review*, 104 (1989), 1–24; reprinted in his *Military Orders and Crusades*, 7

Primary sources in translation (in rough chronological order):

A History of Deeds done Beyond the Sea by William, Archbishop of Tyre, ed. and trans. E. A. Babcock and A. C. Krey (New York, 1943; reprinted 1976)

Arab Historians of the Crusades, trans. Francesco Gabrieli, trans. from the Italian by E. J. Costello (Italian edn, Turin, 1957; English edn, London, 1969, repr. New York, 1989)

The Conquest of Jerusalem and the Third Crusade: Sources in Translation, trans. Peter W. Edbury (Aldershot, 1996)

Ambroise, *The Crusade of Richard Lionheart*, trans. John L. La Monte and Merton Jerome Hubert (New York, 1976)

Chronicle of the Third Crusade: a Translation of the Itinerarium Peregrinorum et Gesta Regis Ricardi, trans. Helen Nicholson (Aldershot, 1997)

The Life of Saladin by Baha al-Din trans. Aubrey Stewart, Palestine Pilgrims' Text Society 13 (1897)

'Imād al-Dīn al-Isfahānī, *Conquête de la Syrie et de la Palestine par Saladin (al-Fath al-qussî fî l-fath al-qudsî*, trans. Henri Massé (Paris, 1972)

Anonymous pilgrim 5, 2 in *Anonymous Pilgrims I–VIII (11th and 12th Centuries)*, trans. Aubrey Stewart, Palestine Pilgrims Text Society, 6 (London, 1894)
Oliver of Paderborn, 'The Capture of Damietta', in *Christian Society and the Crusaders, 1198–1229*, ed. Edward Peters (Philadelphia, 1981)
Roger of Wendover, *Flowers of History, Comprising the History of England . . . Formerly Ascribed to Matthew Paris*, trans. J. A. Giles, 2 vols (London, 1849)
Philip of Novara, *The Wars of Frederick II Against the Ibelins in Syria and Cyprus by Philip de Novare*, trans. John L. La Monte (New York, 1936)
Ibn al-Fūrat, *Ayyubids, Mamluks and Crusaders. Selections from the Tārīk al-Duwal wa'l-Mulūk of Ibn al-Fūrat*, text and trans. U. and M. C. Lyons, introduction by Jonathan Riley-Smith, 2 vols (Cambridge, 1971)
Joinville and Villehardouin, *Chronicles of the Crusades*, trans. M. R. B. Shaw (Harmondsworth, 1963)
Matthew Paris' English History, From the Year 1235 to 1273, trans. J. A. Giles, 3 vols (London, 1889; reprinted New York, 1968)
Brother Joseph of Chauncy, in 'Letter from Sir Joseph de Cancy, knight of the Hospital, to King Edward I', and 'Letter from Edward I to Sir Joseph', trans. W. Sanders, in Palestine Pilgrims Text Society, 5 (London, 1888)
Crusader Syria in the Thirteenth Century: the Rothelin Continuation of the History of William of Tyre with Part of the Eracles or Acre Text, trans. Janet Shirley (Aldershot, 1999)
Letter of John de Villiers, master of the Hospital, describing the fall of Acre, in Edwin James King, *The Knights Hospitaller in the Holy Land* (London, 1931), pp. 301–2
The Chronicle of James I of Aragon, trans. John Forster, 2 vols (London, 1883)

Chapter 3. THE HOSPITALLERS ON RHODES, 1306–1522

Crusade plans:

For James de Molay, see: *Le Dossier de l'Affaire des Templiers*, ed. Georges Liserand (Paris, 1923), pp. 2–14
Pierre Dubois, *The Recovery of the Holy Land*, trans. W. Brandt (Colombia, 1956)
For Fulk de Villaret, see: *Documents on the Later Crusades, 1274–1580*, trans. Norman Housley (Basingstoke, 1996), pp. 40–47

Crisis after 1291:

Alan Forey, 'Constitutional Conflict and Change in the Hospital of St John During the Twelfth and Thirteenth Centuries', *Journal of Ecclesiastical History*, 33 (1982), 15–29; reprinted in his *Military Orders and Crusades*, 10
Anthony Luttrell, 'The Hospitallers in Cyprus after 1291', *Acts of the I International Congress of Cypriot Studies, II* (Nicosia, 1972), 161–71; reprinted in his *The Hospitallers in Cyprus, Rhodes, Greece and the West, 1291–1440* (London, 1978), 2
Anthony Luttrell, 'The Hospitallers' Interventions in Cilician Armenia: 1291–1375', in *The Cilician Kingdom of Armenia*, pp. 118–144; reprinted in his *Latin Greece, the Hospitallers and the Crusades, 1291–1440* (London, 1982), 5
Anthony Luttrell, 'The Aragonese Crown and the Knights Hospitallers of Rhodes:

1291–1350', *English Historical Review*, 76 (1961), 1–19, reprinted in his *The Hospitallers in Cyprus, Rhodes, Greece and the West (1291–1440)* (London, 1978), 11

Silvia Schein, '*Gesta Dei per Mongolos* 1300: the Genesis of a Non-Event', *English Historical Review*, 94 (1979), 805–19

See also:

Papers in *Acri 1291: La Fine della Presenza degli Ordini Militari in Terra Santa e i Nuovi Orientamenti nel XIV Secolo*, ed. Francesco Tommasi (Perugia, 1996)

Conquest of Rhodes:

For the background, see:

Alexis Savvides, 'Rhodes from the End of the Gabalas Rule to the Conquest by the Hospitallers, A.D. c. 1250–1309', *Byzantios Domos*, 2 (1988), 199–232; reprinted in his *ΒΥΖΑΝΤΙΝΟΤΟΥΡΚΙΚΑ ΜΕΛΕΤΗΜΑΤΑ Ανατύπωση άρθρων, 1981–1990* (Athens, 1991), 12

Anthony Luttrell, 'The Genoese at Rhodes: 1306–1312', in *Oriente e Occidente tra Medioevo ed Età Moderna: Studi in Onore di Geo Pistarino*, ed. Laura Balletto, 2 (Acqui Terme, 1997), pp. 737–61; reprinted in his *The Hospitaller State on Rhodes and its Western Provinces, 1306–1462* (Aldershot, 1999), 1

For the conquest, see:

Anthony Luttrell, 'The Hospitallers at Rhodes, 1306–1421', in *A History of the Crusades*, ed. Kenneth M. Setton, vol. 3, *The Fourteenth and Fifteenth Centuries*, ed. Harry W. Hazard (Madison, 1975), 278–313: here 282–6; reprinted in his *Hospitallers in Cyprus*, 1

Sophia Menache, 'The Hospitallers during Clement V's Pontificate: the Spoiled Sons of the Papacy?' in *The Military Orders*, vol. 2, *Welfare and Warfare*, ed. Helen Nicholson (Aldershot, 1998), pp. 153–62

Sophia Menache, *Pope Clement V* (Cambridge, 1998)

Jonathan Riley-Smith, *Knights of St John in Jerusalem and Cyprus* (London, 1967)

The Templars' legacy:

Anthony Luttrell, 'Gli Ospitalieri e l'eredità dei Templari, 1305–1378', *I Templari: Mito e Storia – Atti de Convegno Internazionale di Studi alla Magione Templare di Poggibonsi-Siena (29–31 maggio 1987)*, ed. G. Minnucci, F. Sardi (Singaluna–Siena, 1989), pp. 67–86; reprinted in his *The Hospitallers of Rhodes and their Mediterranean World* (Aldershot, 1992), 3

Criticism and other problems:

For the period before 1291 see:

Helen Nicholson, *Templars, Hospitallers and Teutonic Knights: Images of the Military Orders, 1128–1291* (Leicester, 1993)

For Geoffrey of Paris and John Dupin, see:

Helen Nicholson, *Love, War and the Grail: Templars, Hospitallers and Teutonic Knights in Medieval Epic and Romance 1150–1500* (Leiden, 2001), p. 229

For Marino Sanudo, Piloti and other critics including popes see:

Anthony Luttrell, 'Emmanuele Piloti and Criticism of the Knights Hospitallers of Rhodes: 1306–1444', *Annales de l'Ordre Souverain Militaire de Malte*, 20 (1962), 11–17; reprinted in his *Hospitallers in Cyprus*, 24

Charles Tipton, 'The Irish Hospitallers during the Great Schism', *Proceedings of the Royal Irish Academy*, 69 section (1970), 33–43

Charles Tipton, 'English and Scottish Hospitallers during the Great Schism', *Catholic Historical Review*, 52 (1966), 240–45

The Order on Rhodes:

For an overview in the context of crusading, see:

Norman Housley, *The Later Crusades: From Lyons to Alcazar, 1274–1580* (Oxford, 1992), pp. 218–21

Norman Housley, 'Frontier Societies and Crusading in the Late Middle Ages', *Mediterranean Historical Review*, 10 (1995), 104–19

The standard work on the Hospital for the first century on Rhodes is still Joseph Delaville le Roulx, *Les Hospitaliers à Rhodes (1310–1421)* (Paris, 1913: reprinted London, 1974)

This is being supplemented by the work of Anthony Luttrell. See, for instance:

Anthony Luttrell, 'The Hospitallers of Rhodes Confront the Turks, 1306–1421', in *Christians, Jews and Other Worlds: Patterns of Conflict and Accommodation*, ed. P. F. Gallagher (Lanham, 1988), pp. 80–116; reprinted in his *Hospitallers of Rhodes and their Mediterranean World* (Aldershot, 1992), 2

Anthony Luttrell, 'The Hospitallers' Interventions in Cilician Armenia: 1291–1375', in *The Cilician Kingdom of Armenia*, pp. 118–44; reprinted in his *Latin Greece, the Hospitallers and the Crusades, 1291–1440* (London, 1982), vol. 5

Anthony Luttrell, 'The Military Orders, 1312–1798', in *The Oxford Illustrated History of the Crusades*, ed. Jonathan Riley-Smith (Oxford, 1995), pp. 326–64: here pp. 350–64

See also:

Peter W. Edbury, *The Kingdom of Cyprus and the Crusades, 1191–1374* (Cambridge, 1991)

After 1421, there is no full modern assessment of the Order. The fullest study is still:

I. Bosio, *Dell'Istoria della Sacra Religione et Illustrissima Militia di S. Giovanni Gierosolimitano*, 2, 2nd edn (Rome, 1629). This was one of the sources used by the Abbé Vertot, *Histoire des Chevaliers Hospitaliers de S. Jean de Jerusalem, appellez depuis Chevaliers de Rhodes, et aujourd'hui Chevaliers de Malthe*, 5 vols (Paris, 1726), 2, p. 416 onwards

For modern studies, see:

Norman Housley, *The Later Crusades: From Lyons to Alcazar, 1274–1580* (Oxford, 1992)

Ettore Rossi, 'The Hospitallers at Rhodes, 1421–1523', *A History of the Crusades*, ed. Kenneth M. Setton, 2nd edn, 6 vols to date (Madison, 1969–89), vol. 3, *The Fourteenth and Fifteenth Centuries*, ed. Harry W. Hazard (Madison, 1975), pp. 314–39

For the city of Rhodes, see:

Elias Kollias, *The Medieval City of Rhodes and the Palace of the Grand Master*, 2nd edn (Athens, 1998)

Michel Balard, 'The Urban Landscape of Rhodes as Perceived by Fourteenth- and Fifteenth-Century Travellers', trans. Annette Dulzin, *Mediterranean Historical Review*, 10 (1995), 24–34

Jürgen Sarnowsky, 'Die Kirche auf Rhodes im 15. Jahrhundert', *Ritterorden und Kirche im Mittelalter*, ed. Zenon Hubert Nowak, Ordines Militares: Colloquia Torunensia Historica, 9 (Torún, 1997), pp. 193–224

Nicolas Vatin, *Rhodes et l'Ordre de Saint-Jean de Jérusalem* (Paris, 2000)

On finance, see:

Jürgen Sarnowsky, '"The Rights of the Treasury": The Financial Administration of the Hospitallers on Fifteenth-Century Rhodes, 1421–1522', in *The Military Orders*, vol. 2, *Welfare and Warfare*, ed. Helen Nicholson (Aldershot, 1998), pp. 267–74

L'Enquête Pontificale de 1373 sur l'Ordre des Hospitaliers de Saint-Jean de Jérusalem, ed. Jean Glénisson, vol. 1, *L'Enquête dans le Prieuré de France*, ed. Anne-Marie Legras (Paris, 1987)

The sieges of 1440 and 1444:

For the Burgundian role see Richard Vaughan, *Philip the Good* (London, 1970), pp. 268–73

For Francesc Ferrer's verse account of the siege of 1444, see L. Nicolau d'Olwer, 'Un témoignage catalan du siège de Rhodes en 1444', *Estudis Universitaris Catalans*, 12 (1927), 376–87

For the alleged Genoese co-operation with the Turks in 1444, see Constantin Marinesco, 'Du nouveau sur *Tirant lo Blanch*', *Estudis Romanics*, 4 (1953–4), 139–56, 197–98: here 147, quoting J. Bosio, *Dell'Istoria della Sacra Religione et Illustrissima Militia di S. Giovanni Gierosolimitano*, 3 parts in 2 vols (Rome, 1594–1602), 1, part 2, p. 162

See also Elias Kollias, *The Knights of Rhodes: the Palace and the City* (Athens, 1999) and Elias Kollias, *The Medieval City of Rhodes*

The siege of 1480 and the period 1480–1522:

Norman Housley, *The Later Crusades: From Lyons to Alcazar, 1274–1580* (Oxford, 1992); Kollias, *The Knights of Rhodes*, Kollias, *The Medieval City of Rhodes* and

Ettore Rossi, 'The Hospitallers at Rhodes, 1421–1523', *History of the Crusades*, ed Setton, vol. 3, *The Fourteenth and Fifteenth Centuries*, ed. Hazard

Bosio's and Vertot's histories are very useful for this period.

For the sieges see also Lionel Bulter, *The Siege of Rhodes, 1480*, Order of St John Historical Pamphlets, 11 (1970)

Kenneth M. Setton, *The Papacy and the Levant (1204–1571)*, 4 vols (Philadelphia, 1976–84), 2, pp. 346–59, 3, pp. 198–215

William Eric Brockman, *The Two Sieges of Rhodes, 1480–1522* (London, 1969)

Chapter 4. THE HOSPITALLERS' ORGANISATION AND RELIGIOUS LIFE

Organisation and administration of the Hospital:

For the period to 1310:

Alan Forey, *The Military Orders: From the Twelfth to the Early Fourteenth Centuries* (Basingstoke, 1992), pp. 148–74

Jonathan Riley-Smith, *The Knights of St John in Jerusalem and Cyprus* (London, 1967), pp. 229–340

See also Jochen Burgtorf, 'Wind beneath the Wings: Subordinate Headquarters Officials in the Hospital and the Temple from the Twelfth to the Early Fourteenth Centuries', in *The Military Orders*, vol. 2, *Welfare and Warfare*, ed. Helen Nicholson (Aldershot, 1998), pp. 217–23

Jochen Burgtorf, 'The Order of the Hospital's High Dignitaries and their Claims on the Inheritance of Deceased Brethren – Regulations and Conflicts', in *Autour de la Première Croisade: Actes du Colloque de la Society for the Study of the Crusade and the Latin East (Clermont-Ferrand, 22–25 juin 1995)*, ed. Michel Balard (Paris, 1996), pp. 255–65

Jochen Burgtorf, 'Leadership Structures in the Headquarters of the Orders of the Hospital and Temple (12th Through Early 14th Centuries) – Jerusalem, Acre, Cyprus', in *Expanding the Frontiers of Medieval Latin Christianity. The Crusades and the Military Orders*, ed. József Laszolovsky and Zsolt Hunyadi, Central European University (Budapest, 2001)

For the period after 1310, see:

Stanley Forini and Anthony Luttrell, 'The Italian Hospitallers at Rhodes, 1437–1462', *Revue Mabillon*, 68 (new series 7) (1996), 209–231: reprinted in Anthony Luttrell, *The Hospitaller State on Rhodes and their Mediterranean World* (Aldershot, 1992), 19: on the tongues

Jürgen Sarnowsky, 'The Oligarchy at Work: The Chapters General of the Hospitallers in the XVth Century (1421–1522)', in *Autour de la Première Croisade*, ed. Michel Balard (Paris, 1996), pp. 267–76

Jürgen Sarnowsky, '"The Rights of the Treasury": The Financial Administration of the Hospitallers on Fifteenth-Century Rhodes, 1421–1522', in *The Military Orders*, vol. 2, *Welfare and Warfare*, ed. Helen Nicholson (Aldershot, 1998), pp. 267–74

L'Enquête Pontificale de 1373 sur l'Ordre des Hospitaliers de Saint-Jean de Jérusalem, ed. Jean Glénisson, vol. 1, *L'Enquête dans le Prieuré de France*, ed. Anne-Marie Legras (Paris, 1987)

For the seventeenth century see:

René d'Aubert de Vertot, *Histoire des Chevaliers Hospitaliers de S. Jean de Jérusalem, appellez depuis Chavaliers de Rhodes, et aujourd'hui Chevaliers de Malthe*, 5 vols (Paris, 1726), 5, pp. 180–89, 347–98

See also:

Alan Forey, 'Constitutional conflict and change in the Hospital of St John during the twelfth and thirteenth centuries', *Journal of Ecclesiastical History*, 33 (1982), 15–29; reprinted in his *Military Orders and Crusades*, 10

Organisation and economic policy in the Order in the provinces in the West:

Michael Gervers, ed., *The Cartulary of the Knights of St John of Jerusalem in England, Secunda Camera, Essex* (Oxford, 1982)

Michael Gervers, ed., *The Cartulary of the Knights of St John of Jerusalem in England*, part 2, *Prima Camera, Essex* (Oxford, 1996)

Anthony Luttrell, 'The Hospitallers' Western Accounts, 1373/4 and 1374/5', *Camden Miscellany 30*, Camden Society, 4th series, 39 (1990), 1–21: here p. 2: reprinted in his *Hospitaller State on Rhodes*, 11

Anthony Luttrell, 'Les Exploitations rurales des Hospitaliers en Italie en XIVe Siècle', in *Les Ordres Militares, la Vie Rurale et le Peuplement en Europe Occidentale (XIIe–XVIIIe Siècles)*: *Flaran*, 6 (1986), 107–20; reprinted in his *Hospitallers of Rhodes*, 12

Dominic Selwood, *Knights of the Cloister: Templars and Hospitallers in Central–Southern Occitania, 1100–1300* (Woodbridge, 1999)

The Knights Hospitallers in England: Being the Report of Prior Philip de Thame to the Grand Master Elyan de Villanova for AD 1338, ed. L. B. Larking and J. M. Kemble, Camden Society, lst series, 65 (1857)

Personnel, recruitment and novitiate:

General works:

Alan Forey, *The Military Orders: From the Twelfth to the Early Fourteenth Centuries* (Basingstoke, 1992), pp. 132–47, 174–203

Jonathan Riley Smith, *The Knights of St John in Jerusalem and Cyprus* (London, 1967), pp. 233–46

Particular studies:

Alan Forey, 'Novitiate and Instruction in the Military Orders in the Twelfth and Thirteenth Centuries', *Speculum*, 61 (1986), 1–17; reprinted in his *Military Orders and Crusades*, 3

Alan Forey, 'Women and the Military Orders in the Twelfth and Thirteenth Centuries', *Studia Monastica*, 29 (1987), 63–92; reprinted in his *Military Orders and Crusades*, 4

Alan Forey, 'Recruitment to the Military Orders (Twelfth to Fourteenth Centuries)', *Viator*, 17 (1986), 139–71; reprinted in his *Military Orders and Crusades*, 2

And compare Dieter Wojtecki, *Studien zur Personengeschichte des Deutschen Ordens im 13 Jahrhundert*, Quellen und Studien zur Geschichte des östlichen Europas, ed. Manfred Hellmann, 3 (Wiesbaden, 1971), pp. 78–80, 88–91

For the early modern period, see:

David Allen, '"A parish at sea": Spiritual Concerns aboard the Order of Saint John's Galleys in the Seventeenth and Eighteenth Centuries', in *The Military Orders: Fighting for the Faith and Caring for the Sick*, ed. Malcolm Barber (Aldershot, 1994), pp. 113–20

The Life of Captain Alonso de Contreras, Knight of the Military Order of St John, Native of Madrid. Written by Himself (1582 to 1633), translated from the Spanish by Catherine Alison Phillips with an Introduction by David Hannay (London, 1926)

Vertot, *Histoire*, 5, pp. 319–46

Knightly views of the Hospital:

Helen Nicholson, *Love, War and the Grail: Templars, Hospitallers and Teutonic Knights in Medieval Epic and Romance, 1150–1500* (Leiden, 2001)

The Infirmary of the Hospital (in chronological order):

Benjamin Z. Kedar, 'A Twelfth-Century Description of the Jerusalem Hospital', in *The Military Orders*, vol. 2, *Welfare and Warfare*, ed. Helen Nicholson (Aldershot, 1998), pp. 3–26

Susan Edgington, 'Medical Care in the Hospital of St John in Jerusalem', in *The Military Orders*, vol. 2, *Welfare and Warfare*, ed. Helen Nicholson (Aldershot, 1998), pp. 27–33

Anthony Luttrell, 'The Hospitallers' Medical Tradition: 1291–1530', in *The Military Orders: Fighting for the Faith and Caring for the Sick*, ed. Malcolm Barber (Aldershot, 1994), pp. 64–81; reprinted in his *Hospitaller State on Rhodes*, 10

Fotini Karassava-Tsilingiri, 'The Fifteenth-Century Hospital of Rhodes: Tradition and Innovation', in *The Military Orders: Fighting for the Faith and Caring for the Sick*, ed. Malcolm Barber (Aldershot, 1994), pp. 89–96

Ann Williams, '*Xenodochium* to Sacred Infirmary: the Changing Role of the Hospital of the Order of St John, 1522–1631', in *The Military Orders: Fighting for the Faith and Caring for the Sick*, ed. Malcolm Barber (Aldershot, 1994), pp. 97–102

Paul Cassar, 'Malta's Medical and Social Services under the Knights Hospitallers', in *Hospitaller Malta, 1530–1798: Studies on Early Modern Malta and the Order of St John of Jerusalem*, ed. Victor Mallia-Milanes (Msida, 1993), pp. 475–82

Henry J. A. Sire, *The Knights of Malta* (New Haven and London, 1994), pp. 217–20

Roderick Cavaliero, *The Last of the Crusaders: the Knights of St John and Malta in the Eighteenth Century* (London, 1960), pp. 62–70

See also, for the Hospital's hospital at Genoa, Steven Epstein, *Wills and Wealth in Medieval Genoa, 1150–1250* (Cambridge, Mass., and London, 1984), pp. 149–50, 175–9.

Other charitable work:

R. B. Pugh, 'The Knights Hospitaller of England as Undertakers', *Speculum*, 56 (1981), 566–74

Education:

James Brundage, 'The Lawyers of the Military Orders', in *The Military Orders: Fighting for the Faith and Caring for the Sick*, ed. Malcolm Barber (Aldershot, 1994), pp. 346–57

Alan Forey, 'Literacy and Learning in the Military Orders during the Twelfth and Thirteenth Centuries', in *The Military Orders*, vol. 2, *Welfare and Warfare*, ed. Helen Nicholson (Aldershot, 1998), pp. 185–206

Elias Kollias, *The Medieval City of Rhodes and the Palace of the Grand Master*, 2nd edn (Athens, 1998), pp. 65–73

Anthony Luttrell, 'Fourteenth-Century Hospitaller Lawyers', *Traditio*, 21 (1965), 449–46: here 450; reprinted in his *Hospitallers in Cyprus, Rhodes, Greece and the West (1291–1440)* (London, 1978), 16

Anthony Luttrell, 'Greek Histories Translated and Complied for Juan Fernández de Heredia, Master of Rhodes: 1377–1396', *Speculum*, 35 (1960), 401–7: reprinted in his *Hospitallers in Cyprus*, 20

Anthony Luttrell, 'The Hospitallers' Historical Activities: 1291–1400', *Annales de l'Ordre Souverain Militaire de Malte*, 24 (1966), 1–10; reprinted in his *Hospitallers in Cyprus*, 17

Anthony Luttrell, 'The Hospitallers' Historical Activities: 1400–1530', *Annales de l'Ordre Souverain Militaire de Malte*, 25 (1967), 145–50; reprinted in his *Latin Greece, the Hospitallers and the Crusades, 1291–1440* (London, 1982), 2

Anthony Luttrell, 'The Hospitallers' Historical Activities: 1530–1630', *Annales de l'Ordre Souverain Militaire de Malte*, 26 (1968), 57–60; reprinted in his *Latin Greece*, 3

Disciplinary problems:

Anthony Luttrell, 'Intrigue, Schism and Violence among the Hospitallers of Rhodes: 1377–1384', *Speculum*, 41 (1966), 30–48; reprinted in his *Hospitallers in Cyprus, Rhodes, Greece and the West (1291–1440)* (London, 1978), 23

Victor Mallia-Milanes, *Venice and Hospitaller Malta, 1530–1798: Aspects of a Relationship* (Marsa, 1992), pp. 37–45

Iconography, spirituality and art:

T. S. R. Boase, 'The Arts in Rhodes', in *A History of the Crusades*, ed. Kenneth Setton, vol. 4, *The Art and Architecture of the Crusader States*, ed. Harry W. Hazard (Madison, 1977), pp. 229–50

Mario Buhugar, *The Iconography of the Maltese Islands, 1400–1900: Painting* (Valetta, Malta, 1987)

Jaroslav Folda, *Crusader Manuscript Illumination at Saint-Jean d'Acre, 1275–1291*

(Princeton, 1976), on the work of a master illuminator who accepted commissions from the Hospital at Acre

Jaroslav Folda, 'Crusader Frescos at Crac des Chevaliers and Marquab Castle', *Dumbarton Oaks Papers*, 36 (1982), 177–210

Michael Gervers, 'Rotundae Anglicanae', in *Actes du 22e Congrès International d'Histoire de l'Art, Budapest, 1969* (Budapest, 1972), 1, pp. 359–76

Roberta Gilchrist, *Contemplation and Action: The Other Monasticism* (London, 1995), pp. 94–6

E. J. King, *The Seals of the Order of St John of Jerusalem* (London, 1932)

For the relics after 1291, see:

Anthony Luttrell, 'The Rhodian Background of the Order of Saint John on Malta', in *The Order's Early Legacy in Malta*, ed. John Azzopardi (Valletta, 1989), pp. 3–14: here pp. 12–14; reprinted in his *Hospitallers of Rhodes and their Mediterranean World* (Aldershot, 1992), 18

Anthony Luttrell, 'The Spiritual Life of the Hospitallers of Rhodes', in *Die Spiritualität der Ritterorden im Mittelalter*, ed. Zenon Hubert Nowak, Ordines Militares: Colloquia Torunensia Historica, 7 (Torún, 1993), pp. 75–96; reprinted in his *The Hospitaller State on Rhodes and its Western Provinces, 1306–1462* (Aldershot, 1999), 9

Chapter 5. RELATIONS WITH THE REST OF CHRISTENDOM

Economic activities in the East:

Denys Pringle, *Secular Buildings in the Crusader Kingdom of Jerusalem: An Archaeological Gazetteer* (Cambridge, 1997)

See also: P. Brigitte-Porëe, 'Les Moulins et Fabriques à Sucre de Palestine et de Chypre', in *Cyprus and the Crusades*, ed. Nicholas Coureas and Jonathan Riley-Smith (Nicosia, 1995), pp. 377–510

Anthony Luttrell, 'The Hospitallers in Cyprus after 1386', in ibid., pp. 125–41: here p. 134; reprinted with many corrections in his *Hospitaller State on Rhodes and its Western Provinces, 1306–1462* (Aldershot, 1999), 5

Anthony Luttrell, 'Actividades Economicas de los Hospitalarios de Rodes en el Mediterraneo Occidental Durante el Siglo XIV', *VI Congreso de la Historia de la Corona de Aragón* (Madrid, 1959), pp. 175–83; reprinted in his *Hospitallers in Cyprus, Rhodes, Greece and the West (1291–1440)* (London, 1978), 7

The West:

Michael Gervers, ed., *The Cartulary of the Knights of St John of Jerusalem in England, Secunda Camera, Essex* (Oxford, 1982)

Michael Gervers, ed., *The Cartulary of the Knights of St John of Jerusalem in England,* part 2, *Prima Camera, Essex* (Oxford, 1996)

Anthony Luttrell, 'Les Exploitations Rurales des Hospitaliers en Italie en XIVe Siècle', in *Les Ordres Militares, la Vie Rurale et le Peuplement en Europe Occidentale (XIIe–*

XVIIIe Siècles): *Flaran*, 6 (1986), 107–120; reprinted in his *Hospitallers of Rhodes*, 12

Malta:

Roderick Cavaliero, *The Last of the Crusaders: the Knights of St John and Malta in the Eighteenth Century* (London, 1960), pp. 85–89

Frontiers:

F. L. Carsten, *The Origins of Prussia* (Oxford, 1954)

Walter Kuhn, 'Kirchliche Siedlung als Grenzschutz 1200 bis 1250 (am Beispiel des mittleren Oderraumes)', *Ostdeutsche Wissenschaft*, 9 (1962), 6–55

Anthony Luttrell, 'Feudal Tenure and Latin Colonisation at Rhodes: 1306–1415', *English Historical Review*, 85 (1970), 755–75; reprinted in his *Hospitallers in Cyprus, Rhodes, Greece and the West (1291–1440)* (London, 1978), 3

Helen Nicholson, 'The Knights Hospitaller on the Frontiers of the British Isles', in *Mendicants, Military Orders and Regionalism in Medieval Europe*, ed. Jürgen Sarnowsky (Aldershot, 1999), pp. 47–57

Ann Williams, 'Crusaders as Frontiersmen: The Case of the Order of St John in the Mediterranean', in *The Frontiers in Question: Eurasian Borderlands, 700–1700*, ed. Daniel Power and Naomi Standen (Basingstoke, 1999), pp. 209–27

Relations with popes and kings:

David F. Allen, 'The Order of St John as a "School for Ambassadors" in Counter-Reformation Europe', in *The Military Orders*, vol. 2, *Welfare and Warfare*, ed. Helen Nicholson (Aldershot, 1998), pp. 363–79

Carlos Barquero Goñi, 'The Hospitallers and the Kings of Navarre in the Fourteenth and Fifteenth Centuries', in *The Military Orders*, vol. 2, *Welfare and Warfare*, ed. Helen Nicholson (Aldershot, 1998), pp. 349–54

Karl Borchardt, 'The Hospitallers, Bohemia and the Empire, 1250–1330', in *Mendicants, Military Orders and Regionalism in Medieval Europe*, ed. Jürgen Sarnowsky (Aldershot, 1999), pp. 201–31

B. Bromberg, 'The Financial and Administrative Importance of the Knights Hospitaller to the English Crown', *Economic History*, 4, no. 15 (Feb. 1940), 307–11

Alan Forey, 'The Military Orders and Holy War Against Christians in the Thirteenth Century', *English Historical Review*, 104 (1989), 1–24; reprinted in his *Military Orders and Crusades*, 7

Luis García-Guijarro Ramos, 'Exemption in the Temple, the Hospital and the Teutonic Order: Shortcomings of the Institutional Approach', in *The Military Orders*, vol. 2, *Welfare and Warfare*, ed. Helen Nicholson (Aldershot, 1998), pp. 289–93

Anthony Luttrell, 'Juan Fernández de Heredia at Avignon: 1351–1367', *El Cardenal Albornoz y el Colegio de España*, ed. E. Verdera y Tuells (*Studia Albornotiana*, 11) (Zaragoza, 1972), pp. 289–316; reprinted in his *Hospitallers in Cyprus, Rhodes, Greece and the West (1291–1440)* (London, 1978), 19

Anthony Luttrell, 'The Aragonese Crown and the Knights Hospitaller of Rhodes:

1291–1350', *English Historical Review*, 76 (1961), 1–19; reprinted in his *Hospitallers in Cyprus*, 11

Anthony Luttrell, 'Juan Fernández de Heredia at Avignon: 1351–1367', *El Cardenal Albornoz y el Colegio de España*, ed. E. Verdera y Tuells (*Studia Albornotiana*, 11) (Zaragoza, 1972), pp. 289–316; reprinted in his *Hospitallers in Cyprus*, 19

Victor Mallia-Milanes, *Venice and Hospitaller Malta, 1530–1798: Aspects of a Relationship* (Marsa, 1992)

Helen Nicholson, 'The Military Orders and the Kings of England in the Twelfth and Thirteenth Centuries', in *From Clermont to Jerusalem: The Crusades and Crusaders Societies 1095–1500*, ed. Alan V. Murray (Turnhout, 1998), pp. 203–18

Helen Nicholson, *Templars, Hospitallers and Teutonic Knights: Images of the Military Orders, 1128–1291* (Leicester and London, 1993), pp. 21–2 and notes on p. 143

Jürgen Sarnowsky, 'Kings and Priors: The Hospitaller Priory of England in the Later Fifteenth Century', in *Mendicants, Military Orders and Regionalism*, ed. J. Sarnowsky (Aldershot, 1999), pp. 83–102

Johannes Schellakowsky, 'The Bailiwick of Brandenburg and the Prussian Monarchy 1701–1810', in *The Military Orders*, vol. 2, *Welfare and Warfare*, ed. Helen Nicholson (Aldershot, 1998), pp. 381–9

Myra Struckmeyer, 'The sisters of the Hospital of St John at Buckland', M.Phil. thesis, University of Cambridge, 1999

Charles L. Tipton, 'The English Hospitallers During the Great Schism', *Studies in Medieval and Renaissance History*, 4 (1967), 91–124

Charles L. Tipton, 'The Irish Hospitallers during the Great Schism', *Proceedings of the Royal Irish Academy*, 69 C (1970), 33–43

Charles L. Tipton, 'The English and Scottish Hospitallers during the Great Schism', *Catholic Historical Review*, 52 (1962), 240–5

On lay patrons and religious orders in general, see, for instance:

C. B. Bouchard, *Sword, Mitre and Cloister: Nobility and the Church in Burgundy, 980–1198* (Ithaca and London, 1987)

Emma Mason, 'Timeo Barones et Dona Ferentes', in *Religious Motivation: Biographical and Sociological Problems for the Church Historian*, ed. Derek Baker, Studies in Church History, 15 (1978), pp. 61–75

Chapter 6. THE ORDER OF MALTA, 1530–1798

Background:

Anthony Luttrell, *Medieval Malta: Studies on Malta before the Knights* (London, 1975)

The Order on Malta:

To 1580:

Norman Housley, *The Later Crusades: From Lyons to Alcazar, 1274–1580* (Oxford, 1992), esp. pp. 230–33

Anthony Luttrell, 'The Military Orders, 1312–1798', in *The Oxford Illustrated History of the Crusades*, ed. Jonathan Riley-Smith (Oxford, 1995), pp. 326–64: here pp. 350–64

The main sources are:

Victor Mallia-Milanes, *Venice and Hospitaller Malta, 1530–1798: Aspects of a Relationship* (Marsa, 1992)
Hospitaller Malta, 1530–1798: Studies on Early Modern Malta and the Order of St John of Jerusalem, ed. Victor Mallia-Milanes (Msida, Malta, 1993)

The works of Bosio and Vertot remain valuable (see page 156, above). Bosio ended his account with the siege of Malta, 1565, but Vertot carried his account down to his own day, ending in 1725.
For the period 1725–98 see:

Roderick Cavaliero, *The Last of the Crusaders: the Knights of St John and Malta in the Eighteenth Century* (London, 1960)

See also:

Jonathan Riley-Smith, *Hospitallers: A History of the Order of St John* (London, 1999), pp. 127–8
Michael Galea, *Die Deutschen Ordensritter von Malta* (San Gwann, Malta, 1996)
E. Schermerhorn, *Malta of the Knights* (London, 1929)
Henry J. Sire, *The Knights of Malta* (New Haven and London, 1994), pp. 59–98, 221–42

The Order in the Reformation:

Christoph T. Maier, 'Strategies of Survival: the Military Orders and the Reformation in Switzerland', in *The Military Orders*, vol. 2, *Welfare and Warfare*, ed. Helen Nicholson (Aldershot, 1998), pp. 355–62
Alan Macquarrie, *Scotland and the Crusades, 1095–1560*, 2nd edn (Edinburgh, 1997), pp. 117–18

The Order as a naval power:

David Allen, '"A parish at sea": Spiritual Concerns aboard the Order of Saint John's Galleys in the Seventeenth and Eighteenth Centuries', in *The Military Orders: Fighting for the Faith and Caring for the Sick*, ed. Malcolm Barber (Aldershot, 1994), pp. 113–20
Salvatore Bono, 'Naval Exploits and Privateering', in *Hospitaller Malta*, ed. V. Mallia-Milanes (Msida, 1993), pp. 351–97
M. Fontenay, 'Le Rôle des Chevaliers de Malte dans le Corso Méditerranéen au XIIe siècle', *Las Órdenes en le Mediterráneo Occidental (s. XII–XVIII)* (Madrid, 1983), pp. 369–95
Alexander H. de Groot, 'The Ottoman Threat to Europe, 1571–1800: Historical Fact or Fancy?', in *Hospitaller Malta*, ed. V. Mallia-Milanes (Msida, 1993), pp. 199–254
The Life of Captain Alonso de Contreras, Knight of the Military Order of St John, Native

of Madrid. Written by Himself (1582 to 1633), translated from the Spanish by Catherine Alison Phillips with an Introduction by David Hannay (London, 1926)

Ann Williams, 'Crusaders as Frontiersmen: The Case of the Order of St John in the Mediterranean', in *The Frontiers in Question: Eurasian Borderlands, 700–1700*, ed. Daniel Power and Naomi Standen (Basingstoke, 1999), pp. 209–27

Politics on Malta:

Ann Williams, 'The Constitutional Development of the Order of St John in Malta, 1530–1798', in *Hospitaller Malta*, ed. V. Mallia-Milanes (Msida, 1993), pp. 285–96

See also:

Frans Ciappara, 'Gio. Nicolò Muscat: Church-State Relations in Hospitaller Malta during the Englightenment, 1786–1798', in *Hospitaller Malta*, pp. 605–58

The Siege of Malta, 1565:

Ernle Bradford, *The Great Siege* (London, 1961)

Joseph Ellul, *1565: The Great Siege of Malta* (Zabbar, 1992)

K. M. Setton, *The Papacy and the Levant (1204–1511)* (Philadelphia, 1976–84), 4, pp. 829–81

See also:

Francesco Balbi de Correggio, *The Siege of Malta, 1565*, trans. Henry Alexander Balbi (Copenhagen, 1961)

Vertot, *Histoire des Chevaliers Hospitaliers de S. Jean de Jérusalem* (Paris, 1726), vol. 4, p. 425 – vol. 5, p. 122

The Order and Malta:

Anthony Luttrell, 'Malta and Rhodes: Hospitallers and Islanders', in *Hospitaller Malta*, ed. V. Mallia-Milanes (Msida, 1993), pp. 255–84

See also:

Paul Cassar, 'Malta's Medical and Social Services under the Knights Hospitallers', in *Hospitaller Malta*, ed. V. Mallia-Milanes (Msida, 1993), pp. 475–82

Ann Williams, '*Xenodochium* to Sacred Infirmary: the Changing Role of the Hospital of the Order of St John, 1522–1631', in *The Military Orders: Fighting for the Faith and Caring for the Sick*, ed. Malcolm Barber (Aldershot, 1994), pp. 97–102

On scientific advance:

Roderick Cavaliero, *The Last of the Crusaders: the Knights of St John and Malta in the Eighteenth Century* (London, 1960), pp. 24–5, 123–4

The Order and foreign powers:

David F. Allen, 'The Order of St John as a "School for Ambassadors" in Counter-

Reformation Europe', in *The Military Orders*, vol. 2, *Welfare and Warfare*, ed. Helen Nicholson (Aldershot, 1998), pp. 363–79

Alain Blondy, 'Malta and France, 1789–1798: the Art of Communicating a Crisis', in *Hospitaller Malta*, ed. V. Mallia-Milanes (Msida, 1993), pp. 659–85

Victor Mallia-Milanes, 'Corsairs Parading Crosses: the Hospitallers and Venice, 1530–1798', in *The Military Orders: Fighting for the Faith and Caring for the Sick*, ed. Malcolm Barber (Aldershot, 1994), pp. 103–12

Victor Mallia-Milanes, 'The Price of Hospitaller Crusading Warfare in the Eighteenth Century: the Maltese Consulate on Zante', in *The Military Orders*, vol. 2, *Welfare and Warfare*, ed. Helen Nicholson (Aldershot, 1998), pp. 173–82

Johannes Schellakowsky, 'The Bailiwick of Brandenburg and the Prussian Monarchy 1701–1810', in *The Military Orders*, vol. 2, *Welfare and Warfare*, ed. Helen Nicholson (Aldershot, 1998), pp. 381–9

On the French Revolution:

See Roderick Cavaliero, *The Last of the Crusaders: the Knights of St John and Malta in the Eighteenth Century* (London, 1960), chs 14–15

Chapter 7. THE ORDER OF ST JOHN FROM 1798 TO THE PRESENT DAY

For the beginning of the period:

Roderick Cavaliero, *The Last of the Crusaders: the Knights of St John and Malta in the Eighteenth Century* (London, 1960), pp. 232–70

For the modern day:

Jonathan Riley-Smith, 'Revival and Survival', in *The Illustrated Oxford History of the Crusades* (Oxford, 1995), pp. 386–91

Jonathan Riley-Smith, 'The Order of St John in England, 1827–1858', in *The Military Orders: Fighting for the Faith and Caring for the Sick*, ed. Malcolm Barber (Aldershot, 1994), pp. 121–38

Jonathan Riley-Smith, *Hospitallers: The History of the Order of St John* (London and Rio Grande, 1999), pp. 124–139

Henry J. A. Sire, *The Knights of Malta* (New Haven and London, 1994), pp. 242–79

Index

Abbreviations:

br	brother
gm	grand master
H	the order of the Hospital
m	master
T	the order of the Temple

Personal names for persons living before 1400 are listed under Christian name; those living after 1400 are listed under surname. Figures in bold type refer to illustrations.